Architectural Guide
Sub-Saharan Africa

Volume 6

Central Africa:
From the Atlantic Ocean to the Great Lakes

M000099893

Architectural Guide
Sub-Saharan Africa

Volume 6

Central Africa:
From the Atlantic Ocean to the Great Lakes

Edited by Philipp Meuser and Adil Dalbai

DOM
publishers

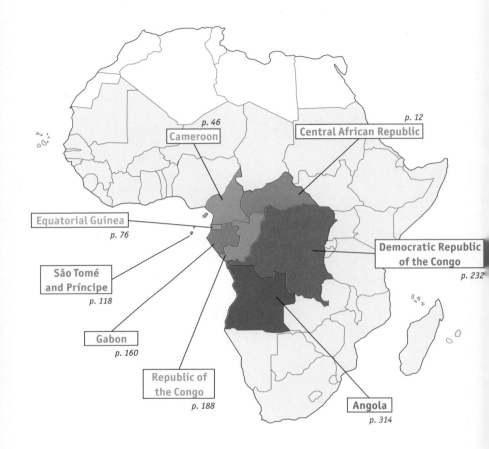

Central Africa:
From the Atlantic Ocean to the Great Lakes

Editors' Introduction

Philipp Meuser, Adil Dalbai

In this compendium of architecture in the sub-Saharan world we aim to celebrate the enormous spectrum of architecture in the region, to share the many stories that architecture tells, so that others around the world may learn of it, as much as from it. Seven volumes with a total of more than 3,400 pages have been produced: a highly condensed knowledge resource. Six of these volumes, each corresponding to a region of the continent, contain the 49 chapters – one country per chapter. The chapters are as diverse as the continent: 49 very different approaches to the subject, united by their structure. Underlying every one, though, is a specific question: what is African architecture? Does such a thing even exist? And if so, how might we understand it? The first volume in this collection deals explicitly with such enquiries. It features introductory essays and statements theorising architecture in sub-Saharan Africa, in which renowned scholars and architects critically inspect the concepts of *African Architectures*. Other subject matter is also pursued there: how to leave behind narratives of deficiency and catching up, ways to formulate the distinction between *African Architecture* and *Architecture in Africa* theoretically, and why the order of the publication itself – by country – is founded on colonial boundaries and what that has to do with architectural identity.

African architecture must be examined for its own sake, rather than viewed as a manifestation of perpetual conflict or romantic transfiguration. Because what the Nigerian author Ainehi Edoro observed about African fiction also applies to non-fiction: 'we – readers, reviewers, publishers – have forgotten how to engage with African novels except from the standpoint of the social or political issues they address.'[1] But, at the same time, we do not want to regard architecture from a purely aesthetic perspective. We tackled this issue by including critical articles, which scrutinise and contextualise the architecture against the background of race, gender, and power, be it colonial, neocolonial, or local.

The idea for a compendium covering the entirety of sub-Saharan Africa dates back to 2014. At that point in time, we had been working as architects for several years on a first project in Western Africa, and the process of finding background information on buildings in sub-Saharan Africa was laborious; by the end, not even a metre of the bookshelf was full.

This scholarly collection was dominated by historical themes, with the main focus on vernacular and colonial architecture and a few titles on the architecture of independence and Tropical Modernism. On the whole, there were far too few in-depth books on contemporary architecture, a theme that was usually represented through schools, nurseries, hospitals. There was a dearth of ambitious surveys of the region, and especially books accessible to those outside the academic sphere. David Adjaye's absorbing, monumental photographic documentation of the continent[2] did not remedy this. And the genre of the architectural guide covers, at best, individual countries or cities. *Architectural Guide South Africa*, for instance, is a drop in the ocean.[3]

So do these monographs really represent the kaleidoscope of architecture in sub-Saharan Africa? If one widens the scope to include popular culture, the outlook is not much better: glossy magazines featuring Africa usually show safari lodges with pseudo-ethnic architecture or fancy resorts on expanses of long, sandy beaches. Delve a bit deeper, into the themed issues of critical periodicals, and reports on the consequences of overpopulation and a lack of education and healthcare dominate tables of contents.

To put it succinctly, there is hardly any reporting on the totality of African architecture, everyday architecture, a 'real' picture of African cities. This is without doubt due to a certain ignorance in intellectual circles outside Africa and as

European editors we are unable to, and do not want to claim to fill this gap. Nevertheless, we have ventured to compile this vast work, which brings together texts by 338 authors. Half of these contributors have African roots, and more than 180 are based on the continent. Alongside fact-finding in international publications, online, and in European archives, extensive on-site research conducted by architects and authors in each individual sub-Saharan country forms the basis of this publication. A scholarly approach was sought – as far as this was possible.

Here the truism of Africa's diversity applies: the spectrum of research methods runs from well-catalogued and air-conditioned state archives to discussions with local residents through oral history methodology or even just small talk. While in one country there was a national association of architects who chose the featured projects via member surveys, in the neighbouring country, a nation with just ten registered architects, there were dedicated researchers or one-person NGOs and their personal collections but not a single published study on the country's recent architecture. Political and economic situations – all nations are represented, from democratic constitutional states to nations in the midst of civil war – as well as secretiveness in the face of cultures not particularly shaped by architectural criticism, set clear limits for research, as did bans on photography and the ensuing detentions. The individual country chapters are thus often the result of the activities of local architects and researchers, who take every opportunity to present the architecture of their country. Various actors have their say: scholars, practising architects, journalists, architecture critics, architectural historians, art historians, lecturers, architecture activists, monument conservationists, photographers, students, landscape architects, designers, engineers, urban planners and urbanists, anthropologists, social scientists, and many

others besides. Authors from Europe, the Americas, Asia, and Australia, as well as the worldwide African diaspora broaden the local perspective.

To set an academic impulse in this context was therefore a challenge. How can one give 49 countries an architectural face in a single publication? Where do you start? Where do you stop? From the beginning it was clear that the gap on the architectural map could only be filled by directing attention to a subjective selection of buildings. That meant walking the tightrope between academic norms and opening up the subject to a wider audience, and in doing so, to avoid producing a book ridden with clichés of war-torn Third World territories or one designed to sit passively on coffee tables. Social, political, cultural, economic, and historical dimensions should, according to our claim, by no means be omitted – the book is inconceivable without them. After all, the built environment can always be read as a mirror of a society, and consequently, architectural criticism understood as a tool for socio-cultural analysis.

Hence, we are well aware that in this field of topics, complete editorial coherence is not possible. On the one hand, this is down to the extremely wide range and diversity of content. And on the other, it is because this publication deliberately gathers together a variety of voices from both Africa and the rest of the world, spanning the spectrum from craftspeople to post-colonial theorists. Nor did we intend to smooth out this diversity – polyphony was a principle that accompanied us in this mammoth editorial task.

This volume covers the countries in Central Africa running from the Sahel region at the northernmost tip of Cameroon, over the rainforest of the Congo Basin (the largest part of the region), and all the way down to the Namib Desert in southern Angola. Because of the climatic conditions, the proportion of wooden constructions in traditional architecture is much higher here than in other parts of

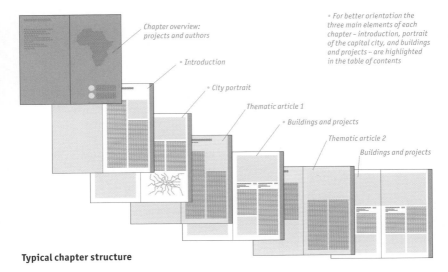

Chapter overview: projects and authors

• Introduction

• City portrait

• For better orientation the three main elements of each chapter – introduction, portrait of the capital city, and buildings and projects – are highlighted in the table of contents

Thematic article 1

• Buildings and projects

Thematic article 2

Buildings and projects

Typical chapter structure

the continent. The featured buildings are as varied as the geography, and regional differences are marked: crisis-hit nations such as the Central African Republic are described, as are the glittering skyscrapers of Luanda, Angola, a city considered one the most expensive in the world.

The differences within nations are also stark: the Democratic Republic of the Congo (DRC), for instance, has contemporary works built amid the rainforest using local materials, while showy glass towers populate its capital, Kinshasa. Cutting-edge works by post-war modernists, both African and European, such as Jean Prouvé's steel houses, are present in neighbouring Congo-Brazzaville.

Angola was, and still is, a laboratory of architectural innovation. During the colonial period Portuguese architects created expressive projects such as open-air cinemas, and civil war was only a temporary interruption to the continuing ingenuity of practitioners in the country. In recent years new large-scale Chinese-built residential developments have sprung up, sparking debates on appropriateness. Examinations of informal housing have also provided windows into inventive thinking. Next to Angola and the DRC, which dominate both economically and architecturally, there are also smaller countries whose buildings are well worth exploring: Gabon has its own expressive modernism, and Cameroon has a diverse architectural palette, which includes Mousgoum dwellings and which has always played a

central role in the construction of social-cultural identity. On the island of São Tomé, the ambivalent history of the colonial plantation system is still highly visible, as the roças illustrate. The oil boom in Equatorial Guinea, the only Spanish-speaking country in sub-Saharan Africa, brought about large-scale international undertakings as well as ground-breaking smaller projects and heritage initiatives. The structure of the individual chapters in the book follows a uniform scheme. At the beginning of each chapter we introduce the authors through short biographies. A general introduction to the architectural context, the history of construction, and the current situation of building culture in the respective country is followed by alternating descriptions of buildings and articles on pertinent topics.

Working in collaboration with local experts, we aimed to both pick out the architectural highlights and to offer a more or less representative cross-section of the respective built environment. With a selection of ten to thirty buildings per country, it is by no means possible to speak of an encyclopedic completeness. Absolute objectivity was never the goal; rather, each country chapter has its own thematic or regional focus, depending on the author and the specific local situation. Themes which were too extensive to squeeze into the short building descriptions are discussed in greater detail in the thematic articles,

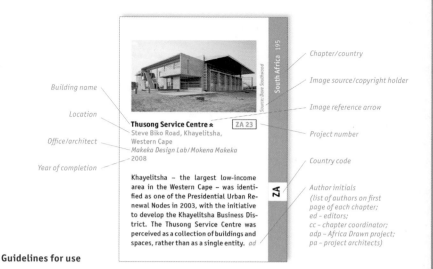

South Africa 195

Source: Dave Southwood

Chapter/country

Image source/copyright holder

Image reference arrow

Building name

Location

Thusong Service Centre ⚓   ZA 23
Steve Biko Road, Khayelitsha,
Western Cape

Project number

Office/architect

Makeka Design Lab/Mokena Makeka
2008

Country code

Year of completion

Khayelitsha – the largest low-income
area in the Western Cape – was identified as one of the Presidential Urban Renewal Nodes in 2003, with the initiative
to develop the Khayelitsha Business District. The Thusong Service Centre was
perceived as a collection of buildings and
spaces, rather than as a single entity. *ad*

ZA

Author initials
(list of authors on first
page of each chapter;
ed – editors;
cc – chapter coordinator;
adp – Africa Drawn project;
pa – project architects)

Guidelines for use

interviews, photo essays, and so on, thus revealing the architectural, spatial, social, and historical contexts of the featured buildings.

Individual countries, seen alone, are by force of circumstance only partially documented (the architecture of each country could fill its own book), but together the 49 chapters and 850 building descriptions give a broad overview and a substantial picture of the architecture of sub-Saharan Africa. The result is an architectural kaleidoscope of an area that is greatly underrepresented in comparison to the rest of the world. It is a kaleidoscope that incorporates the area's contradictions, many facets, diversity, and multiplicity.

Given the fast pace of change on the African continent, as well as the scope and duration of this project, some information will be out of date at the time of publication. That said, one of the main aims of the project will have been achieved if it succeeds in widening the critical debate on architecture in Africa, by identifying aspects that have been less investigated or even unexplored so far, and encouraging young scholars and authors to take an even closer look at the theory and reality of African architecture, past and present.

We would like to take this opportunity to extend our thanks to the more than 650 authors, photographers, architecture practices, and supporters, most of whom have offered their help in order to create a broader foundation for future studies of African architecture. The team around South African urban designer Bouwer Serfontein kindly provided the fascinating hand-drawn city maps and many informative city-portrait texts from the book *Africa Drawn: One Hundred Cities*.[4] Ingrid Stegmann established initial contact with authors in the early days and edited some chapters. In more than three years of work, our in-house editors, in particular Amy Visram, have proofread, translated, and standardised the texts, and checked their plausibility. Special thanks are owed to Anaïs Dresse, who contributed many ideas, and to our associate editor Livingstone Mukasa. Livingstone, an essential part of the editorial team, provided invaluable advice, support, and connections, all in the cause of furthering literature on African architecture. Without him the final publication would not have been of such high quality.

Notes
1 Ainehi Edoro 'How not to talk about African fiction',
   6 April 2016, *The Guardian*, https://www.theguardian.
   com/books/2016/apr/06/how-not-to-talk-about-
   african-fiction, accessed 10 January 2020.
2 David Adjaye and Peter Allison (eds), *Adjaye Africa
   Architecture: A Photographic Survey of Metropolitan
   Architecture*, 7 vols (New York, 2011).
3 Nicholas Clarke and Roger Fisher, *Architectural Guide
   South Africa* (Berlin, 2014).
4 Gary White, Marguerite Pienaar, Bouwer Serfontein,
   Africa Drawn: One Hundred Cities (Berlin, 2015).

Central African Republic

Thierry Bangui, Central African-French architect, urbanist, and international development consultant. Holds a PhD in urbanism and planning. Taught at various French higher-education institutions. Author of several books. He is currently head of an international development firm in Bangui, CAR. *(tb)*

Winfried Bullinger, German artist and laywer, born 1965 in Munich. Graduated from the Universität der Künste, Berlin, in 1993. Studied at Michaelis School of Fine Art, Cape Town, South Africa, in 1987. Completed many photographic projects in Africa. Author of the book *At the Edges of Power* (2017).

Editors' note:
Because of the unstable political situation in the Central African Republic (CAR) since the outbreak of violence in 2015, it has unfortunately not been possible to check and confirm all of the details in this chapter of the book.

CF

Anaïs Dresse, Belgian development practitioner, born 1986. Studied sociology, peace and conflict studies, and human rights law. Worked for several international and non-governmental organisations in various African countries for many years, including Benin, Central African Republic, and Guinea. *(ad)*

Mesmin Guenguebe Mbari, architect and urbanist, born 1986. Graduated from the Ecole Africaine des Métiers de l'Architecture et de l'Urbanisme, Lomé, Togo. Works at the Ministry of Urbanism, City, and Habitat. Currently head of technical services at the Fonds d'Amenagement et d'Equipement Urbains.

Riccardo Vannucci, PhD, Italian architect, born 1958. After twenty years of varied professional experience, in 2006 he established FAREstudio, an organisation involved in planning and building projects for UN agencies and non-governmental organisations in various developing countries.

Introduction

Mesmin Guenguebe Mbari

The history of architecture in the territory of the Central African Republic (CAR) has, of course, been strongly influenced by the phases in the country's history. The two principal ethnic groups that compose the population of the CAR – the Banda and the Gbaya peoples – settled in the area in the nineteenth century. The Banda, who originate from Sudan, and the Gbaya, from Nigeria, were both fleeing tribal wars and slaver raids. These peoples were semi-sedentary (settled for part of the year but otherwise nomadic), because of the hostile climatic conditions. They were in perpetual movement: firstly, because of their activities of fishing, hunting and gathering; secondly, because of pandemics of malaria, yellow fever, and African trypanosomiasis (commonly called sleeping sickness).

The region's indigenous population – Aka Pygmies, also known as Central African Foragers or Forest People of Central Africa – were nomads. Determined by their culture, their architecture was respectful of the environment and had a seasonal and ephemeral character. Their temporary constructions were made of perishable materials: branches, twigs, leaves, etc. The Central African Republic is not believed to have had a prosperous ancient kingdom, like those of the Mossi people in Burkina Faso and the Yoruba and Hausa peoples in Nigeria. However, this assumption does not completely rule out the presence of chiefdoms and sultans who had their fortunes seized by the colonisers. When the indigenous Central African societies settled, they were organised around the residences of the chiefs, who had vast courts where members would gather, either for festivities, public sentencing, or other events. The palaver tree was the main place for public dialogue. Shrines were built to venerate deities. Each group was constituted of castes, including griots

Source: Brice Blondel

Aerial view of a typical village in the CAR

(musicians or storytellers), blacksmiths, hunters, fishers, healers, and builders. Anyone who aspired to join a caste had to go through initiatory rites. In most cases, the transmission of knowledge within a caste passed through families. The grouping and settlement depended on sociocultural and socioeconomic interests. Because of its semi-sedentary, temporary character, which did not require a great deal of financial or material resources, the architecture of these pre-colonial societies did not withstand the test of time. Equally, the chosen materials – such as earth, untreated wood, or straw – were not resistant to climatic conditions. The systematic destruction of the traces of leaders who were hostile to foreign occupation was another contributing factor in the obliteration of this architecture.

Though the CAR did not inherit monumental buildings from its pre-colonial past for the aforementioned reasons, one can note that vernacular constructions today are respectful of their environment and emphasise the use of local techniques and resources. However, profound improvements need to be introduced. The country's vernacular architecture showcases many interesting themes and is a rich source of inspiration.

Bangui on the banks of the Ubangi River, with Bongo Soua Island

Source: Private collection

N'Bougbou house (1945), Mobaye, Basse-Kotto Prefecture

With its imported techniques and materials, colonisation bequeathed the CAR (which was the French colony of Ubangi-Shari from 1906 to 1958) a composite architectural style. Constructions from that time were well adapted to their environment. The era of the rationalisation of space and the use of pure shapes and volumes began. Locally available materials were processed before being used for construction: for instance, instead of adobe and twigs, fired bricks were used to build walls. Dry, treated wood was introduced into buildings. Concepts answered usage needs and functions. Administrative, commercial, industrial, harbour, and residential structures differed from one another. Houses were mostly rectangular or square and surrounded by wide verandas supported by posts. These structures protected the walls from hot sun and heavy rainfall. The walls – which were load-bearing – were of consequent width. The roof was usually made of corrugated metal and

steeply pitched on two or four sides in order to maximise rainwater drainage. Administrative and commercial buildings were conceived in Art Deco style, with thin, double-slab roof terraces for waterproofing and cooling, natural ventilation systems, and concrete awnings above the treated wood shutters. These conceptual and technical choices provided a pleasant thermal environment and minimised energy consumption.

Throughout the CAR today, most of the built heritage from the colonial period is used either as offices or as residences for local officials. It is only in the capital, Bangui – created in 1889 on the Ubangi Rock, where one of the highest buildings in the city, the thirteen-storey Hotel Oubangui, now stands – that we can identify many architectural works that answer to the various urban needs. These include those of state or social services, but also residential, commercial, and industrial requirements.

Bangui's colonial architecture is an inheritance that needs to be preserved. However, it must be underlined that this heritage is subject to daily transformations that put it in danger. The recurring crises that the country has undergone have brought forth the partial destruction of this heritage.

The CAR's independence in August 1960 marked the beginning of another period for architecture in the country. Modern sovereign infrastructure was required alongside that inherited from the colonial administration. And one must not forget that during colonisation Bangui depended on Brazzaville, which was then the capital of the colony of French Equatorial Africa. After independence, the infrastructure of this provincial city had to be reinforced in order to turn the

Source: Philippe Hecquet (left and right)

Ornate vernacular homes near River Mbi in Bossembélé, Ombella-M'Poko Prefecture, in 1989

Source: Ilya Varlamov

The National Assembly (Palais de l'Assemblée Nationale), the seat of the parliament of the Central African Republic, was built with the help of South Korea and inaugurated in 1993

location into a capital. And so, during the years following 1960, a series of construction projects ensued: the Building Administratif (which burnt down in 2003 but was rehabilitated in 2017), the Uzès Tower (a residential compound of average density, originally aimed at expatriate executives and development workers, the renovation of which is about to start), the Cité des Ministres across from the Alliance Française of Bangui, as well as various others.

During the late 1960s and throughout the 1970s, the CAR gained a number of buildings for institutions, including the University of Bangui, M'Poko Airport, the Ministry of Foreign Affairs, the Arc de Triomphe, the Banque Centrale d'Afrique, CAR Television, the Court of Appeal, and the Omnisport Stadium. In the period from the 1980s to the present, another generation of public and private infrastructure edifices can be identified. The most important among these are the National Assembly (Palais

de l'Assemblée Nationale), the Sahely Building, the Ledger Plaza Hotel, and the 20,000-seat stadium named after Barthélemy Boganda, a politician considered the founding father of the CAR.

Currently, Bangui's architecture remains predominantly horizontal: the highest buildings never go above fifteen floors, with most barely reaching ten storeys. The country's continuing instability is an obstacle to real-estate investment, particularly in the private sector. This 'instability factor' could be compared to the semi-sedentary characteristics that once created an unfavourable climate for architecture's emergence and development. Over the last few years, Bangui and the entire country have known profound crises, which have led to destruction on a massive scale and increased demand in almost every sector. If post-conflict reconstruction opportunities could be seized, then there could be a very different kind of architectural production in the future.

Source: Ilya Varlamov (left); CCTV Africa (right)

Courthouse in Bangui

'Building Administratif' before renovation

Rainforest Constructions: Buildings of the Baka

Winfried Bullinger

The following pictures were taken in 2008 in the Central African Republic (CAR), near the borders with Cameroon and the Republic of the Congo. This jungle region, which is crossed by the Sangra River, is inhabited by the Baka people. The ethnic group live in the southwest of the CAR, and in Cameroon and the north of Gabon and the Republic of the Congo (in the latter they are known as the Bayaka). Some groups live nomadically in the forest, while others settle around villages in the region. The forest is their livelihood: they hunt there with their traditional nets and spears and their staple food is a type of forest antelope, the blue duiker. Their buildings are created from the materials they take from the forest. In a short time, women build a framework of branches, which is then filled with leaves and sealed. Where available, the Baka also integrate industrial materials such as blankets and pieces of plastic. Their buildings, however, usually follow the same basic scheme. Unfortunately, the region is ravaged by illegal logging, violence, and poachers seeking elephants for ivory.

Source: Winfried Bullinger (all pictures; image on left page is cropped)

Building in a jungle village (left page). Temporary Baka buildings: women construct the structure and cover it with leaves and other forest materials (above and following pages).

Source: Winfried Bulinger (cropped image)

Bangui

Aerial view of Bangui towards Zongo (Democratic Republic of the Congo) on the other side of the Ubangi River

Source: Kalyan Neelamraju

Source: Africa Drawn Project

Bangui's rectilinear street grid reflects its past as a colonial trading post

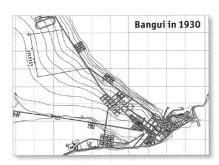

Bangui in 1930

Source: Private collection

Bank of Central African States (BEAC)

Source: Flickr/Kayikwamba

The CAR's capital has seen better days

Once described as La Coquette, a name expressing its beauty, the capital of the Central African Republic (CAR) has in recent decades become a face for rebel activity and political upheaval, being named as the most dangerous city in the world in 1996. Originally established as a trading post in the French colony of Ubangi-Shari, the city lies on the banks of the Ubangi River, with rolling green hills behind it. In and around the urban area are Iron Age archaeological sites, some as close as 800 m to Avenue de l'Indépendance, a main city boulevard.

As the administrative, trade, commercial and transport hub of the turbulent CAR, it continues to draw migrants every day. Entry points include M'Poko Airport and a river port that handles the country's international trade. All of the main roads – mostly dirt, with only toll roads paved – originate from the Place de la République, connecting the city to urban centres elsewhere. The colonial city centre features an arch (the Arc de Triomphe) and wide boulevards leading to a central market square. Administrative and institutional buildings, mostly from the Modern Movement period, are scattered around the centre of the city. Permanent buildings are generally of cement blocks, while sun-dried brick walls and thatched roofs are reserved for increasingly densely scattered dwelling houses,

Source: iStock/mtcurado

Skaiky Ouday Centre (2016) is, at fifteen storeys high, one of Bangui's tallest buildings

rendering a strong horizontal character to the expanding city. Traditionally, village space is completely open, with no enclosures, as indigenous Central Africans consider concealment a violation of cultural norms. Like village layouts, streets in the city are extensions of communal space, where all activities are visible to passers-by. The Muslim religion, with an ever-increasing presence in the local, mostly Christian communities, culturally requires enclosures. The KM5 Neighbourhood, roughly five kilometres from the physical city centre (Bangui's districts are often named after their distance from this point), is considered by many to be the real Bangui, with its mix of ethnic groups and religions. The Church of Fatima and the Notre Dame d'Afrique are in KM5, as are the city's largest mosque and market.

Resources are becoming progressively scarce as urban growth increases, and the intense rebel activity in recent years (there were coup attempts in 2013 and 2015) has led to destruction in the city. Deforestation and loss of agricultural land around the urban periphery, along with lack of infrastructure, sanitation, electricity, running water, access to roads, drainage and lack of housing, all contribute to a difficult situation. *adp*

Source: Ilya Varlamov

Street scene in Bangui: a few high-rises stand out in an otherwise low-rise city

Bangui's Colonial Architecture: Urban Heritage in Decay

Thierry Bangui

Many sub-Saharan African cities – especially the larger ones – were constructed from scratch during colonial times. Bangui, the capital of the Central African Republic (CAR), is one of them. After independence, the African states inherited the material traces of colonisation – a coherent urban fabric, with a particular type of architecture. These remains were sometimes considered objects that formed part of the apparatus of domination by a foreign power and so in some cases fell victim to vandalism and abandonment. This was not so in the CAR, though, and since the country's independence, in Bangui – the location of many colonial buildings – these structures have been home to ministries, administrations, and other public services, and serve as private residences for a particular social class (the elite, expats, and so forth).

Figures such as administrators and/or individuals with specialist technical skills (architects, urban planners, engineers) brought about most colonial urban projects. For instance, Joseph Simon Gallieni, the governor general of Madagascar from 1896 to 1905, left a number of traces in Antananarivo and many other cities in Madagascar. Likewise, governor generals of French Equatorial Africa (AEF),[1] such as Émile Gentil, Martial Henri Merlin, Raphaël Antonetti, and Félix Éboué,[2] all made their mark on the region. Indeed, most of the infrastructure and colonial urban superstructure of the CAR were, like those in the other countries of the former AEF, the work of administrators.

The Creation of a Capital: From Colonial Times to Today

'Bangui was founded in 1889 by Michel Dolisie' is a sentence that any person finishing secondary school in the CAR can recite. The history books in the country note that on 10 May 1889 Michel Dolisie,

Colonial-era buildings around Point Kilomètre Zéro, in Bangui city centre

a French explorer, decided to set up a trading post at Bangui, and on 26 June that same year, he and Alfred Uzac founded the city on the slopes of a steep hill along the banks of the Ubangi River. The objective for creating this trading post was to open up roads to Chad and the Nile. Two years later, Victor-Emmanuel Largeau arrived as an administrator to run the city. In 1903, a decree created the Ubangi-Shari colony, and another in 1906 made Bangui the capital of the territory. The building of Bangui illustrates the advantages of being able to build *ex nihilo*: a general concept can be followed through and a certain homogeneity can be created.

Today, the city consists of the administrative, commercial, and residential areas that were established on the site of the former colonial trading post, as well as unplanned working-class neighbourhoods, which are sometimes several kilometres away from the city centre, where most of Bangui's population lives and works. The city centre is essentially made up of colonial architecture inherited from the days of Ubangi-Shari. This built heritage, shaped by seventy years of history, bears the hallmarks of France. In terms of architecture and urban planning, the colonial period from 1889 to 1960 is marked by various achievements: administrative and utility buildings (housing, schools, hospitals, etc.), structures for commercial or industrial use, religious buildings, roads, electricity and water distribution supply systems, and others.

The urban fabric that makes up Bangui's old colonial district – the current city centre – is the most urbanised section of the city. However, it is now very much in decline: most buildings and streets are dilapidated; certain edifices are in ruin. Furthermore, many buildings still carry the scars (the vestiges of bullets and looting) from the violent political crises that the city has endured in recent years.

The colonial urban structure – a combination of rectangular plots and radial roads – is still visible in the centre of the CAR's capital

1. Point Kilomètre Zéro
2. City Hall
3. Presidential Palace

Source: Africa Drawn Project

Bangui's Buildings: Types and Uses

Unlike many French colonies in Africa, Ubangi-Shari, and in particular the city of Bangui, did not have any fortifications; it also had very few grandiose buildings. Instead, it was home to many classical colonial constructions: houses or buildings with verandas. Even though Bangui depended, for its big decisions, on Brazzaville – the capital of the AEF, where the higher echelons of the AEF colonial territories' administration resided (the governor general, inspector generals, and such) – the city had its own administration in charge of managing the colony. Indeed, Ubangi-Shari had a governorate and an array of services (public works, customs, treasury, town hall, finances, post and telecommunications, etc.), all based in its capital. In line with this, the city's more prestigious buildings are mostly administrative – the former Governor's Residence (Hôtel du Gouverneur) or the present city hall. The public buildings constructed by the administration (housing, schools, hospitals/dispensaries, etc.) are on the whole standard, of simple style, with an emphasis on comfort and functionality. Essentially, the administrative buildings in Bangui are houses – there were no apartment buildings like in other African colonial cities. These homes have verandas and are adapted to the city's tropical climate. The residences were destined not only for European officials, but also clerks and local auxiliaries, whose housing was smaller that that of the officials. These staff lived in smaller, simplified buildings, with only one or two rooms. For European officials, the size of their house also depended on their rank; they always had houses on their own plots.

Scholastic and medical infrastructures are part of the colonial architectural achievements in Bangui. The buildings from that period were constructed for utility, with up to three floors, and verandas and balconies on those with more than one storey. On some, the roofing is made from slabs and on others corrugated metal, upon metal or wood structures. These buildings answer to strict technical requirements. The vocational schools in certain regional cities (such as Bouca, Bangassou, Boali, and others) were based on the Bangui model: standard buildings of 36 × 14.25 m (verandas included) and three classrooms separated by load-bearing walls. One example of this, the Centre Hospitalier Universitaire de Bangui (CHUB), Bangui's teaching hospital, is today in ruins.

The erection of commercial buildings was important in Bangui during the colonial period. An essential part of today's city-centre commercial infrastructure comes from that time. These buildings are mostly two storeys high, with the ground floor used for shops and storage, and the upper level for housing. The functions are separated in the one-storey buildings. All of the buildings give directly onto the street, and starting at the Rond-Point de la République, line three main arteries for several hundred metres over the Avenue de l'Indépendance, Avenue Barthélemy Boganda, and Avenue David Dacko. They were the property of economic operators and French and Portuguese companies (such as the famous Moura et Gouveia shops, which not only existed in Bangui but in many of the regional cities as well). These shops mainly specialised in general commerce. On the level of architectural constraints, the constructions for commercial and private use did not have to respect the same layouts imposed upon the administrative buildings. They therefore had scope to create more original decor and a more varied urban landscape. At the end of World War II, the colonial administration started to worry about the living conditions for indigenous people. The period between 1945 and 1960, described as the 'march towards independence', brought forth the restructuring of the African neighbourhoods and the building of houses of a higher standard in those locations. The Fonds d'Investissement pour le Développement Économique et Social (FIDES – Community Economic and Social Development Investment Fund) was created and was used to finance various constructions, in particular for housing in the French colonies. FIDES existed from 1947 to 1958. In 1949, the restructuring of the Lakouanga District and the Cité Christophe, adjacent

Source: Private collection (all pictures)

Point Kilomètre Zéro and wide boulevards

Bank building in Bangui

Cinéma Le Club

Société Générale

Courthouse (Palais de Justice)

Le Rock Hotel (1950s)

Treasury (Trésor) in 1950

Source: Private collection (all pictures)

to the European neighbourhoods, took place in Bangui. The Christophe Company built seventy-five houses from earthen concrete for the African population. These houses (including a living room, one or two bedrooms, a kitchen, a squat toilet, a tap, and a septic tank nozzle pending installation) were built with 25 cm thick walls. The walls were coated with a Tyrolean finish made of coarse sand; the roof was constructed of corrugated metal and the ceilings of plywood; and the exterior featured a roughcast finish applied with a ram press. On a financial level, though, it was reported that the Cité Christophe was unsuccessful and that the earthen houses were not cheaper than those made of cement conglomerate. This high cost was the result of various factors, but the main problem was that it was impossible to absorb this cost when building such a restricted number of houses in the specified materials.

The Former Colonial Districts: An Important Inheritance

In a city like Bangui, where housing and urban planning today exist in name only, it is not trivial to underline the decent character of housing and the coherent urban planning seen in the time before the country's independence. The cubic houses (built on a square or rectangular base) are organised along streets. Ubangi's indigenous villagers were forced by the colonial authorities to abandon their traditional round huts for these cubic constructions.

The European neighbourhoods were supposed to represent colonial modernity and had to have all the telltale signs. The division of land is generally defined by an orthogonal grid of rectangular plots – often in groups of four and separated by streets that regularly cross at right angles. Many of the streets are paved with asphalt and lined with trees (mostly mango). Individual houses are on different-sized plots. The neighbourhoods do not constitute a homogenous whole. The commercial centre stands out, thanks to its activity and location; it is made up of one- and two-storey buildings which stand along the streets. Both today and during colonial times, administrative personnel lived and worked in districts far from the commercial centre. The 'European City' is composed of the Hospital District (around the CHUB), the Aviation District (around the current Police Headquarters), and the Industrial District on the edge of the Ubangi River.

Present-day Bangui: An Urban Fabric in Decline

The buildings in Bangui's former colonial neighbourhoods (the current city centre) served various functions, and consequently, their owners are just as diverse. Today, the state is in possession of many of these buildings. The municipality also holds some of this built heritage, as do private persons, the Church, and others. These individuals and organisations have different financial resources at their disposal, as well as varying attachments to their heritage. There is every reason to believe that, for these owners, the utility and functionality of these buildings count more than their upkeep, revalorisation, preservation, or conservation.

Present-day Bangui's city centre is mostly composed of derelict buildings, and the public roads are in a state of disrepair. All one needs to do is stroll around this area to instantly notice the presence

Chamber of Commerce in the 1950s

Moura et Gouveia premises in the 1960s

of a heritage – a witness to the past – in ruins. The buildings, be they for office, residential, or commercial usage, are very dilapidated. Their solid structures remain (walls, posts, beams, etc.) – a result of colonial architecture's technical rigour – but some elements are in a process of decay: tiles and cement flooring have been removed; doors, windows, ceilings, and wooden structures have rotted; paint and coatings are impaired; and rainwater seeps through degraded roofs. All of these factors depreciate this part of the city, which is not only a showcase for the capital, but also an inheritance that needs to be preserved. The situation can be explained by the lack of interest that the owners have in their heritage. This applies first and foremost to the state, and they are not fully aware of what they own. The public buildings that house the ministries and other official functions are incredibly rundown. Private owners of houses seldom live in them. They let out the homes and receive their rent, but care little about performing the necessary upkeep. The rare buildings that are kept in good condition are those occupied by foreign embassies and representatives of international institutions based in Bangui. Some buildings for commercial use are also well kept, but that is something necessitated by competition with commercial rivals.

In the end, one cannot help but wonder about the place public authorities – and the Central Africans – hold for their architectural heritage and history, because the issues raised here not only concern the urban fabric (or the buildings) but also history, and in particular, memory: colonial architecture is, in Bangui, a testimony to the past. It appears that the question that arises from this analysis is

not of interest to the various owners, the first being the state. It may be argued that the CAR – a poor country – has other priorities. That may be true – especially in times of crisis – but it comes down to a matter of volition.

The authorities should put an end to the indifference to and neglect of this part of the city. For this, it is necessary to inscribe the preservation of this heritage among their priorities and to dictate clear regulations concerning the upkeep of the buildings within a specified area, and then to make organisations and individuals comply with these rules – starting with the public authorities (state and municipality). There is no doubt that these old colonial neighbourhoods display the capital, because apart from these districts, neighbourhoods that are the product of such coherent urbanism are rare. The neighbourhoods are both a showcase and a memory.

To sum up, well maintained colonial architecture in Bangui would elevate the image of the city centre, attract more people (businesses, residents, and in particular tourists), and thus generate economic benefits. The maintenance of colonial architecture means the preservation of a heritage for generations to come. And we must therefore acknowledge it.

This text is adapted from: Thierry Bangui, 'L'architecture coloniale du centre-ville de Bangui (Rép. Centrafricaine): Essai sur un patrimoine urbain en décadence', Les Cahiers d'Outre-Mer, 261:1 (2013), pp. 105–122.

Notes
1 Ubangi-Shari (present-day Central African Republic) constituted – with Cameroon, Gabon, Middle Congo (present-day Republic of the Congo), and Chad – the colony of French Equatorial Africa (Afrique Équatoriale Française, AEF).
2 Émile Gentil, Martial Merlin, Raphaël Antonetti, and Félix Éboué were General Governors of French Equatorial Africa, respectively from 1904–1908, 1908–1918, 1924–1935, and 1940–1944.

Notre-Dame Cathedral   CF 01
Rue Joseph, 1ᵉʳ Arrondissement, Bangui
Jean-Marie Flour
1934–1937

The first Christian religion in Bangui, Catholicism was established in the city almost concomitantly to the town's creation. Monsignor Augouard, Vicar Apostolic of Upper French Congo, arrived in Bangui in 1893, and chose the site of the future Saint Paul Mission, which would be founded the following year. The Saint Paul Church is located in the southeast of the city, in the Ouango District, on the banks of the Oubangui River. The Saint Paul Mission was followed, a few years later, by the construction of a second church, the current cathedral, located near the hospital, in the heart of the 'European' city. Consecrated to Our Lady of the Immaculate Conception, it is the country's main Christian church and the official seat of the Metropolitan Archdiocese of Bangui (although the archbishop traditionally resides at the Saint Paul Mission compound). Like many religious buildings in Bangui, the cathedral is constructed of red, uncoated fired bricks. This is perhaps a result of the work of the French missionary Brother Jean-Marie Flour, who worked as a mason as well as

an architect, and besides the cathedral designed and built many schools and chapels in the French colony of Ubangi-Shari. The cathedral has space for 1,500 people (during holidays up to 3,000) and features an imposing neo-Gothic main façade, flanked by two large towers. Its floor plan follows classical examples and is essentially a basilica with two side aisles on either side of the central nave and a semicircular choir. The original choir with its tall, narrow arched windows was later significantly altered and the solid brick walls replaced with partly coloured translucent glass bricks. The Central African Republic's recent history

of violence has not spared the cathedral: in 2013, it was looted by the Séléka rebel militia, and a year later, dozens of people were killed or wounded by radical Islamist terrorists. In November 2015, Pope Francis visited the cathedral on his African tour. *tb/ed*

Source: Flickr/Kayikwamba

Source: Private collection

Governor's Residence ⌇ ⌐   `CF 02`
Avenue du Colonel Conus,
1er Arrondissement, Bangui
Victor Henri Sisson
1920

The former Governor's Residence in Bangui (Hôtel du Gouverneur) was the most imposing building of the colonial era. Indeed, it was intended to impress the public and to represent France's dignity and superiority in the Ubangi-Shari colony. In common with the majority of stately buildings from the colonial era, the building was symmetrical, with the main entrance at its centre and wings situated on either side. All four façades were surrounded by 2.8 m deep verandas, adorned with arcades and balustrades. The parapets – also balustraded – separate the central section's hipped roof and the side wings' gable roofs from the verandas' roofing. The gable roofs end in gently inclined crow-stepped gables, giving the building a Gothic aspect. The entire building sits around 1 m proud of ground level, so an outdoor staircase of six steps affords access to the surrounding terrace. After the CAR's independence in 1960, the building became the residence of the president of the young republic. It suffered major disfigurement following significant conversion work under president and self-declared emperor Jean-Bédel Bokassa around 1970. Modernist concrete arcades completely hid the old residence and ultimately formed an entirely new building, which is now known as the Presidential Palace or Palais de la Renaissance.   *tb/ed*

Bangui City Hall ⌆   `CF 03`
Avenue du Colonel Conus,
1er Arrondissement, Bangui
ca. 1947

Bangui's colonial City Hall (once known as 'Mairie') was a typical Art Deco style building in the heart of the city, right next to Point Kilomètre Zéro roundabout. With its sober and plain façade surfaces and centrally located main entrance, the two-storey building showcases perfect geometrical rigor and symmetry. The large entrance hall leads to the central staircase, from where the upper floors and the building's two wings are accessed. In recent years the building has been renovated and 'adorned' with neo-classical ornamentation and columns.   *tb/ed*

Governor's Residence

Presidential Palace

Source: Private collection (left); Alain Nzilo (right)

Source: Private collection (left); Bruno-Serge Gersil Piozza (right)

Barthélemy Boganda National Museum ≈ CF 04
Avenue Boganda,
2e Arrondissement, Bangui
1950s

After it was built as a hospital in the 1950s, this two-storey Tropical Modernist building soon became the residence of the prime minister Barthélemy Boganda. It consists of a central staircase, a loggia around the upper floor, and a rectangular pediment on top of the main balcony. The mobile vertical shutters built around the loggia for natural ventilation were later replaced by glass windows. In 1964, the building was turned into a museum by ethnomusicologists Simha Arom and Geneviève Dournon. The museum, inaugurated two years later, was initially dedicated to music, including instruments and an oral literature sound archive. Its collection was later widened to encompass rites and customs, work and domestic tools, as well as ornaments, furniture, and toys. These ethnographic objects were displayed in six rooms until the museum was closed to the public in 2012, after a wave of violent clashes. The attacks left the building shattered, and weather conditions and its unstable foundation on marshland have led to further damage. The museum is currently under renovation, though a number of objects were lost as a result of the violence and looting. *ad*

Bangui University ≈ CF 05
Avenue des Martyrs,
1er Arrondissement, Bangui
1969

The University of Bangui Campus is centrally located on the northern part of the Barthélemy Boganda Sports Complex. It was created in 1969 and hosts around 6,500 students. The main entrance is gated by a distinctive fence, which is highlighted by four triangular concrete panels that form a sluice-like architectural element. The compound comprises several buildings of different heights and styles, and hosts five faculties and four institutes. The modernist façade of the main building is layered with vertical concrete elements. The Health Science Faculty contrasts with this style with its stilt structure and yellow panels. *ad*

Ministry of Foreign Affairs ⌣ ≈ CF 06
Avenue des Martyrs,
1er Arrondissement, Bangui
1960s–1970s

The compound is made up of two main structures: a rectangular office block accessible via a covered gate and decorated by concrete elements, and a circular annex resembling a macaroon. The latter is no longer in use, but is an interesting example of African futurism, with its round top and bottom halves surrounded by several staircases. *ad*

Source: Bruno-Serge Gersil Piozza (left); Ilya Vartamov (right)

Source: Bruno-Serge Gersil Piozza

Source: Ilya Varlamov

aptly named Quartier Combattant, a popular neighbourhood marked by recurrent violent outbreaks during the recent civil unrest. Following the outbreak of civil war in December 2012, the airport was bordered by Bangui's largest internally displaced people camp. Over the next years, the unofficial M'Poko camp stretched up and down along the landing strips, hosting up to 100,000 people fleeing the violence at the height of the conflict in abandoned hangars, plane carcasses, and tents. People began arriving at the camp in December 2013, after clashes between ex-Séléka (Muslim majority) and anti-Balakas (Christian majority) factions hit Bangui, marking a high point of the third Central African civil war. The camp was closed in 2017 and plans for a new airport were mooted.   *ed*

M'Poko Airport ⩘ ⩘   CF 07
Avenue de France,
5ᵉ Arrondissement, Bangui
1967 onwards

The core of Bangui's civilian airport is made up of a rectangular, two-floor main building, entered through a large hall. With a current annual passenger flow of around 120,000, its initial capacity of 10,000 is greatly exceeded. The CAR's aerial transport has massively increased since the airport's conception in the years following independence in 1960. The airport is located on the city outskirts, beyond the

Barthélemy Boganda Stadium ⮎   CF 08
Avenue de France/Avenue des Martyrs,
1ᵉʳ Arrondissement, Bangui
Complant
2006

This stadium is part of the Barthélemy Boganda Sports Complex (built in 1977), which is named after the founding father of Central African independence. The construction of the 20,000-seat venue was funded and carried out in 2006 by the Chinese development and construction company Complant. It consists of a circular structure with two VIP seating

Internally displaced people camp at M'Poko Airport (November 2016)

Source: touriste.ru/dk1974

Source: Jean-Pierre Ramazani

Source: Louisa Lombard

areas facing each other and further seating areas around a grass football field and running track. It hosts sports but also political and cultural events, such as Pope Francis' mass in November 2015. *ad*

Ledger Plaza Hotel » ↵   CF 09
Avenue de l'Indépendance,
1ᵉʳ Arrondissement, Bangui
2012 (renovation)

Located a few kilometres down from the Notre-Dame Cathedral, along the Avenue de l'Indépendance, and a few minutes away from the University of Bangui, the Ledger Plaza is the Central African capital's most prestigious hotel. The renovated building was inaugurated in 2012 as part of the Laico Hotel Group. As it is separated from the main street by a monumental gate and driveway with numerous parking spaces, it is also one of Bangui's safest spots, and has been spared from the numerous attacks that have shaken the capital over the past years. As such,

the building contrasts with its surroundings: low-rise gated compounds and official buildings. Visitors enter the four-floor building through a large hall with a reception desk. The two perpendicular L-shaped wings that form the ground floor host a gym and spa complex, as well as a restaurant bordering the outdoor swimming pool at the centre of the building. In Bangui's current context, the hotel has become a popular meeting place for the expatriate community and humanitarians who work in the CAR. It also regularly hosts events in its three conference halls. *ad*

Source: Bruno-Serge Gersil Piozza

Source: Bengt Hildebrand

Source: Studio TAMassociati

Emergency Paediatric Centre CF 10

Avenue de l'Indépendance,
1er Arrondissement, Bangui
Studio TAMassociati
2008

After the completion of the Salam Centre for Cardiac Surgery in Sudan, satellite clinics were planned in the nine bordering countries, among them the Central African Republic. Bangui, the capital of a country where the life expectancy averages around fifty years for men and fifty-five for women, was the site of the first of these clinics. This building with a covered area of about 430 m² was assigned to a Central African contractor who was selected through a tendering process. The costs amounted to 515,000 euros.

The Bangui Paediatric Centre is a one-storey building with a courtyard typology and central patio made of quarry brick and a traditional wooden ceiling. Great attention was paid to the materials and heat liabilities of the building. To increase energy performance, the clinic was provided with a high insulating wall, a natural ventilation system of the roof, insulated low-emission glass, and shielded walls. Within the courtyards are a series of sculptures designed and built by local artisans – together with games made from rattan to entertain young patients. The Emergency Paediatric Centre in Bangui offers health assistance to children under the age of fifteen and also provides educational courses on hygiene and health. On average, one hundred children

and twenty pregnant women are treated there every day. The Centre is also equipped with two cardiology stations, where international medical staff periodically screen patients suffering from cardiac problems. Those who require treatment are transported free of charge to the Salam Centre in Sudan. After surgery, patients are given post-operative treatment at the Centre in Bangui, where they receive all of the necessary medicines free of charge.

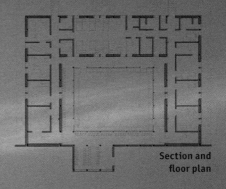

Section and floor plan

Building at a Time of Crisis

Italian architect Riccardo Vannucci on architecture as international cooperation and FAREstudio's experiences in the Central African Republic

Rendered view towards the kitchen block

Over the past few years, building activity in Africa, particularly in the field of social programmes related to international cooperation, has gained increasing attention from the media. This interest is important, but it should be accompanied by a clear definition of the circumstances of the projects so as to avoid reducing the information to a collection of stylish images. Africa is an entire continent, and so some degree of precision should be introduced into discussions about it.

In fact, a combination of geographical and historical facts delineates various regions that are larger than and different from the borders introduced by colonial powers. One of these macro regions includes a number of countries located in the belt between the Sahara Desert and the Gulf of Guinea: Mali, Burkina Faso, Niger, Chad, and the Central African Republic (CAR) all have a legacy inherited from the days of French colonisation, which includes a multi-ethnic and multi-confessional composition, a fragile environment, extreme poverty, social instability, language, and political vulnerability. These countries partially depend on foreign aid, and are therefore involved with international cooperation.

International cooperation operates, among other segments of the economy, in and with the construction industry of the country it supports. These structural conditions are not easy to overcome. In the aforementioned countries, the building industry has a very large informal sector. The system is by definition labour intensive, with low capital investment, and is extremely basic in technical terms. The combination of a few 'modern' products and the remnants of colonial technologies leaves little space for variety in production: the ubiquitous association of concrete structural frames, hollow block masonry, and corrugated iron (or aluminium) sheet roofing abounds. The market is largely based on imported materials and therefore basically unpredictable – particularly with regard to the stability of prices.

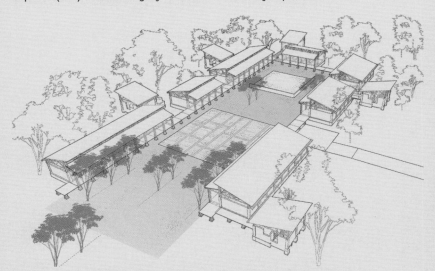

FAREstudio's design for a youth training centre in Sassara, Ouham Prefecture

Source: FAREstudio (all pictures)

Module of FAREstudio's training centre – the only one completed before work ended

CF

All of this conflicts with the procedures for the procurement of constructions (and the related technical services, which include design) adopted by international organisations in response to a logic of accountability, transparency, and equity, within an overall emphasis on decentralisation and capacity building. The result is that the general attitude tends to be conservative (and not only in the construction industry). Both international organisations and local contractors are very reluctant to defy conventional practices, and so combine an excessive realpolitik of the former entities with the intrinsic rigidity of the latter ones. In such a scenario, the CAR holds a particular position. In the 2016 Human Development Index, the country ranked 188th out of 188, and it has been unstable since its independence from France in 1960. Decades of insecurity – particularly between 2004 and 2008, and again more recently with the violent outbreaks of 2015 – have undermined the economy and the structure of society in general. The CAR possesses substantial agricultural and mineral resources, but corruption is widespread and destabilises any potential production.

During the rainy season, the road to the small village of Sassara often becomes impassable

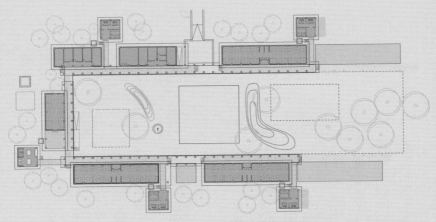

Master plan of the U-shaped configuration and key design strategies (below)

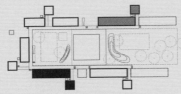

Connection and integration

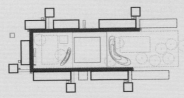

Public and shared space

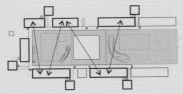

Gender separation and protection

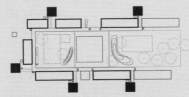

Washing and sanitation

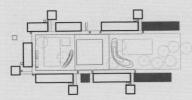

Future expansion potential

FAREstudio's Project

In the CAR in early 2011, a UN agency initiated a project for a training centre for the rehabilitation and social reintegration of children and teenagers with problematic social and cultural backgrounds. In a post-conflict rural area, the project was to work through agricultural and pastoral activities, and its users would include former child soldiers. The scheme was to take advantage of a period of (relative) calm and was located 350 km north of Bangui in the isolated village of Sassara, in Ouham Prefecture. Conditions for building in the location can be extreme: during the rainy season many of the roads deteriorate, making transportation of materials potentially hazardous or simply impossible.

The aim was to provide schooling and training while giving students housing facilities that would allow them to avoid daily back and forth walking trips from their home town or village. The project was supposed to be integrated into a social programme where various activities, from education to entertainment, are combined. The centre was to be run by the Jeunesse Pionnière Nationale (JPN), a local governmental organisation. It was intended as part of a network of similar centres in the rest of the country – a scheme reminiscent of a constellation of training centres for young people which were set up before and after independence in some countries of the former French Equatorial Africa and French West Africa. The programme envisaged

Source: FAREstudio (all pictures)

Rendering of the courtyard space

Inside one of the classrooms

space for 192 youths – male and female students aged between fourteen and twenty-one – and four to six JPN staff. Besides the managing of a large congregation of teens with a particular combination of needs based on traumatic experiences, gender segregation was an issue that had to be taken into consideration in the building. Given the nature of the community and the local culture (not necessarily only related to religious background), it is common that boys and girls do not share the same spaces at the same time. In general, they are required to be strictly separated. The staff normally insist on being clearly detached from the centre's other residents, and they pay special attention to mutual distance as a sign of respect.

Design Strategy

FAREstudio's design strategy was based on a couple of main assumptions. The first was that, in contrast to the layout commonly adopted in such centres, where every function is housed in a detached building and the whole appears as a scattered collection of heterogeneous volumes, the complex should embody and enforce the idea of community, with a strong formal and spatial identity. This is by far the main characteristic of the project. As a consequence, the complex is made up of separate pavilions, which are arranged so as to form a unique entity. One continuous passage connects all the buildings. The resulting shape is an elongated 'U' with a central courtyard.

One end of this yard is open for future extension and for direct contact with the landscape, while the other is reserved for shared facilities. Future expansion of the complex can take place by filling the gaps between buildings or by extending the structure. In terms of safety and security, monitoring is much easier when every part of the location is in sight.

The second assumption concerned the construction technique. A sense of unity was stressed through the use of a single spatial module that was repeated in order to form the entire building. The mode of production was based on standardisation and, to a certain degree, prefabrication, because of various considerations, which were primarily economic, but also aimed at implementing a form of quality control throughout the process. The replicability of the solutions was part of the architects' own agenda and was added to the official (very vague) programme.

A further consideration for the project was sanitation. Bathrooms and kitchens were included in an integrated network

Visualisation of the proposed prototype to test all main elements of the construction

Source: FAREstudio (all pictures)

Wooden trusses make up the module's roof **Earth bricks were produced on-site**

aimed at optimising the use of water while impacting on the personal behaviour of the users. The bathrooms and kitchen blocks are the only elements that were not part of the main volume, although they originated from the use of the same components.

Critical Issues

The project was beset by many difficulties. Initially, the complexity of the building was underestimated, and the construction was possibly regarded as a sort of annoying obligation rather than an opportunity – to the point that the training centre was designed without a comprehensive functional and pedagogical programme; these two aspects were seen as mere quantities to put together. Innovation was far from being welcomed by those involved in the process – this applied to the local beneficiaries and to the system as a whole, and concerned every aspect of construction, typology, technology, and morphology.

In these circumstances a powerful aesthetic prejudice can easily be experienced. A disproportionate consideration can also be given to some features such as air conditioning – (often) a status symbol more than a real need – or the use of corrugated aluminium roofing as a demonstration of 'modernity'. The realisation of a full-scale mock-up to test the proposed solutions, which would have been decisive in terms of planning, was rejected, because it was not included in the original scope of work. Procurement turned out to be a very complex matter, as it was stretched between the formal obligations of an international

organisation and the reality of a contractor who was not properly equipped to face those obligations.

From the beginning of the project it was thought that JPN would act from a favoured position – a feeling that was confirmed by the results of the tendering phase. From this point of view, the process was managed 'according to the rules' but substantially driven from above. This fact was particularly relevant with regard to the duration of the tender process, which greatly exceeded what was originally planned – to the extent that the start date for the work was shifted to a period that was not exactly suitable for construction: May, the beginning of the rainy season.

After the commencement of building work in July 2012, a first module was realised in order to verify the consistency and feasibility of all of the technical options. Activity on site turned out to be easier than envisaged, and the product was largely satisfactory. Unfortunately, in November 2012, soon after the completion of the module, work stopped due to the uprising of Séléka, a coalition of rebel groups that took over towns in the central and northern regions of the country, where Sassara is located. Since then, the construction site has been abandoned and nothing has been heard from there in the last years. Only a few low resolution images, taken before evacuation, are available to testify to the situation. A ghost town surrounded by forest, the site is a sad metaphor for the uncertainty and ambiguity that control international cooperations, and possibly even the meaning of design activity, in an age of improper globalisation.

Construction of the first wall of the first and only module built in Sassara, Ouham Prefecture

Foundations for the module; part of the project's goal was to train and employ local workers

Cameroon

The coordinators of the Cameroon chapter, Diane Chehab and Epée Ellong, would like to thank: Amélie Essesse *(ae)*, architect and expert in African traditional architecture and heritage, and women builders – she provided the information and the photos of Mousgoum architecture in northern Cameroon; Jean Ngougo, deputy government delegate in the urban community of Yaoundé, who provided insight into Yaoundé's contemporary architecture; Théodore Moluh, head of the architecture department of the Fine Arts Institute of Foumban, who provided much insight into Foumban, as well as Bandjoun; and Stéphane Akoa, sociologist, who provided the history of Yaoundé.

Epée Ellong, architect, born in Douala, Cameroon, in 1952. Graduated from the École Nationale Supérieure des Beaux-Arts, Paris, France, in 1980. In 1983 he and Diane Chehab opened an architecture firm in Douala, Cameroon. He has completed many building projects in Africa and the USA. *(ee)*

Diane Chehab, architect, born 1954 in Brookline, Massachusetts, USA. Graduated from École Nationale Supérieure des Beaux-Arts, Paris, in 1980. In 1983 she and Epée Ellong opened an architecture firm in Douala, Cameroon. She has completed many building projects in Cameroon. *(dc)*

Mark D. DeLancey, American scholar, born 1973. Graduated in 2004 with an MA and a PhD from Harvard University. Researches Cameroonian architecture and Mauritanian manuscripts. Associate professor of History of Art and Architecture at DePaul University, Chicago, Illinois, USA.

The Reunification Monument in Cameroon's capital, Yaoundé (Armand Salomon, 1974)
Source: Mark Fischer

Introduction

Diane Chehab, Epée Ellong

Cameroon, like many African countries, was created through European decisions. In 1884 chunks of Africa were cut up to divide and conquer. This makes it difficult to write about the evolution of Cameroonian architecture as a whole. Traditionally, climate and culture determined architecture and types of construction. Traditional Cameroonian architecture has rich and varied styles.

The country has a diverse landscape and is known by many as 'Africa in Miniature'. The north is dry, with a mostly Muslim population, and the south is tropical, with a majority of Christians, alongside followers of traditional religions. Traditional architecture reflects this dichotomy. In the north, earth walls are covered with straw, or structures are completely made of earth, and round shapes prevail. In the south, walls are built with woven palm fronds, pisé, and bamboo, and often covered with a second layer of palm fronds.

Western Cameroonian construction uses similar materials to the other southern Cameroonian regions: palm fronds, bamboo, and mud brick. However, each specific region of the country has its own shapes. Bamileke traditional architecture – in what was called the 'Grasslands' by the Germans, for its lush landscape – is particularly noteworthy for its beauty. Bamileke traditional architecture is renowned for its soaring structures and high roofs, made of bamboo lattices, covered by woven straw, and mud brick walls. Intricately carved wood columns support and surround the homes of Cameroonian dignitaries. As time went on and new construction materials appeared, the soaring roofs became metal pyramids; the higher the number of pyramidal roofs, set over a concrete block structure, the higher the rank of the occupants in the society.

To the north, the most striking architecture belongs to the Mousgoum ethnic group. They created giant cone-shaped,

Source: Diane Chehab

Modern architecture in Douala

self-supporting domes made of successive mortar rolls (clay earth mixed with water, straw, and dung). Each dome forms one room – one for each family member – with a chimney on at the top for ventilation. These structures are fast disappearing; today there are a couple of copies that have been built just for tourists. Europeans started trading in Cameroon in the seventeenth century. In the nineteenth century, having settled, they brought along their construction methods and lifestyles. Cameroonian territory became a German colony in 1884, at which point several towns were built. The most distinct architecture came from the Sito in Buea (near Mount Cameroon, around an hour's drive from Douala). Walls and roofing were made of corrugated metal, but the homes looked very similar to the European houses.

Roads created by European settlers disrupted traditional life. The three original villages of Douala only contained courtyards through which goods and people circulated, and these same courtyards were used for ceremonial purposes such as funeral wakes. Nowadays the wakes still take place, and are known for blocking the roads.

Source: iStock/Micky Wiswedel

Urban landscape of Douala, Cameroon's largest city and commercial capital

In around 1910, the Germans built the Woermann House, as well as the Mandessi Bell Villas in Douala. Both are surrounded by covered galleries with open walls, for ventilation and protection from the hot and humid climate. King Manga Bell also built a palace, nicknamed La Pagode, in 1905 in Bonanjo, Douala. The layered structure resembles its namesake, a pagoda. The Bell family lived in it until 1914, when Rudolf Duala Manga Bell, the German-educated heir to the throne, was hanged by the Germans. La Pagode still belongs to the Bell family, and is now one of Douala's architectural icons.

After Germany's defeat in World War I, Cameroon became a French and British protectorate. Amongst other buildings in Douala, the French built the Trésor Public (1920), the Palais de Justice (1920), the Chambre de Commerce (1928); in Yaoundé, they built the Dispensaire de Yaoundé (1930) and the former Presidential Palace (1932). They also built the Centre Climatique de Dschang (1942), in western Cameroon. Americans also contributed to colonial construction and built the Foulassi Presbyterian Church (1944) in Ebolowa – birthplace of the Cameroonian national hymn.

Colonial houses were differently arranged than traditional African ones, and gradually, some of the organisational features were adopted by the local European-educated population. Cameroonians began building with concrete blocks and metal roofing, or if there were insufficient funds for concrete, they used *kalabot*, leftover wood from shipping containers; the word may have been derived from 'car aboard', in relation to the containers of imported automobiles.

The National Order of Architects of Cameroon (ONAC) was founded in 1962 by a group of Cameroonian architects who had studied at the École des Beaux-Arts in Paris, France. The first official Cameroonian architects, registered from 1962 to 1969, were Jacques Nsangue Akwa, Richard Bebey Black, Armand Salomon – a French-born architect who spent his entire career working and living in Cameroon – and J. William Noumbissi. Today the ONAC includes ca. 300 members. Cameroon has two architecture schools: the École Supérieure Spéciale d'Architecture du Cameroun (ESSACA) in Yaoundé (founded in 2011 by Jean-Jacques Kotto), and the Architecture Department of the University of Dschang.

The city plan for Yaoundé, Cameroon's capital, was drawn up in 1962 by Armand Salomon. Douala, the economic capital and main port, located at the estuary of the Wouri River, was subject to several government planning commissions over the years. However, the influx of populations from all over the country saw the city grow increasingly larger, its unorganised boundaries extending ever further from the city centre.

Officially, every building has to be designed and stamped by an architect listed on the Cameroonian Board of Architects. In reality, however, the general population often relies on draftspeople, or contractors, as they are less expensive, and then have the drawings signed by registered architects. In the higher spheres, foreign architects often design large buildings – especially those financed by overseas sources – that are then signed by Cameroonian architects for a fee. The architects who are not interested in making a living by signing other architects' projects keep their practices going with government contracts – which unfortunately do not all go to Cameroonian architects, and invoices are not always paid – or with smaller private clients. Some have emigrated for other opportunities or for a chance to make a better living.

A movement towards more climate-oriented construction is afoot. Progress is slow. Research is happening at grass roots level and in architecture school workshops, in order to find inexpensive ways to design and work with the climate.

Source: Carsten ten Brink

Central Station, Ngaoundéré (1974)

It is difficult to say where Cameroonian architecture is headed. However, the number of national architects is rapidly increasing, especially with the advent of local architectural degrees from local architecture schools. The presence of these architecture schools, albeit with their reputation still in the making, should help reach out to better educate the public as to the role of architects and the general profession, but the question of whether there will be enough available work with decent wages remains.

Source: Ollivier Girard/CIFOR

Construction works in downtown Yaoundé in 2013

Yaoundé

Cameroon's capital is situated on a hilly plateau between two rivers and within a rainforest which is quickly receding
Source: Ville Miettinen

Yaoundé is the capital of Cameroon, and unusually, is situated some distance from the country's coast. Known as the Town of Seven Hills, it is located on a hilly plateau between the Nyong and Sanaga rivers, and amid a rapidly disappearing tropical rainforest. The city's amorphous urban structure is largely a result of its topography. Its centre is characterised by a number of atypical administrative buildings,

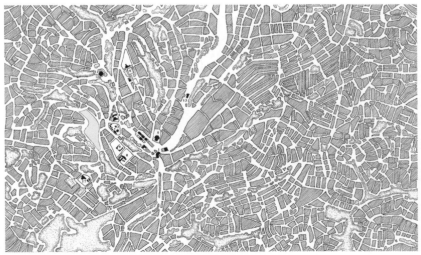

Source: Africa Drawn Project

Yaoundé's amorphous structure stems predominantly from its topography

arranged along central axes that flow from Place Ahmadou Ahidjo. From there, the nebulous urban form is organically shaped and limited by the natural topography.

Originally, the city was an outpost called Jaunde (the name came from a misunderstanding of the local ethnic group's name), created in 1889 by the Germans Richard Kund and Hans Tappenbeck for scientific observation purposes and as a starting point for further expeditions. After Germany's World War I defeat, part of Cameroon became a French protectorate. Yaoundé became Cameroon's capital in 1921.

During the colonial period, Yaoundé was divided between a 'White' and a 'Black' neighbourhood. The White area was well equipped and organised, and strategically situated on the two hills on either side of the Abiergue River. In 1923, the non-White parts that had been located in the 'White' defined area were relocated elsewhere. A camp for the indigenous civil servants, named Madagascar, was created to the northwest. The Black neighbourhood was left to be managed by its local population. Yaoundé became an important administrative region, and grew rapidly in the postwar period, as workers were needed for the public projects launched under the French development scheme. Around the time of independence in 1960, Armand Salomon created the first city plan, and Yaoundé experienced a second growth phase, reflected in its rapid present-day increase in population density. The city has expanded as an administrative, service, and commercial centre. It has a number of small manufacturing and processing industries, including tobacco, dairy, and lumber, and is an important market for the country's agricultural production. The 1980s economic crisis saw the layering of the informal sector affect the sprawling urban form. Thus there are many randomly built neighbourhoods without basic infrastructure. *dc*

Written with input from:
  Stéphane Akoa, Olivier Iyabo Mandjek, Marie Morelle

Douala

Douala is the largest city in Cameroon, the commercial capital, and the capital of the Littoral Region. This economically influential port city is located on the banks of the Wouri River. It was initially three villages established by Douala families along the river banks, as the ultimate settlement factor in Douala was water – a source of life, wealth, trade, and fishing. The villages of Bell (*Bonandjo*), Akwa (*Bona Ku*), and Deido (*Bona Ebele*) followed the course of the left bank.

The name 'Cameroon' originates from the arrival of the Portuguese – the first Europeans – in the fifteenth century, at the Wouri River estuary. As there was an abundance of crustaceans, known as *mbea towe*, the river was named *Rio dos Camarões* (River of Prawns). With the arrival of the Portuguese, British, and Germans, this area became the headquarters for colonial enterprises over several centuries. The city rapidly developed as a commercial and political hub for the German administration during their settlement; and was eventually renamed Douala. Douala is divided into seven districts: Akwa, Bassa, Bonabéri, Bonapriso, Bonanjo, Deïdo, and New Bell. Akwa is the business district and Bonanjo is the administrative district (historically referred to as Plateau Joss). The Dorian Plan (1959) provided Douala with a framework for improvement. It was designed for an urban population of 300,000 inhabitants, and primarily focused on the highway, remodelling some of the areas and creating new neighbourhoods in order to enhance the city's use of space and make it more breathable. The establishment of a network of roads was planned to enable inter-district communication; the railroad was moved to the eastern part; a major road was created from east to west between Douala and Bonabéri; and industries were clustered around the port where a second dock was built. Both riverbanks are linked by the Wouri Bridge, which also gives access to all the western points. However, Douala is poorly equipped to accommodate the rapidly increasing urban population, affecting the city's services provision. In 2015, Douala officially had a population close to four million. Formerly empty neighbourhoods are now bustling; sidewalks have been taken over by microstores and food stalls. A few multistorey buildings have started to sprout up, but most of the growth has been horizontal, transforming the commercial capital into a sprawling city. *dc/ee*

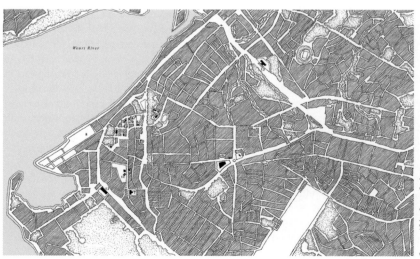

The sprawling city of Douala on the Wouri River

Source: Africa Drawn Project

CM

Contrasts between low and multistorey buildings in Douala

Source: Alvise Forcellini

View over one of Douala's business districts

Source: iStock/Mtcurado

King Njoya's throne room in the Palace of the Bamoun Sultans,
which still serves as the royal residence today

Modernity and Tradition in Cameroonian Architecture in the Colonial Period

Mark D. DeLancey

In the study of African architecture, the term 'traditional' is frequently elided with 'pre-colonial'. However, as Shirine Hamadeh has made clear in the case of North African cities, these two terms are quite distinct, as the concept of the 'traditional' lacks any relation to time, while the 'pre-colonial' focuses on a time, albeit with the further implication of some sort of culture purity.[1] The pitfalls of these terms are nowhere made clearer than in the study of the colonial period in which 'modernity' is just as problematically equated with the colonising power. Yet colonial architecture must be considered in light of the context of the colony just as the architecture of the colonised also reflects contemporaneous circumstances. As was the case in the pre-colonial period, Cameroonian rulers continued to play the role of intercessor with the outside world, bearing primary responsibility for innovation through selective adoption of the foreign. This essay focuses on Cameroonian responses to colonial architecture, particularly as seen in the palaces of local rulers.

One especially striking example is the Palace of the Bell Kings, often referred to as La Pagode, built in the coastal city of Douala in 1905. Douala was the early political capital of the German colony of Kamerun, and to this day remains Cameroon's main port and its economic capital. This multistorey building towered over its surroundings, including a German prefabricated structure created for King Rudolf Duala Manga Bell's father, King August Manga Ndumbé Bell.[2] The use of durable material, arches on heavy pillars on the ground floor, and slender columns on the upper floors, the absence of an internal courtyard, and a cupola at the apex all spoke the language of German colonial architecture, yet in an ensemble clearly distinguishable from colonial examples. These features served to display the ruler's familiarity with the architectural language of the coloniser, yet at the same time also indicated his independence from its rote copying.

Only a few years later in 1908, King Ibrahim Mbombuo Njoya, ruler of the powerful inland Bamoun Kingdom, had

Source: Mark D. DeLancey (all pictures)

The Palace of the Bamoun Sultans in Foumban (1917–1922)

Source: Mark D. DeLancey (all pictures)

New palace added by King Achirimbi II, Bafut (ca. 1940s)

a residence in the European style constructed behind the palace of his father in Foumban. Unfortunately, this palace from 1908 no longer stands, but it is known from a few rare photographs that depict a multi-storey brick structure with heavy pillars on the ground floor and slender columns on the upper storeys.[3] Just like for the Palace of King Manga Bell in Douala, the use of galleries which completely surrounded the exterior of the building was an element borrowed from German colonial architecture developed for the tropics. This building was erected after a trip that King Njoya took to the coast to meet with the German colonial governor. The multiple hipped roofs, projecting masses, and heavy multi-storey brick construction of the palace appear to be modelled specifically on the old governor's residence in Douala, which later served as the District Office and which is now destroyed. In the book that he wrote entitled *History and Customs of the Bamoum*, King Njoya described the two metal conduits leading from the upper floor to the lower into which he could pour water for his servants to wash with or palm wine to fill their cups. This architectural experiment was clearly designed to astonish both his subjects and the colonial officials as King Njoya declared that, 'All, great and small will say, "King Njoya surpasses all men in intelligence."'[4]

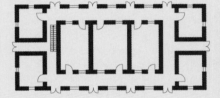

Palace of Achirimbi II: ground floor plan

In 1917, King Njoya initiated the construction of a new palace, which is still standing and serves as the ruler's residence to this day. The courtier Ibrahim Njoya was in charge of its design and construction. This building was a much more sophisticated response to not only the German style, but also local architecture and that of the Islamic polities to the north. Once again, brick, heavy pillars and arcades, external galleries, tripartite massing, employing towers and a lack of interior courtyards, all pointed to the European model. On the other hand, the semicircular eave of the audience courtyard in his father's palace was reflected in the central tower. Likewise, the tripartite division of the façade recalled the previous palace's similar division into a central royal axis with entrances to either side for royal and nonroyal courtiers. The four columned throne room behind the central tower on the one hand frequently evokes a sense of the Romanesque in European viewers, perhaps attributable to models taken

Palace of the Bell Kings in Douala, which is also known as La Pagode (1905)

from illustrated magazines that King Njoya had seen.[5] On the other hand, this hall reflects a type of entrance, known as a *sooro*, employed in architecture of the Islamic polities to the north, signifying King Njoya's conversion to Islam, his alliance with the Islamic state of Banyo, and his desire to obtain the more *laissez-faire* relations that the Germans held with Islamic rulers in northern Cameroon.

Just as astonishing and complex, a relationship between the colonial and traditional architecture is displayed at the nearby kingdom of Bafut in the Northwest Region. A German attack in 1907 resulted in the destruction of the Bafut palace and its king being exiled one year. In 1908–1910, at the same time that King Njoya was building his first brick palace, the Germans came to an agreement with the exiled king of Bafut and rebuilt his palace out of brick, with a tile roof. The long, low, brick structures, with porches made of broad eaves set on pillars, were soon after emulated in wood and thatch construction at the nearby kingdom of Kom, and numerous other regional palaces thereafter. In the 1940s, King Achirimbi II of Bafut added a new two-storey structure with a hipped roof and a central lantern on a hill overlooking his German-built palace. The interior features a hallway on both levels that completely surrounds three chambers, and two more chambers at either end on both levels. The plan is essentially that of many German colonial structures in Douala which were designed to protect central rooms from the harsh sun. Indeed, it is so closely related to its models that most have assumed that it was in fact built by a German architect.

These few examples are illuminating because of the degree to which a style of architecture developed for colonial authorities was adopted and turned to new purposes by local elites. These rulers at times sought to meld local with colonial architecture, at other times created structures that seem entirely novel in their expressions, or wholly adopted the colonial style hook, line, and sinker. This diversity in fact points to the extraordinary complexity of Cameroonian responses to the colonial situation, a complexity which has only just begun to be explored with any seriousness.

Notes
1   Shirine Hamadeh, 'Creating the Traditional City: A French Project', in Nezar AlSayyad (ed.), *Forms of Dominance: On the Architecture and Urbanism of the Colonial Enterprise* (Aldershot, 1992), pp. 241–259.
2   Michel Viallet, *Douala autrefois: Recueil de cartes postales anciennes de Douala* (Biarritz, 2002), p. 56.
3   See for example Christraud M. Geary and Adamou Ndam Njoya, *Mandou Yénou: Photographies du pays Bamoun, royaume ouest-africain, 1902–1915* (Munich, 1985), p. 71.
4   Sultan Njoya, *Histoire et coutumes des Bamum [History and Customs of the Bamoum]*, trans. Henri Martin (Dakar, 1952), p. 66.
5   Christraud M. Geary, *Images from Bamum: German Colonial Photography at the Court of King Njoya, Cameroon, West Africa, 1902–1915* (Washington, DC, 1988), p. 69.

Mousgoum Dwellings CM 01
Maroua, Far North Region

The traditional architectural structure of the Mousgoum people is known as a *teulek*. These structures are mostly located in the north of Cameroon, near the city of Maroua. They are built as a community effort, by men, women, and children, each participating in a specific aspect of the construction. The building technique is similar to pottery. There is no foundation, and no framework. Earth, a grass called *souksouky*, cow and/or goat dung are mixed with water and made into balls. A perfect circle is drawn on the ground, using a spike and string; the circumference can run from 3 m to 20 m and determines the height of the dome, between 5 m and 15 m. The dome is built, row by row, along a slope decided upon by the builders and influenced by the base, the directions of rains, with the goal of creating a stable structure. As the structure rises, the slope becomes sharper. At the top is a small round opening used as a lightwell and for evacuating smoke. A rope attached to a cap allows occupants to close the opening from inside. Another rope, on the outside, is used for assistance when climbing the dome. Construction takes about six months, as when the wall is 1.4 m high, the builders let the structure rest for about a month, so the earthen mix can settle. The *teulek* is a handmade masterpiece. Unfortunately, there are few left standing. *ae*

Source: Amélie Essesse (all pictures)

Chefferie de Bandjoun CM 02
Bandjoun, West Region
2015 (renovation/rebuilding)

The traditional Chefferie de Bandjoun (the homestead of a Bandjoun chief), located in the western highlands of Cameroon, consists of a group of generally square houses with a single habitable unit. After the colonisation of the territory, houses began to have multiple rooms (living room, dining room, and bedrooms), replacing the single room house. The builders of the traditional house showed ingenuity in using the square shape at the base, and fitting a circular roof on top of the walls. The roof also has a very high peak to facilitate the flow of rainwater, since rainfall in western Cameroon can be very heavy. A thick layer of straw – about 30 to 50 cm – covers the roof structure, preventing water infiltration during heavy rainfall. Carved columns are positioned directly underneath the roof eaves and follow the circumference of the roof. The Bandjoun are part of the larger Bamileke ethnic group. In Bamileke everyday life, the spiritual dimension has always been important. Therefore, carvings on the pillars are made by professionals who know which signs to use (or not) in order to bless the house and its occupants. These professional wood craftsmen recount stories about the group's ancestors, describe the general social activities, such as hunting, or the women's activities between their kitchen and the river. These sculpted pillars also helped determine the inhabitants' level of nobility.

Nobles and dignitaries lived relatively far from the king, but the architecture of their huts remained similar to his: generally a one to three bedroom hut. The foundation was laid dry with cut stone. The walls were usually made of bamboo panels woven together with ropes. Traditional houses usually have a life span of forty to fifty years, when they are well built. Maintaining the building generally consists of replacing the worn out straw on the roof. A new palace was built at the Bandjoun Chefferie, but has nothing in common with traditional architecture, since it was also built with modern construction materials. A few traditional houses are being rebuilt as well, after some of the original ones caught fire in 2004. A new banquet hall was designed by Théodore Moluh. At the time of writing, construction of these buildings was expected to be finished shortly. *dc/ee*

Source: Carsten ten Brink (all pictures)

Source: iStock/Mtcurado

Palace of the Bell Kings CM 03
Administrative District, Bonanjo
Quarter, Douala, Littoral Region
1905

The Palace of the Bell Kings was designed
to be the residence of the Manga Bell
family, a family of traditional kings in
Douala. King August Manga Ndumbé Bell,

who had the house built, had studied in Bristol, England, at a time when
Orientalist architecture was in vogue;
hence the pagoda shape. The building
was composed in layers, and its nickname,
La Pagode, was used by the French author Louis-Ferdinand Céline who visited
Cameroon in 1916. It is a historical landmark building, and is situated in what is

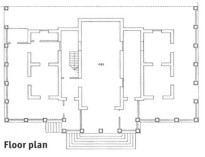

Floor plan

Section

Source: Wolfgang Lauber (left and right)

1966

Source: Jean-Marie Bidaux

Source: Diane Chehab

Centre Climatique de Dschang CM 04
Dschang, Ménoua, West Region
1942

The Centre Climatique de Dschang was built in 1942 as a holiday resort for French soldiers and colonial government employees. Dschang is located in West Cameroon, in territory historically inhabited by the Bamileke ethnic group, so the roof is modelled after traditional Bamileke roofs. This area, at an altitude of 1,380 m, was chosen because the climate is cooler and drier than in many other regions. It is as close as the Cameroonian climate can be to a temperate, European-style climate – the bungalows even include fireplaces. The main building houses the restaurant, kitchen, and administrative offices. It is accompanied by a series of round bungalows, a pool, and gardens. Nowadays, the Centre Climatique is a hotel, with fifty rooms distributed among twenty-three bungalows, and used by business travellers or tourists. It is located close to the University Centre of Dschang, a school specialised in agriculture, and partnered with universities in other countries, such as the Florida Agricultural and Mechanical University in the USA.   *ee*

now the administrative centre of Douala. The palace is constructed in brick, which is covered in cement. Its roof and floor tiles are green. King Ndumbé Bell died in 1908, after having lived in his palace for only three years. He was followed by his son and heir, Rudolf Duala Manga Bell, who rebelled against the Germans, who in turn hanged him in August 1914. Later, his son, Alexander Douala Manga Bell, opted not to live in the palace. The treaty signed by the Manga Bell rulers and the Germans in 1884 had confirmed land ownership by the original local population. Today, the building is still the property of the Douala Manga Bell family, and an architectural icon in Douala. The compound is known as Le Parc des Princes and it today serves as a restaurant and an art space.   *dc*

Source: Carsten ten Brink

Palace of the Bamoun Sultans `CM 05`
Foumban, Noun Department,
West Region
King Njoya
1917

The Bamoun people, originally from the Tikar ethnic group, formed their own kingdom about 500 years ago. Upon contact with the German colonisers, the seventeenth *mfon* (meaning king in the Bamoun language) decided to give his people additional tools by creating an original alphabet and even a new language that was in use for specific rituals, in 1895. In 1917, the *mfon* built a new palace with sturdier materials than the wood and bamboo originally used, similar to materials used to build other chiefdoms in Western Cameroon. The palace is built primarily with brick (made locally) and is three levels high. The central royal hall, used as throne room, but also for ceremonial functions and large meetings, is two levels high, with large brick columns covered with cement (the bottom part wrapped in a traditional blue and white fabric), and a wooden staircase on each side of the room leading to other parts of the building. Intermediate floors are also made of wood, whereas the ground floors are covered in terracotta tiles. The roof was originally covered with tiles, but crows created too much damage and the roof is now protected with painted metal. Photography is now forbidden inside the palace, because photographs were used to plan a robbery in 1997. The third level of the palace runs the entire length of the building and currently hosts the museum, showing artefacts from the past three sultans. Njoya converted to Islam around 1918; Foumban is mostly Muslim, but there is a substantial Christian population, as well. In a few years' time, the museum is slated to move next door to a new building which is currently under construction. In the front yard, a painted wall shows the history of the kingdom: the rulers are all listed, and so are the colonial administrators from Germany and France. *dc*

Source: Mark D. DeLancey

List of rulers in the Bamoun dynasty

Source: Diane Chehab

Yaoundé City Hall CM 06

Place de l'Indépendance, Yaoundé
Armand Salomon
1982

Yaoundé City Hall (Hôtel de Ville de Yaoundé) was built in 1982 on a large plot of land of approximately 8 ha, which lies to the north of Independence Square. The building's structure is of reinforced concrete. It is composed of an elongated rectangular slab connected to a circular volume. The façade is punctuated by thin, vertical concrete ridges, decorated with red marble fragments, and an acrylic glass mosaic – designed by

Source: iStock/Bob Scuff

the architect – set on an aluminium structure, which serves as solar protection. The wide terraces that line the first floor protrude from the façade in such a manner that they serve as an awning for the ground floor entrance. The interior walls are polished raw concrete. Columns in raw concrete achieved via a laminated hull, or covered with stone, and sculpted wood panels add to the interior decor. Hall lighting is provided by transparent globe lamps. There are several entrances and grand halls leading to the various government offices. Each end of the building seems to be standing in rectangular pools of water, which provide a cool exterior atmosphere. The vast marching grounds, long rows of trees, and large planted spaces that stand to the south of the city hall's estate are accessed by an imposing iron gate and add a certain baroque style to the whole. The building's French architect, Armand Salomon, arrived in Cameroon for the first time in around 1956, when Cameroon was still under French rule. He was the only foreigner to ever be a licensed architect in Cameroon. Although of European descent, he felt it was important to create architecture that was inspired by African design. The Hôtel de Ville was one of the most successful examples.   *dc*

Douala Train Station

CM 07

Bessengue-Deido, Douala,
Littoral Region
*Jacques Nsangue Akwa,
Emilien Doualla Bell*
1980

Douala Train Station was inaugurated in
1982, and is located in the Bessengue district of Deido, Douala. Bessengue-Deido
is not part of downtown Douala – in other
words, not part of the colonial administrative neighbourhood. However, it is increasingly central, due to the city's horizontal expansion. The architects are
Jacques Nsangue Akwa, the first architect registered in Cameroon, and Emilien
Doualla Bell. The central space is the

main concourse, which runs almost the
entire length of the building. Ventilation
was an important factor in a hot and humid city; air conditioning was ruled out
because of the cost implications. Thus
the air flow was carefully studied to keep
the temperature and humidity comfortable. The front façade is mostly glass. An
exterior clock tower shows the time on all
four sides. Construction is concrete, with
wood and tile, and below the concourse's
ceiling are decorative aluminium slats.
The ground floor contains the cafeteria,
a newspaper kiosk, a small police station,
and the ticket counters. The floor tiles
change colour a metre before the counters to indicate where the queue starts.
The offices are on a mezzanine floor.   *dc*

Source: Mark Fischer (all pictures)

Source: Diane Chehab (all pictures)

BEAC Building   CM 08
Boulevard du 20 Mai, Bafoussam
Armand Salomon
1985

The Cameroonian BEAC headquarters are in Yaoundé, but the iconic building of the Bank of Central African States (BEAC), was built in Bafoussam, in 1985, when offices were decentralised (there are also offices in Limbe and Garoua). Annual meetings are held in a different BEAC building every year. The material used for the building's structure is reinforced concrete. The façade is decorated with different types of marble, mainly shaped in an African style; the fence's ironwork discretely replicates this theme. The rooftop solar protections resemble an inverted Bamileke style, on slim columns, carrying the gourd-shaped structures, as they traditionally carry the roofing of the Bamileke chiefs' huts. There are two levels, and an accessible upstairs terrace with gardens. On the ground floor is a large reception hall for the public, as well as space for the technical services (bill sorting), and safes (one third of the surface). The executive offices are on the upper level. Interior decoration consists of tropical wood plywood marqueterie for the conference room, in themes designed by the architect. On the upstairs patio stands a sculpture of a traditional king, made by the Tikar people (who also come from Western Cameroon). The BEAC was intent on showing local and foreign art in all of their buildings. *dc/ee*

CCEI Bank ⋩   CM 09
Douala (demolished)
Epée Ellong
1993

The CCEI Bank's first national head offices in Yaoundé was designed in 1993, by Epée Ellong, to resemble the Douala headquarters owned by Cameroonian business people. Bank tellers and public spaces used to be on the ground floor, and the administrative offices and meeting rooms were on the first floor. For the bank it was a question of pride to have its buildings designed by Cameroonian architects, in an African style. The façade was made of reinforced concrete, with brise-soleil in the shapes of stylised Bamileke statue motifs. The headquarters were located in the banking neighbourhood of downtown Douala. In 2013, twenty years after it was constructed, the building was torn down to make space for a much larger edifice, as the bank had expanded its operations since its inception. *dc*

Source: Epée Ellong (all pictures)

CM

Nzeulie Residence
Bandja, West Region
Epée Ellong
1994

CM 10

Many Cameroonians who have made their livelihood in Douala or Yaoundé build a residence in their home village; the size of this house depends on their means and family circumstances. Gabriel Nzeulie is a Cameroonian businessman and entrepreneur, based in Douala. His home village is Bandja, near Bafoussam in the west of Cameroon. In his case, it was important to be able to have several spaces in which to receive visitors from the village. For this, there are two round living rooms at the entrance of the house, on the ground floor. The main portion of the ground floor includes a large living area, a central kitchen, and on each side, a separate home for each of the owner's two wives. The upstairs is reserved for the homeowner's bedroom and personal living area. In the back, in a partial basement facing the valley, is a large vault for the family graves. The residence spans 1,600 m²; its structure is in tremor-resistant reinforced concrete. The shape of the house, from the front, is reminiscent of a person opening his arms to welcome life and humanity. The exterior wall coverings are tiled in a pattern similar to Dogon lizard shapes: a symbol of intelligence and astuteness. Interior floor coverings are imported Italian marble; the outside doors are bulletproof glass with aluminium frames. At the gate to the compound, there are two contemporary guard posts in the shape of traditional Bamileke architecture. *dc/ee*

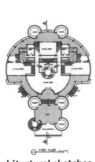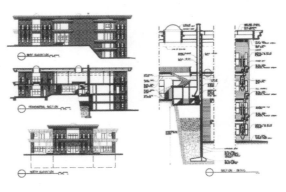

Architectural sketches

Modern façade in Douala
Source: iStock/Mtcurado

Source: Isabelle Ngoundo Black

Indigo Building ⌃ | CM 11 |

Rue Toyota/Rue Tokoto, Bonapriso
Quarter, Douala, Littoral Region
Isabelle Ngoundo Black
2011

This building was initially required to host commercial spaces and offices on the first two levels, and apartments on the four higher levels. This was later changed to offices on all floors, which explains why the building has balconies on the upper levels as well as an atrium connecting the ground and first floor levels. The building has tiled floors and suspended plaster tile ceilings, with all the included electronic cabling, as well as optical fibre, television cabling, and so forth, giving each tenant the flexibility to lay out the space according to their needs. The structure is concrete with concrete block walls. The aluminium roofing is supported by steel framework. The façade that faces the street is covered with flat aluminium composite panels that are lacquered in an indigo blue. The less visible walls are painted. Side and rear walls are covered in glazed tiles. Much thought was put into the main doors – aluminium frames – the same colour as for the double-glazed window frames. Structural interior columns were covered with fibre cement in order to hide the electric and digital cabling. The common areas, such as elevator banks, were covered in wood-style panels with aluminium junction points. *pa*

Source: Diane Chehab

OAPI Building ⌃ | CM 12 |

Place de la Préfecture, Yaoundé
Muhamad Machia
2015

The new Organisation Africaine de la Propriété Intellectuelle (OAPI) headquarters are in Yaoundé. This building marries tradition and modernity through its shape and the construction techniques, and materials used. It covers 9,600 m², and includes three basement levels, with 120 parking spaces, a ground floor and seven upper levels. The central vertical core houses a staircase and two elevators, which offer a view of the hanging gardens located on the west side of the building. The exterior finishes are tile and glass. Visitors enter through a grand hall, and the conference room has 200 seats. Offices are located on levels two through six, while levels seven and eight are reserved for the executive management and the High Commission of Appeal. *dc*

Equatorial Guinea

Laida Memba Ikuga, expert on development and execution of infrastructure and urban planning projects in Equatorial Guinea. Holds an MSc in architecture. Has documented and made interventions in historical heritage sites in Equatorial Guinea. Co-director of the Patrimonio Guinea 2020 project. *(cc)*

Montserrat Villaverde Rey, lecturer at La Salle School of Architecture, Ramón Llull University, Barcelona. Expert in research and management of architecture and urban heritage. Head of research at the RehabiMed Association and co-director of the Patrimonio Guinea 2020 project. *(cc)*

Dominica Nchama Minang Ntang, architecture graduate of the Universidad Politécnica de Madrid, Spain. She began practising in Madrid in 2005 and then in Equatorial Guinea in 2011. She currently works at Atland Global and is one of Equatorial Guinea's few young female architects.

78

Torre de la Libertad (Freedom Tower) in Bata (Horizon Construction, 2011)
celebrates the independence of Equatorial Guinea from Spain in 1968

Introduction

Laida Memba Ikuga, Montserrat Villaverde

Equatorial Guinea is one of the smallest countries on the African continent, with a surface area of 28,000 km². Geographically it occupies a continental area and the islands of Bioko, Annobón, Corisco, Elobey Grande, and Elobey Chico. Its present-day architectural and urban heritage is the result of fusion between native cultures (Fang, Bubi, Ndowe, Annobón, and Bissio) and the successive colonising cultures (English, Portuguese, and Spanish). The diversity of traditional tangible culture can be seen in the different ethnic groups. Their vernacular settlements and architecture are examples of constructions that maintain their utility and meaning, and tell of the origins of these groups and their adaptation to Equatorial Guinea's environment.

Source: Patrimonio Guinea 2020

Example of traditional Fang architecture

The period of occupation by the English (1827–1834) and the founding of the city of Port Clarence (later Santa Isabel, today Malabo) saw the start of Western-style urban development, based on a grid of street blocks containing detached single-family dwellings set in gardens. Decades later, colonial houses were built, either constructed on site or imported from Europe, using prefabricated elements of iron and timber. English occupation brought with it Methodist churches, which, with their work setting up schools and places of worship, marked the beginning of Christian religious architecture in the country. Spain took effective possession of the territories in the Gulf of Guinea in 1858. Taking as its basis the urban planning of the *Laws of the Indies*, it formed centres of power around the Plaza España (today's Independence Square, Malabo) and extended the Ensanche (area of the city for new buildings) with larger street blocks. That same year, the Jesuits settled in Santa Isabel with the aim of founding a mission for the purpose of converting and educating the native population (1858–1868). They built the first Catholic church (ca. 1861) and the Mission, both in Plaza España.

As of 1883, the Claretian missionaries took on a fundamental role in the Spanish colonial undertaking, on the island and on the mainland, organising many aspects of colonial intervention as part of the Indigenous People's Board (1904), which was set up to manage all Equatoguinean heritage. With the aim of creating a homogenous national identity, they settled throughout the territory, following the model of the Banapá Mission, where the subjects taught included construction-related crafts. They built schools and churches, leaving behind them traces of neoclassicism and neo-Gothic architecture. This form of architecture evolved in the course of the twentieth century and laid the bases for construction throughout the country.

The Treaty of Paris of 1900 defined the area of Spanish influence on the mainland, delimiting the territory we know today as Equatorial Guinea. Spain aimed to turn the colony into a huge estate for the production of cassava, palm oil, coconuts, rubber, coffee, and cocoa. Cocoa production increased from the 1880s to the mid-1920s. On the island, cocoa became the principal economic activity, establishing a model of plantation estates with a structure and organisation similar to US colonies and the neighbouring islands of São Tomé and Príncipe. The import of labour and the construction of accommodation for the workers (*braceros*) marked the start of industrial architecture, drastically modifying the lifestyle of the Bubi people on the island of Bioko.

In the 1920s, especially under the government of General Miguel Núñez del Prado (1925–1931), the concentrations of settlements were grouped into villages, located on flatter land in more strategic areas. This gave way to the gradual substitution of vernacular architecture built using local materials (timber, nipa palm, etc.) with a residential architecture characterised by constructions using cement blocks and other imported materials, and different typologies, a phenomenon that intensified in the 1940s. Similar examples can be found the length and breadth of the country, using the same composition and materials. In this period, the Urban Constructions Service of the Equatorial Region, directed by the architect Antonio Román Conde (1940–1948), stood out for its work designing colonial facilities such as hospitals, schools, housing for civil servants, and urban projects such as the layout of the city of Bata. Pressure from the UN on countries that still had colonised territories led in 1959 to the territory being converted into two Spanish provinces: Fernando Póo and Río Muni. Town and provincial councils were set up throughout the territory. From 1963 the provinces had autonomous ruling bodies – the result of a referendum. Between 1964 and 1967, the Equatorial

Bank of Central African States (BEAC) Building in Bata
(Société française des dragages et des travaux publics, 1972)
Source: iStock/Alarico

Guinea Economic Development Plan was implemented with the aim of improving public services, health, education, and housing. The plan also favoured private production sectors, such as farming. It was in this period that the role of architects such as Ramón Estalella y Manso de Zúñiga stood out for the design of model villages under the umbrella of the late Modern Movement, adapting to the country's environment and cultures.

Independence was declared in 1968. In the early years, infrastructures were built, such as some of the bridges on Bioko and service buildings. However, the economy plummeted, leading to the degradation of these infrastructures. After striking oil in the 1990s, Equatorial Guinea started to experience new economic growth. The national census showed that the population had doubled in the period from 1994 to 2001. Several international firms have designed and built infrastructures and modern buildings using new technologies, with the aim of placing Guinean architecture within a more global context. Urban development plans have been designed for Malabo, Bata, and Luba, and new neighbourhoods such as Malabo II have been constructed. Today, the country is undergoing a process of definition and construction.

Façade detail (left) and wall decoration in the lobby (right) of the Sipopo Congress Centre near Malabo (Tabanlıoğlu Architects, 2011)
Source: Emre Dörter (all pictures)

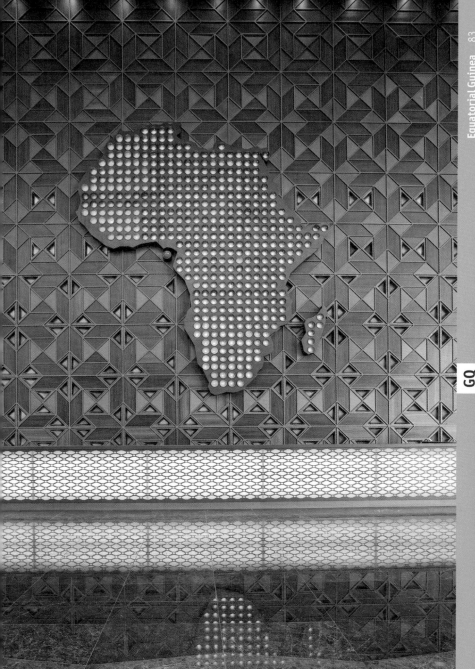
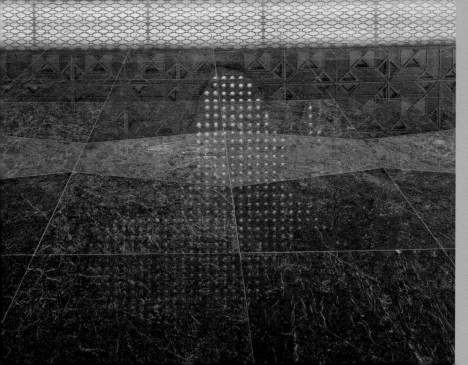

Malabo

Malabo, Equatorial Guinea's capital and main port, is situated on the northern coast of Bioko Island, in the Atlantic Ocean, south of Nigeria and west of Cameroon. The city, formerly Port Clarence and then Santa Isabel, lies on the rim of a sunken volcano. The island of Bioko was inhabited by the Bubi people when the Portuguese explorer Fernão do Pó arrived in 1472. It was later named after Fernão (Fernando Póo) and colonised by Portugal. In 1778, the island, nearby smaller islands, and commercial rights to the mainland between the Niger and Ogooué rivers were handed over to Spain in return for land on the American continent. The strategically important city settlement arose as Port Clarence in 1827, after the British leased Bioko Island from the Spanish to establish a naval base in order to help fight slavery. The city became the capital

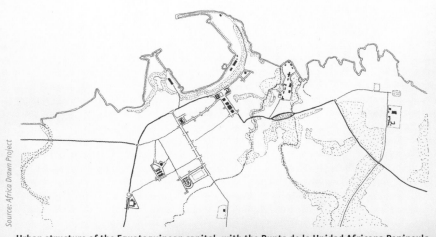

Source: Africa Drawn Project

Urban structure of the Equatoguinean capital, with the Punta de la Unidad Africana Peninsula

View of the Malabo President Palace Hotel (now demolished), Malabo Cathedral, and the palm trees of Independence Square from the port
Source: Flickr / Embassy of Equatorial Guinea

PLANO
DE
SANTA ISABEL
FERNANDO POO
AÑO 1946

Islotes Henriquez

Punta Cristina

Punta Fernanda

GUARDIA
COLONIAL

Barrio Yaunde

Barrio Hausa

RIO

REGISTRO TERRITORIAL

SECCIÓN DE TOPOGRAFÍA

Levantado por el Ingeniero Industrial D. Ricardo Ispizua Achútegui
y el Topógrafo Don Luis Sánchez Monge y Cruz.

El Gobernador General é
Inspector General

Source: Flickr/Wapster

Aerial view over the capital of Equatorial Guinea and the Bay of Malabo

of Equatorial Guinea in 1968, and was renamed Malabo in 1973 under a campaign by President Francisco Macías Nguema to replace European place names with African ones. Though the city resembles a formal grid, its structure is predominently influenced by the natural topography of the volcanic rim and Atlantic coast. Malabo's street network is poorly developed, with few paved roads leading into the city. The heart of the city is the colonial Cathedral of Santa Isabel at Independence Square. Other buildings in the capital reflect the influence of the Spanish colonial era, such as the Casa Verde, a prefabricated construction by the Barcelona-based firm Ribas y Pradell in ca. 1908. The south of Malabo is bounded by the Cónsul River, and just over the river, to the city's southwest, lies the General Hospital. The northern coast features headlands and bays, and the largest peninsula is the half-moon-shaped Punta de la Unidad Africana (Tip of African Unity), which curves up from near the Cathedral of Santa Isabel.   *adp*

GQ

Source: Private collection (all plans)

Map of Santa Isabel de Fernando Póo, today's Malabo (1890)

Bata

Source: iStock/Alarico

Clock tower and commercial centre in Bata

Bata, a former Spanish colonial city, is the largest city on the mainland of Equatorial Guinea, with a population of 250,770 (according to the 2012 census). It operates as a port and a centre for transport, such as ferries to the country's capital, Malabo. The urban landscape reflects this small country's tumultuous past, lacking basic infrastructure, public amenities, and urban planning. Though it is one of the deepest seaports along the coast, Bata does not have a natural harbour. A jetty was therefore built so ships could deposit their cargoes. The sprawling city takes its form from the coastline, and development continues along its feeder roads from the mainland. Independence was proclaimed in 1968 and the country became the Republic of Equatorial Guinea with Francisco Macías Nguema elected as first president. Following anti-Spanish riots in 1969, the numbers of the European population dropped, and subsequently the economy stagnated, which greatly affected the city during the 1970s and the beginning of the 1980s. The regime abolished all government functions, apart from internal security, which was carried out using terror. This resulted in the death or banishment of up to a third of the country's population. Even today, the vast streets along the coast of the city of Bata seem deserted. Along with the rest of the country, Bata's infrastructure, electricity, water, roads, transportation, and healthcare fell into ruin. Religion was repressed and education ceased, which explains the lack of landmarks in Bata compared to other cities. All schools were ordered to close in 1975, and the country's churches were closed in 1978. Following a coup in 1979, Teodoro Obiang Nguema Mbasogo assumed the presidency. The oil

Source: iStock / Atomic

boom in the country in the 1990s boosted Bata's development and put underway several infrastructure projects. New buildings, roads, and streetlighting, and a well-kept waterfront are all testimony to the fresh influx of funds from overseas. The Torre de Libertad (Freedom Tower), built by Horizon Construction in 2011, is one of the new buildings; it stands on the renovated waterfront, celebrating Equatorial Guinea's independence. Past the main roads that follow the coastline lies a sprawling urban conglomerate with small markets and small-scale residential developments. Beyond the affluent regions on the coast, a heterogeneous urban structure represents the majority of the local population.   *adp*

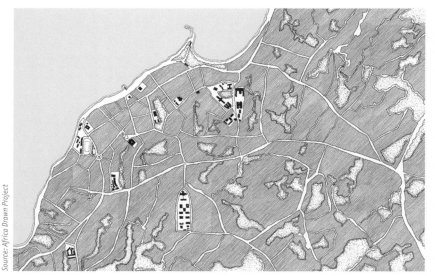

Source: Africa Drawn Project

The irregular street grid of Bata, the largest city in mainland Equatorial Guinea

Ribas y Pradell:
Prefabricated Colonial Constructions

Laida Memba Ikuga, Montserrat Villaverde

In the nineteenth and early twentieth centuries, the metropolises developed a type of colonial architecture with the collaboration of firms specialising in prefabricated construction, using a framework of different metals and wood. Their sales catalogues listed all manner of constructions: houses, churches, haciendas, hospitals, factories, schools, theatres, hotels, stores, cocoa and tobacco dryers, and provisional train and tram stations. They were made in the metropolises and transported to the colonies, where they were assembled, often by the firm's workers who were shipped out for that purpose. The great acceptance of prefabrication was based on two main premises: the light weight of the construction that made it easy to transport, and the speed and simplicity of assembly. In the late nineteenth century, this type of construction was so novel that the firms producing it showed them at the world fairs. In France, a model of a colonial house by the Moreau Brothers firm was presented; this building with an iron structure, metal sheet and wooden cladding was displayed at the International Exposition of 1889. The Belgian firm Aiseau, based in Antwerp, presented some of its iron constructions at the 1897 International Exposition in Brussels. In 1889, the Ministry of Overseas of the Spanish Colonial Government in Equatorial Guinea purchased one of their buildings, a church with a steel structure designed by the engineer Manuel Forreto Paniaigua, which was assembled in Malabo. It weighed 39,000 kg and cost 26,800 pesetas. The firm sent an official to direct assembly, though discontent with the result was repeatedly expressed by those responsible, due to the deficient assembly of the parts. In Spain, the leading firm in prefabricated constructions was Ribas y Pradell, based in Barcelona and founded in 1845 by Damián Ribas and Francisco Pradell. Starting in 1900, it developed an exclusive section of prefabricated constructions under the direction of the architect Simón Cordomí y Carrera (1873–1937). In 1900, Cordomí, who had qualified as an architect in 1895, patented a system to assemble timber buildings with metal reinforcements and a catalogue of prefabricated timber buildings

Casa-finca (estate house) in Basilé, Fernando Póo (Ribas y Pradell, 1913)

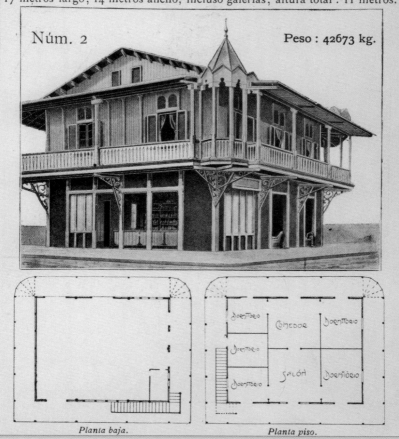

Factoría y habitación en Santa Isabel de Fernando Póo.

Montada sobre cimientos de hormigón. — Cubierta y paredes de los bajos, de hierro ondulado galvanizado.—Puertas de hierro ondulado, sistema silencioso. — Rejas de hierro en las ventanas de los bajos. — Madera pino tea. — 17 metros largo; 14 metros ancho, incluso galerías; altura total : 11 metros.

Núm. 2   Peso : 42673 kg.

Planta baja.   Planta piso.

Source: Private collection (all pictures)

Factory and house in Santa Isabel, Fernando Póo, with floor plans (Ribas y Pradell, 1913)

that he had designed. The *Official Gazette of Intellectual and Industrial Property* approved the two patents, which provided the basis for collaboration between Simón Cordomí and Ribas y Pradell. From that moment on, the firm produced prefabricated constructions for the whole of Spain and exported over a hundred buildings to the island of Bioko during the early decades of the twentieth century.

The firm had various departments (ironmongery, masonry, metal constructions), including the packaging section, directly linked to dismountable iron and timber constructions, and were for years suppliers to the Spanish Ministry of State's Colonial Section. Its advertising highlighted the buildings' solidness, comfort, the quality of their spaces, and the

precision of assembly and ease of transport. The robustness was provided by the metal frame, which ensured slender elements with no risk of collapse. In addition, most of the timber used was yellow pine, for its resistance to rodents and the atmospheric variations that are habitual in Bioko, responding to the dilatation and

Factory on Fernando Póo (1913)

Núm. 21

Negociado de Colonización y Obras

Propiedad del Gobierno Español.

Ground floor

1. Vestibule
2. Office
3. Hallway
4. Dining room
5. Hallway
6. Bakery
7. Toilet
8. Dormitory
9. Kitchen
10. Cooking class rooms

Ground floor

**Colonial and Public Works Department,
Fernando Póo (Ribas y Pradell, 1913)**

Source : Private collection

contraction of the wood. The comfort and inside spaces were further surpassed by the buildings' excellent ventilation and versatility of spatial layout. In almost all the constructions in Malabo, Luba, and Batete, the ground floor housed stores and shops, with the dwelling on the upper floor. Malabo's Casa Verde is the most important restored house still existing. Transport was undertaken with utmost care, protecting the parts from damage during the voyage. The firm always asked for the orientation of the site on which the building was to stand and adapted the models designed by Simón Cordomí to each. Ribas y Pradell, like other

licas. Emplazado en Fernando Póo.

metros largo por 16 metros ancho; altura de los pabello-
es bajos, 5'50 metros; altura pabellones pisos, 10 metros;
pabellón cocina aislado, 6 metros por 6 metros.

Peso : 140740 kilogramos
Cubierta de hierro ondulado galvanizado

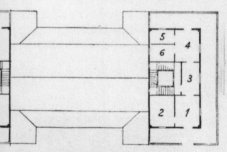

Upper floor

Upper floor
1. Living room
2. Bedroom
3. Hallway
4. Living room
5. Bathroom
6. Bedroom

Kitchen building

international firms specialising in pre-fabrication, published yearly catalogues in which they specified the characteristics of their constructions. They began to incorporate photographs of assembled houses and floor plans to illustrate how adaptable this type of architecture was. It was displayed and received awards at national and international exhibitions, particularly the 1929 International Exposition in Barcelona, showing models of many of the buildings on Bioko. When Ribas y Pradell celebrated their centenary in 1945, it was the printer Oliva de Vilanova, specialised in artistic editions, that published their catalogue.

Source: Patrimonio Guinea 2020 (all pictures)

Ròhiáa (Sacred House) GQ 01

Moka, Bioko Sur Province
2000s

Moka is a town in the south of the island of Bioko with a built landscape that is deeply rooted in the tradition of the Bubi people. One of its outstanding constructions is the *ròhiáa*, designed for uses related with communication with spirits and other traditional Bubi ceremonies. The *ròhiáa* has a rectangular floor plan of ca. 4.5 × 5 m with a symmetrical layout. It comprises ferns placed around the perimeter as uprights, directly anchored to the ground, which are joined using rope or wire to the vertical wall structure. In some cases they are reinforced on the inside by bamboo laths or other plant elements. The construction always has a ridge roof, one possible solution being a king post and three trusses resting on a sleeper on the walls of fern. The trusses are positioned in two of the façades and one at the centre of the space, topped by the ridge pole. The roof is completed by posts called *ripétyòo* that cross over the ridge pole. They are attached by rigid elements that join them crosswise to strengthen the two planes of the roof. The gable end and the roof are covered with *tyerú*, sheets of cladding which in this case are made of palm leaves. Each *tyerú* is made by a man and a woman. The sheets are woven of palm leaves folded over a long rigid frame. The first stitching to join all the palm leaves is the task of the men. The second stitching, underneath, is done by the women. In this way, the piece is thought to maintain its stability and last longer. Occasionally, the outer walls are also clad with *tyerú*, mounted vertically to protect the indoor space from rain and northeastern winds. The *ròhiáa* has just one door situated on the axis of symmetry. Various symbols and elements are arranged inside the *ròhiáa* to hold ceremonies. There are subspaces for women and for men. At the far end is what might translate as the altar, which is subdivided into compartments housing special and ritual objects. The slight separation between the vertical ferns of the wall allows daylight to filter into the space. *cc*

Traditional Benga Settlement GQ 02

Corisco Island, Litoral Province
ca. 1980s

The island of Corisco (or Mandji) is the natural territory of the Benga people, extending along the Muni River estuary and the coasts of Cameroon and Gabon. The Benga are part of the Ndowe people, an ethnic group in Equatorial Guinea. Mandji is occupied mainly by the Benga, who mostly inhabit the west and southwest coasts of the island, living in vernacular settlements built over the years according to the traditions of the place. Spatial organisation is governed by the Ndowe social structure. The social organisation of the Ndowe people, passed down orally through generations, comprises large groups, in Ndowe called *etùnggu* (pl. *betùnggu*), which translates as 'large family'. The *betùnggu* are made up of family units characterised by marital units, polygynous marriages, patrilocal residence and patrilineal descent. Each *ettùngu* has its own story of the occupation of space and remembers the first ancestor to settle in the territory it currently occupies. The *ettùngu* consists of extended family units called *jànga* and lives on a tract of land called a *kòdo*, which is considered the land of their ancestors, belonging exclusively to their descendants. Each *etùnggu* has its *kòdo* and only those with a family tie to the *etùnggu* can build on or use it. Individuals belonging to the *etùnggu* build their houses on this *kòdo*, each forming a *jànga*, or a marital unit, the smallest household for the Ndowe. Each *jànga* is organised in what

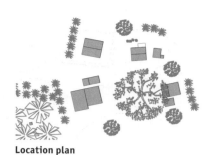

Location plan

translates as a family patio. The structures required for life are built in relation to these concepts. An outstanding characteristic of these family patios is the organisation of constructions around a central space and the planting of vegetation according to meaning and functions; trees like the mango tend to occupy the centre of these yards, whereas bananas grow to the rear of the houses, where organic waste is disposed of. Every element, whether planted or built, has its function and meaning. The circulations created between these elements and the relations between what is inside and outside the yard constitute a system according to kinship and the spaces occupied. The inhabitants of Mandji occupy space according to this system, in which the different family patios making up the island's *betùnggu* can be distinguished. Family patios are characterised as spaces that respond to basic physical needs and allow the development of the Benga's values, economic system, and lifestyle. Settlements are community built and the materials used depend on what is available, usually within the immediate vicinity.   *cc*

Source: Patrimonio Guinea 2020

Abáá Meeting Hut `GQ 03`
Kié-Ntem Province
2000s

The *abáá* is a construction associated with Fang tradition. It was central to the social and cultural life of the settlement, and found in the continental area of Equatorial Guinea. Historically, according to Günther Tessmann, the *abáá* was laid out perpendicular to the family settlement, delimiting the inner and outer spaces. In this position, it commanded views of people entering and leaving, as this was the place where visitors were received. It was a space fundamentally for the men, hosting rituals associated with their lives and with activities associated with traditional production such as nipa palm materials, and acting as a festive venue. The *abáá* was built at the initiative of the head of the household; all the men in the settlement would help in its construction. It had a rectangular floor plan and was symmetrical, with one or two central entrances. It comprised a structure of wooden posts, supporting a framework of wooden rafters that formed the roof structure. The roof and sides were covered with matting woven of bamboo strips and nipa leaves, leaving an opening all the way around. In some cases, the end walls were completely filled in. Inside, a bamboo bench was constructed around the edge. Another representative element, though not every *abáá* had one, was the central column, a structural

Sketches

Source: Patrimonio Guinea 2020 / Rafel Serra Torrent

support for the ridge pole, from which all kinds of objects and hunting trophies were hung. Social and cultural transformations in the twentieth and twenty-first centuries have adapted the *abáá* to contemporary lifestyles. In colonial times, it became known as the palaver hut, a name still used today. Since the 1920s, village structures have changed and many now no longer have an *abáá*.   *cc*

Teodolita House `GQ 04`
Calle del Botuku Luba, Malabo,
Bioko Norte Province
ca. 1902

Ground floor plan

This detached building in the former Ensanche Fernandino is named after the first daughter of Joseph Walter Dougan, known as Teodolita. The Dougan family is well known in Fernandino culture, and this house is one of the culture's key constructions. According to oral tradition, Teodolita House is a point of social reference. The children of other families received cultural and social education here, and the house produced important professionals for Equatoguinean culture and society, such as the first lawyer and the first pianist. The house has a ground floor, main floor, and attic. It was built with a mixed structural system: the ground floor uses a grid of pillars and concrete blocks, and the first floor features light wood-frame walls. It has a ridge roof. Outside, the façades vary on each floor: on the ground, is a gallery with five heavy concrete arches; on the first, a sequence of windows occupies the façades; and two openings on the attic floor ensure cross ventilation of this space. At the time of construction, all the floors were residential and laid out around the central salon, with direct access from the outside, which in turn was used as a hall providing access to the spaces beyond. This was a habitual arrangement at the time, based on symmetry along the central axis of the main salon. Today, interventions have turned the gallery on the upper floor into an extension of the residential spaces. In terms of finishes, the house is exceptional, retaining original features. The ground floor façade is painted stucco and the floors are hydraulic cement tiles. The upper floor façade presents painted timber and the flooring is timber throughout. Remarkable artisan work still exists today: for instance, the tops of the partition walls are fitted with latticework to aid ventilation, decorated with intertwining floral motifs worked in wood. Another outstanding feature is the coloured glass of the skylights.   *cc*

Source: Patrimonio Guinea 2020 (all pictures)

GQ

Banapá Seminary GQ 05

Banapá, Malabo,
Bioko Norte Province
Lluís Sagarra Llauradó
1884, 1918

Banapá Mission was the centre for the Claretians in Equatorial Guinea and an example for all the missions built there. It served as a model for all the timber constructions built on Bioko in its first twenty years. The Mission was set up in 1884 and the first construction was built of timber by the Claretian brothers with the help of carpenters from Accra, Ghana. One wing of the building was given over to the School of Arts and Crafts. There was also an experimental farm to develop different crops. In 1903, Lluís Sagarra Llauradó came to the School of Arts and Crafts and, with his projects, promoted the construction of altarpieces and churches for the whole island, as well as setting up a magazine, *La Guinea Española*, and conducting the Mission's band. In 1903, Sagarra designed the new Mission building according to previous guidelines, using the classical language that characterises the whole: a rectangular floor plan, two storeys and a roof terrace, and three vertical volumes (one in the centre and one to either side) to highlight its verticality. The initial roof unified the whole, adapting to the difference in level of the roofs of the various volumes. The façade comprises a ground floor with a great porch of semi-circular arches supported by pillars from which the vaults spring and that continue in the form of pilasters to the volume above. The windows were set in segmental arches, with oculi at the top. On the first level, the window openings were semi-circular. When work was complete, Guinea's first printing press was set up on the ground floor, and magazines such as *La Guinea Española* and all government documents were edited there. Sagarra also designed the church and promoted the New House; this building with a gallery running round it was constructed by the students, under the guidance of the teachers, as a dwelling prototype for all of Guinea. In 1913, the cross he designed was constructed, and his project was completed in 1918. Interventions in the 1940s modified the floor plan of the roof terrace, and another floor was built in the 2008 to 2009 works by PAC International. This latest work modified the entire complex: seminary, church, school, and gardens. *cc*

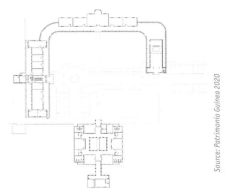

Floor plan

Source: Patrimonio Guinea 2020

Source: Arturo Bibang

Source: Patrimonio Guinea 2020

National Library `GQ 06`
Calle Hipólito Michá Eworo,
Malabo, Bioko Norte Province
*Makinen Venture Corporation/David
Gaggero, Daniele Marafetti
(intervention and extension)*
1916, 2009

The house stands on Calle Hipólito Michá Eworo and is a symbolic representative of the various constructions developed by the Fernandino businessman Maximiliano Cipriano Jones. Although designed as a dwelling, it has never been used for this purpose. According to oral tradition, it was built for Mildred, one of Jones's daughters, who died of tuberculosis. Trinidad Morgades, a specialist in Fernandino culture, dubbed it 'Palacete Mildred'. After their bereavement, the Jones family never lived in the building, giving rise to many legends. The dwelling is a fine example of the buildings developed by Fernandino families, such as the Showers, Granges, Cawens, Linslagers, and Raigts, who were wealthy and socially mobile. It comprises three floors and a mansard roof. In elevation it is quite different to the city's other dwellings. The Jones's social and economic standing led Maximiliano to construct buildings that were different to the rest, with European influences. In this case,

the reference is French historicist architecture. It was designed as a family residence, with a main street frontage and the remainder of the façades overlooking the garden. The windows combine various classical elements: mullions, semicircular and round. An outstanding feature is the balcony at cornice level that runs all around the façades except the side. The balusters and decorative sculpture around the openings are all artificial stone. Iron is only used for the balcony railings. All the walls are stuccoed, imitating natural stone masonry. Entrance is via a classic tripartite opening leading into the hallway and the main staircase. On each floor, the hall leads to the domestic spaces which, on the *belle étage*, have fine finishes, such as marble floors. At the rear, a doorway leads to the garden, with its pergolas and a small outbuilding. The complex was surrounded by a wall delimiting the property. Over the years, the building has had various uses and, in the 1940s, it was the headquarters of the Spanish Falange of the National Syndicalist Offensive Assemblies, Spain's fascist party. *Ébano* newspaper and the Santa Isabel radio station, the Falange's media, were housed there. In 2009, remodelling work was carried out on the house and a new building was constructed in the garden to accommodate the National Library of Equatorial Guinea. The new building stands out for its iron structure and language: markedly industrial with absolutely transparent spaces. The new part currently houses the public areas of the library, such as the reading rooms and some of the offices, and the historic building holds the library's offices, research rooms, and multipurpose work spaces.   *cc*

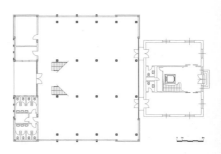

Floor plan

Sampaka Cocoa Dryers

Sampaka, Malabo,
Bioko Norte Province
1906

During the early nineteenth century, the Portuguese brought cocoa plants from Brazil to their colony of São Tomé, and it is estimated that, by the mid-nineteenth century, the first seeds of this product had reached Bioko Island. During the Spanish occupation, the idea was to convert Equatorial Guinea into a great plantation of agricultural products, which included cocoa. Production of cocoa developed most intensely on the island of Bioko. However, it was one of the industries to have the greatest effect on the lifestyle of the inhabitants of Bioko and the transformation of their built environment. One of the biggest cocoa farms, still in operation today, is the Sampaka Estate. The estate has an inscription that dates the farm back to 1906 and, in the early decades, it was the property of landowner Mariano Mora and his wife Antoñita Llorens, and was run by Antonio Azcón. Its rail connection with Santa Isabel facilitated the transport of cocoa to the port. Its growth and consolidation as a cocoa producing company played a fundamental role in positioning Guinea as a major exporter of cocoa. In 1923, it had 300 workers. The approach to the estate is impressive. The road leading to the gate is flanked by the remaining royal palms. The owners' house was built on a site with privileged views, alongside small residential constructions and auxiliary buildings. The Sampaka Production Plant is the country's finest piece of industrial architecture. It has five mechanised dryers, each 30 m long. The basic machinery of each dryer comprises a large platform of slate on which the cocoa beans are spread to dry. The slate trays rest on a structure of T-joists laid out along the dryer and built into its side walls. This produces a strong, smooth, uniform surface. Beneath the slate trays, at a distance of around 0.8 m, is the duct, a dome clad with firebricks, through which the slate surface is heated. The tunnel of firebricks runs lengthwise through the dryer, branching into three or four crosswise tunnels to ensure optimum distribution of heat. The flues are positioned at the end of the heating tunnels to create a draught and evacuate the smoke produced by combustion. The fuel used to produce heat is usually wood cut on the estate. To move the cocoa on the slate surfaces, a rake is positioned across the dryer. A couple of metal wheels at each side allow the rake to slide lengthwise. The movement of the carriage is powered by a mechanical pulley and winch system. *cc*

Source: Patrimonio Guinea 2020 (all pictures)

Malabo Cathedral   GQ 08

Plaza de la Independencia, Malabo,
Bioko Norte Province
Lluís Sagarra Llauradó
1916

The Cathedral of Santa Isabel was built in the eastern sector of Plaza de la Independencia as a symbol of Catholic power in the colony. Construction work was financed by the faithful, with the collaboration of the colony's foremost entrepreneurs and the colonial government. The initial project dates from 1897, with construction beginning in 1899. In 1901, Claretian father Lluís Sagarra Llauradó completely changed the initial proposal. Sagarra's project was considered very bold and excited doubts as to its construction. It was Father Coll, a recently appointed bishop in Barcelona, who showed the project to Antoni Gaudí. The architect who was directing work on the Sagrada Família positively endorsed Sagarra's initiative. Years later, it was Jeroni Martorell i Terrats, an architect who was active in the restoration of monuments, who acted as consultant on constructive issues. The neo-Gothic cathedral is a mixed construction of rubblework and ashlars. It has a basilica floor plan with a well-defined transept, an octagonal presbytery, a nave and two aisles. Three large rose windows stand out in the main façade and the façades of the transept. The nave comprises cross vaults with pointed arches separated from the aisles by slender iron pillars clad with cement. In the transept and presbytery, the columns are fasciculated columns of artificial stone. In the presbytery, at a height of 3 m, there are six large tribunes with parapets ornamented with Gothic chequered fretwork. The side aisles are fitted with large leaded stained-glass windows that draw daylight inside. The choir, at the foot of the cathedral, occupies two stretches of vaults in the nave and one in the aisles, supported by two elliptical and six semi-circular arches. Particular mention should be made of the brick, marble and marble-stucco finishes of the vaults. The Claretian brothers took part in the construction. Under Sagarra's guidance, Brother Jaime Miquel directed the construction, Brother Ramón Ollé built the vaults, Brother Ignacio Meabe built the roofs and Brother Diego Rubio was responsible for the finishes. This team was completed by German brothers recently arrived from Cameroon and joiners such as Juan Henseler. The richness of its finishes is surprising in comparison with other constructions of the time, and most of the elements were imported, having been produced by Barcelona's prestigious artistic industries: the stained-glass windows in the presbytery by Rigalt, Granell i Cía; the hydraulic mosaic tiles by Butsems i Cia; altars by Francisco Rifà; religious carvings by José Rius; the iron railings of the side chapel and presbytery by Damians, and so on. Construction was completed in 1916, though the great 40 m high towers crowning the façade were added in 1927. Between 1928 and 1932, the Archbishop's Palace was built according to Sagarra's design. In 1954, major interventions were carried out to the side chapel, using different types of marble for the finishes. Restoration work began in 2013.   *cc*

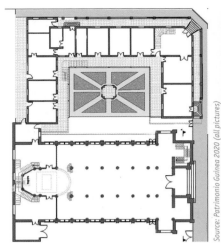

Source: Patrimonio Guinea 2020 (all pictures)

Site plan

GQ

Source: Arturo Bibang

Source: Patrimonio Guinea 2020

Casa Verde

GQ 09

Calle 3 de Agosto/Calle del Presidente
Nasser, Malabo, Bioko Norte Province
Ribas y Pradell
ca. 1908

Casa Verde, as it is popularly known, is the most representative example of the wooden prefabricated buildings imported between 1890 and 1920 by the Barcelona-based company Ribas y Pradell. As of 1875, part of the firm specialised in the production of prefabricated buildings, included in the iron and timber section. These buildings were sometimes built with air cavities made of a special tongue-and-groove system to prevent air or water seeping through the joints. This also facilitated transport and assembly according to detailed plans for easy installation at their definitive location. They could be assembled on concrete foundations; columns and iron platforms or brick piles. The roofs were zinc or galvanised iron and pitch pine or red pine timber. In Santa Isabel (now Malabo), some fifty of these buildings were constructed. Many were factory-houses, and others stand on properties all over Fernando Póo Island. Casa Verde stands on a concrete footing. The columns are cast iron, and the outer railings are wrought iron. Originally the ground floor was clad with corrugated galvanised iron sheet, as this floor was meant for use as a shop and store. The second level had a brief for a complete dwelling housing three bedrooms. Here, the facings were pitch pine timber. The roof was finished with corrugated galvanised iron sheet. A building 20 m long, 16 m wide, 13 m high marked the start of what used to be Sacramento Street (now President Nasser Street), leading to what is today Independence Square in Malabo, which was known as the setting for parades and events during the colonial period. Casa Verde has been reconstructed conserving some of its original elements, such as the iron pillars and beams. *cc*

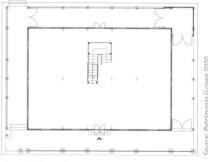

Ground floor plan

Source: Patrimonio Guinea 2020

Batete Church

GQ 10

Batete, Bioko Sur Province
Lluís Sagarra Llauradó
1926

Situated on a small hill, beside the River Okohoko, the Claretian church in Batete is the only neo-Gothic church built of timber that still stands today. Though the Claretian mission was established in 1887, it was not until 1893 that the first timber church was constructed, designed by Brother Ginestá, with the help of the joinery and carpentry workshops at Banapá. This construction was almost entirely remodelled in the 1920s. In 1922, Lluís Sagarra Llauradó drafted a project for a church with a basilica floor plan comprising a single nave, transept, and choir, and a slender tower standing almost 30 m high with a rose window, crowned with a clock. The church is built on a small concrete platform to address the sloping site and structurally it comprises cross vaults supported by slender columns. Being situated at the edge of the hill, the entrance is in the second stretch of vaults, leading into the church via a small porch. This entrance links directly to the road. In all the façades, wooden cresting decorates the walls and tower. Inside are four altars, all carved in wood in Barcelona; hydraulic tile floors reproducing mosaic patterns by the Butsems company and leaded grisaille windows by the Barcelona firm Rigalt, Granell i Cía. Other elements, like

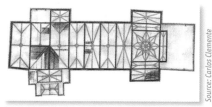

Floor plan

Source: Carlos Clemente

the bells, were cast in Barcelona and Olot. Sagarra himself contacted the artistic workshops and designed the altars and stained-glass windows. The great windows have metal frames, like the ones he fitted in the Cathedral of Santa Isabel. Sagarra was assisted by students at the School of Arts and Crafts in Banapá. The polychromy is noteworthy: the exterior is a sandy yellow, with structural and ornamental elements picked out in blue, while inside, blue is used for the walls and webs, and toasted, sandy tones highlight the ribs and pillars as far as their bases. In the present day, the church has serious structural problems and displays a general lack of maintenance. *cc*

GQ

Source: Patrimonio Guinea 2020 (all photos)

Source: Patrimonio Guinea 2020 (all pictures)

Independence Square `GQ 11`
Plaza de la Independencia, Malabo,
Bioko Norte Province
1863 onwards

This urban space open to the sea is the place where the most representative buildings of the colony's religious and governmental power were concentrated. Today, it is Independence Square, and bounded by three streets. At the centre of the plaza stands a monumental fountain, an allegory of Equatorial Guinea. The space has been a place for human interactions since the urbanisation of the settlement began. First it was the venue for the market. The initial urban development by Governor John Beecroft turned it into a plaza. In 1863 the area was levelled, and big interventions took the form of construction of the various plots bounding the square, the path down to the bay, and the subsequent urbanisation of Punta Fernanda. In the early twentieth century the cathedral was constructed and the square started to materialise with the incorporation of wooden seats and neoclassical-style flowerbeds. In 1906, a drinking fountain was inaugurated to mark the advent of piped water. With the completion of Government House in 1915 and the first phase of the cathedral in 1916, the square was paved, incorporating a curved stairway at the corners to connect the different levels. In 1926 the square was repaved and the palm trees that are still one of the features were planted. The tiles that formed part of the street furniture featured images linked to the colony and the territory, and seat backs commemorated key events in colonisation. Today, after further work, all that remains of the original space are the palm trees.   cc

Malabo President Palace `GQ 12`
Hotel » ↵
Plaza de la Independencia, Malabo,
Bioko Norte Province
Antonio Román Conde, Makinen Venture
Corporation (renovation)
1946, 2007, demolished in 2018

Situated in one of the façades that make up Independence Square, this building is the result of rehabilitation work carried out in 2007 by Makinen Venture Corporation to turn the former Catholic Mission into Malabo's most prestigious hotel. The plot occupied by this complex was the first part of the city to be developed, with the construction in 1859 of the Catholic Mission. In 1889, when a chapel on the site opposite the Mission was destroyed by fire, the Ministry of Overseas bought, from the Belgian firm Aiseau, a church with a steel structure and wooden floors, designed by the engineer

Manuel Forreto Paniaigua, which it put up on the site where the hotel now stands. In 1946, the old Mission was renovated and the architect Antonio Román Conde designed the new building, which was built by brothers Diego Rubio and Antonio Cabrera. Román Conde designed various building types across the country, from public facilities such as Bata and Malabo Hospital, and Malabo market, to private dwellings such as the home of the Governor of Bata. The Mission was a neoclassical complex standing two storeys high, with two taller volumes at the centre and sides. The main façade overlooked the bay and stood perpendicular to Independence Square. The 2007 intervention modified the orientation, creating an entrance from Independence Square and building new volumes around the different patios, using the same compositional language as the original building. The finishes have been restored, recovering the textures of the walls and the sgraffiti on the central pediment. *CC*

Magazine Patio ≫ ≫

GQ 13

Avenida del 3 de Agosto, Luba, Bioko Sur Province
ca. 1940

Maximiliano Cipriano Jones was one of the most influential Fernandino merchants on the island of Bioko. Episodes of his life have produced many oral stories that are often associated with the places he lived in and built – as with Magazine Patio in Luba, where he built one of his residences. Luba was a crucial point for the exchange of goods and trade. The house is a detached single-family residence of great spatial quality. The dwelling consists of a ground floor, first floor, and walk-on roof. It was built with a mixed system of bearing walls and pillars, and uses a platform to adapt to the site's topography. The façades are marked by great dynamism, shunning the concepts of symmetry previously employed in dwellings. The first floor has two clearly differentiated areas: night and day. The daytime space comprises two large, light lounges and the kitchen. The night-time space has four bedrooms and bathrooms. The flat roof with its railings, circular windows, and terraces suggests the image of a ship, embodying an essentially rationalist architecture, of which this house is one of the most important examples in Equatorial Guinea. *CC*

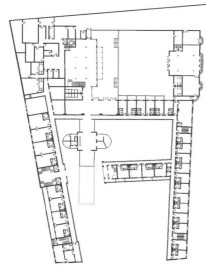

Malabo President Palace Hotel: floor plan

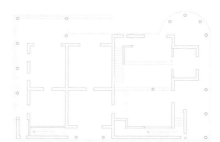

Magazine Patio: floor plan

imported from Barcelona, metal elements, and modern door and window frames with louvered shutters. The outer facings preserve the original stucco work that frames the doors and windows with sinuous patterns and imitates stone blocks. In 1942, the estate was a strategic site controlling access to the town. It now forms part of the installations of Luba Freeport.   *cc*

La Barcelonesa ⌅   GQ 14
Luba, Bioko Sur Province
Luís Subirana
1913

In the 1910s, the local government of San Carlos (present-day Luba) undertook a series of major interventions to restructure, plan, and improve public space and construct new buildings with the aim of increasing its importance in relation to the capital, Santa Isabel. This initiative came in response to the requests of important merchants and landowners, including the master builder Luis Subirana, of the firm Rius y Torres, which owned La Barcelonesa, an estate where cocoa and coffee were grown. In 1912, under the supervision of Sebastián Delcor, work began on a residential building on the La Barcelonesa estate, and was completed in late 1913. With excellent views of the bay, this villa, as it was popularly known, was a flagship building of the time. Worthy of note was its masonry construction with the incorporation of metal pillars in a town where most of the constructions were timber and rather precarious. This detached building is three storeys high and has a hipped roof, with masonry columns and a structure of bearing walls, pillars, and metal girders. The composition is marked by large galleries in all four façades and on the three levels. These galleries, together with the prominent cornice, accentuate the house's horizontality. The gallery is supported by metal pillars and enclosed by a cast-iron ornamental railing. Exceptionally for the time, bathrooms and modern showers were also built on the different floors. The in- and outdoor finishes are especially rich for the time and geographical context: floors of hydraulic mosaic tiles,

Equatoguinean   GQ 15
Arts Centre
Avenida de la Independencia, Malabo, Bioko Norte Province
Pedro Gragera
1956

The Equatoguinean Arts Centre forms part of the seafront of the Bahía de Venus and occupies the former Cardenal Cisneros Cultural Board for Secondary Education, which was first opened on 18 July 1956. The project was commissioned in 1954 to the engineer Pedro Gragera and built by the construction company Andujar, occupying a total of 1,000 m². The ground floor housed eight classrooms of varying sizes, a gymnasium, and an events hall, in addition to two large covered courtyards. The top floor held the library, the archives, the Colonial Museum and offices. The building is designed in the Herrerian style and conveys a sense of monumentality. The high plinth course of bossage runs around the façade and places two turreted volumes at the corners, which rise three storeys and are crowned by Herrerian pinnacles. The indoor spaces are laid out around two covered courtyards. The smaller of the two was situated at the entrance to the building and covered by a large stained-glass window, supported by a colonnade, two Tuscan capitals with superposed shafts and stilted arches, a solution that fosters verticality. The second courtyard, at the centre, was larger with a fountain in the middle, and rose another level. On the ground floor, the outer gallery reproduced the elements of the entrance court, and the upper floor has segmental arches. A gallery opens onto the courtyard and two of the side façades. In the 1960s it became the Cardenal Cisneros National Institute and,

Source: Patrimonio Guinea 2020 (all pictures)

in the 1970s, the Rey Malabo Institute. As of the 1980s it was known as the headquarters of the Hispano-Guinean Arts Centre and, in 2009, remodelling and rehabilitation work began, according to a project by Makinen Venture Corporation and carried out by PAC International. This included the roof of the central courtyard, the construction of a floor over the entrance courtyard and a new distribution of uses. Since 2012, it has been the headquarters of the Equatoguinean Arts Centre of Malabo. *cc*

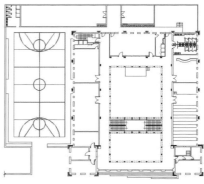

Floor plan

Source: Patrimonio Guinea 2020 (all pictures)

Floor plan

Damián Roku Epitie Monanga GQ 16
Regional Hospital
Calle Organización Unidad Africana,
Bata, Litoral Province
Julio Santacana Fernández
ca. 1957

The original project for this hospital was designed by Julio Santacana Fernández, quantity surveyor of the Delegation of Indigenous Affairs of the Continental District in the late 1950s. Santacana designed a facility of detached pavilions in keeping with the hygienist tendency that emerged in the nineteenth century. This hospital typology has a functional organisation and specific orientation with highly detailed relations and connections between the buildings. They were conceived as small garden cities, where separation of the genders and different illnesses was reflected in the subdivision of the pavilions and their arrangement between large open spaces that served to provide ventilation. Implementing the complex in the site meant clearing a large esplanade, which involved the movement of 25,000 m³ of earth, significantly modifying the local topography. The original hospital project comprised fifteen pavilions organised along a central axis of symmetry and joined by a covered walkway through the centre. Unlike European hospitals, no admissions pavilion was initially designed; two main pavilions, the pharmacy and the convent, being built instead at the entrance. In the space between these two buildings stands the operating theatre and the central axis that arranges the rest of the hospital complex. The remainder of the gender-segregated pavilions are laid out to either side of this central walkway. The rear of the site was set aside for storage or pavilions that called for isolation. Each of the pavilions had a rectangular floor plan, symmetrical distribution, and two storeys. Entry was via the central axis, where the two entrance doorways were situated, forming a well-ventilated foyer, with the foot of the three-run stairway leading to the foyer on the upper floor. The foyers on the two storeys were communicated by galleries or corridors running along the floor. Construction began in June 1953. In the course of building, some modifications to the original project were introduced, leading to the construction at the entrance of a pavilion to house general administration. Recently, the hospital was rehabilitated, with connections modified with covered outdoor walkways to facilitate communication between pavilions. It is the referral hospital for the entire continental area. *CC*

Source: GAMUC Research Group

GQ

Model Villages GQ 17

Nkimi, Centro Sur Province, et al.
Ramón Estalella y Manso de Zúñiga,
Alberto Ripoll Fajardo,
Ignacio Prieto Revenga
1962–1967

The 'model villages' built in the 1960s were promoted by the Instituto Nacional de Vivienda de España (Spanish National Housing Institute) and directed by the architect Ramón Estalella y Manso de Zúñiga. They formed part of the Development Plan for Equatorial Guinea, representing the design of housing developments and communal buildings for the indigenous population. These interventions began at the urban scale and worked towards the detail with the aim of adapting to the natural and social environments into which they were inserted. Altogether, eleven villages were built: Campo Yaoundé (Los Ángeles), Ruitché (Las Palmas), West Basakato, Sácriba, Moeri, San Carlos (Luba), Bikurga, Nkimi, Bidjabidjang, Machinda, and Lea. The team of architects made proposals based on a number of typologies and categories, grouped differently according to the topography and space where they were to be located. The architecture was guided by some principles of the modernist movement: simplicity of composition, use of contemporary materials and techniques, and emphasis on natural cooling systems, employing cross-ventilation and door and window frames in accordance with the area's climate.

The basic elements in the layouts were dwellings and a series of complementary buildings: the church, the palaver hut, stores, a post office, and a fountain. All the sites were made up of a combination of these elements, excluding the occasional complementary building according to the case. Although the dwellings in, for instance, Los Ángeles were designed according to Western parameters, residents appropriated the spaces and projected the living area beyond their homes, while respecting the limits of each family's space and implanting their way of understanding the act of dwelling. Special mention should be made of the treatment of urban space in all the complexes, in the form of transitional spaces between the buildings for family or collective use. In the palaver hut, the idea is to adapt an international architecture project to traditional culture. It occupies the largest plot and is the building with the best situation; it is airy and positioned at the complex's centre of gravity. As in the original typology, part of it stands open to the outside, blurring indoor-outdoor limits. The building in the complex that is most highly regarded by the architects is the church; they note that for a religious building it is small, yet stands out through its verticality. The building was flexible: in the event of a large attendance the altar could also be seen from outside. Though not defined as educational facilities, many of these buildings are, at the moment, also used as classrooms. *CC*

Source: Arturo Bibang

GE Proyectos Headquarters ⩘ ⩗ GQ 18
Ncuantoma, Bata, Litoral Province
China Dalian International Cooperation
2011

In 2003, the National Office for Planning and Administering Projects in Equatorial Guinea, or GE Proyectos, was set up. Its headquarters in Bata is in Ncuantoma, an area that has been addressed by a global strategy of cutting-edge modern buildings and infrastructures. The intervention occupies 7,200 m² and the building has a gross floor area of 6,500 m². The project is inserted on a previously unbuilt site, and the floor plan was therefore laid out according to a functional arrangement of the parts in relation to the entrances, green areas, and car parking. The brief is laid out over five storeys. The ground floor holds an auditorium for 500 people and a cafeteria, and the other floors house the offices and meeting

rooms for civil servants. The overall volume comprises a series of planes that rise from the ground to generate an interplay of empty spaces and volumes with large translucent surfaces that give the indoor spaces a special quality of light. The entire façade is clad with dark grey natural stone, giving it a solidness and force that make it stand out from its setting in Ncuantoma. *cc*

Ministry of Mines, GQ 19
Industry and Energy »
Malabo II, Malabo, Bioko Norte Province
Saraiva + Associates
2014

The Ministry of Mines, Industry and Energy is situated on the Malabo II expressway, in the recently named area of Nuevos Ministerios (New Ministries). The aim of the project was to produce a solution that was not only modern but also enhanced the built complex. It prioritised the use of contemporary materials and technologies, and incorporated state-of-the-art technical solutions. The result comprises two blocks that are interconnected by elements to facilitate communication and circulation. The complex was designed as a whole, using the same architectural language in formal and material terms. The two blocks are set on a shared base, arranged on an axis with a separation between the two of approximately 15 m, generating open-air spaces that help integrate them into

Source: China Dalian International Cooperation

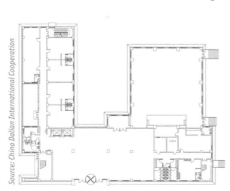

Floor plan

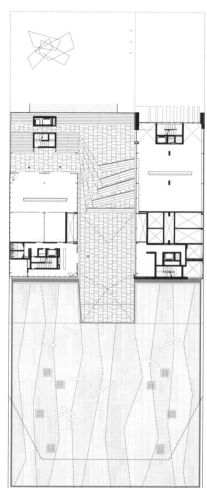

Source: Saraiva + Associates (all pictures)

the setting. The façade treatments of the blocks combine transparency and opacity. Transparency takes the form of dark glazing, and opacity is achieved using very bright materials; the result is a dialogue between the skins of the two volumes, which are set very differently into the site. One volume stands out for its façade, emerging directly from the ground and enveloping the great glazed plane visible from the entrance. The other is raised a complete level above the shared platform and apparently supported by a glazed surface. The main entrance to both of the blocks is from the plaza.   *cc*

Floor plan

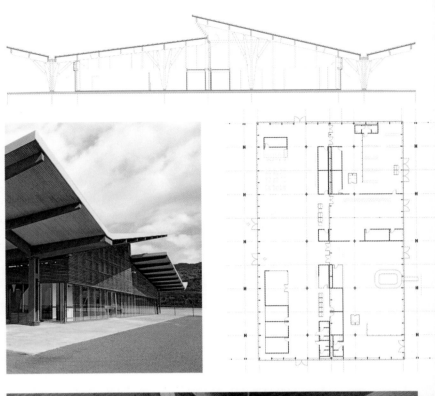

Annobón Airport

GQ 20

San Antonio de Palé, Annobón
Building for Climate/
Nicolas Jobard, Ning Liu
2011

To help develop tourism on the small volcanic island of Annobón, a new airport terminal was designed and built within a period of just ten months in 2011. In the equatorial climate, humidity, rainfall, and the amount of sunshine are all important considerations, and the island's current infrastructure struggles to provide abundant electricity for its needs. Taking into account these environmental factors, the architects, Building for Climate, based their construction on bio-climatic principles. The rectangular plan of the airport terminal makes economic use of the circulation space. Outside the building, the overhanging roof provides covered space for users. The architects imagined two tilted forms as the structure's main roof. Their folded shapes are designed to give the impression of being lifted up by the tropical wind. The two parts do not meet at the top; instead they allow space for hot air to leave the building. The asymmetry reinforces the dynamic character of the volume. The terminal is almost entirely built in wood. Weight-supporting posts are cross-shaped at the base and become arborescent. Both the tree-like forms and the ebony tones of the structure are intended to evoke a forest atmosphere. The use of other materials is limited: only the continuous footings in the foundations are concrete and steel. Wooden ventilation louvres sit on the higher part of the façades, providing natural ventilation and sunlight to the interior. Thus, no air conditioning is required in the main spaces, saving electricity. Double-glazing ensures thermal comfort inside and offers views to the island's horizons. The contemporary building uses high-tech prefabricated processes and has a flexible and resistant structure. *pa/ed*

Source: Building for Climate (all pictures)

Interventions in Public Space

Interview with Dominica Nchama Minang Ntang, one of Equatorial Guinea's
few young female architects

Source: Patrimonio Guinea 2020

Dominica Nchama Minang Ntang

*The National Economic and Social
Development Plan was adopted at the second National Economic Conference, held
in the city of Bata in 2007. Many foreign
companies went to Equatorial Guinea to
be part of this strategy, intervening principally in the construction of infrastructure.
The Local Urban Development Plan (PLU) of
the city of Malabo was presented that same
year and, since then, has been gradually
implemented in the form of multiple projects of urban planning and architecture.
Dominica Nchama Minang Ntang, born
in 1978, is one of Equatorial Guinea's few
young female architects. She gained her
architecture degree at the Universidad
Politécnica de Madrid, and started practising in Madrid in 2005 and in Equatorial
Guinea in 2012. She currently works at
Atland Global, a firm that provides coordination and consultancy for infrastructure projects of the Equatoguinean
Administration, and develops projects for
facilities in the city of Malabo.*

*Interview conducted by Laida Memba
Ikuga and Montserrat Villaverde*

*What is your work with the Administration
made up of? What are the main areas you
are coordinating?*

It's a multidisciplinary project that brings
together architects, technical architects,
and engineers in different fields. We work
for the council, principally for bodies involved in construction. We carry out re-
views of the Local Urban Development
Plan of Malabo, and projects that are underway and at the approval stage. We co-
ordinate, together with the council, the
creation of infrastructures in accordance
with urbanistic growth and compliance
with regulations. And recommendations
are constantly being made about interventions that are underway, ranging from
the extension of green areas, spaces ear-
marked for potential public use, protection of riverbeds, the choice of appropriate vegetation for the climate, and
improved street design in keeping with
present-day needs, including parking
areas, street furniture, trees, etc.

*What effect does your work have on the
architecture, urban planning, and overall
landscape of the city of Malabo?*

The results are significant, even if only
at neighbourhood scale. We make more
green spaces and trees for the city. It's
incredible that in a city that is surrounded by nature, like Malabo, it can be hard
to find somewhere to sit and rest under
the trees! We also try to make sure that
new projects take porches into account,
with the aim of improving the quality of
life of the population, or consider parking spaces, which are very necessary.

*As well as working on coordination, you
have considered specific actions of urban*

GQ

Source: Patrimonio Guinea 2020

Malabo's key urban space of Plaza E'Waiso, which is, among other things, a gathering place

intervention, such as the project for Plaza E'Waiso. Why was it decided to intervene in this square?

Plaza E'Waiso is a key urban space in social and cultural terms. Its very name shows us how important it is: it is the name of the neighbourhood, and it's named after E'Waiso Ipola school (in the Bubi language, 'Woman, stand up!'). It is also a crossroads and a boundary between neighbourhoods. It's Malabo's only plaza and the venue for street fish vendors; the schools' sports activities take place there, there are bars with terraces, and it's also a meeting place for many of the city's young people. The Insituto Cultural de Expresión Francesa (ICEF) asked us to draw up a project for the rehabilitation of the plaza, for the eco-carnival that was being prepared. Three architects were involved in the design: Danila Columbu, Arturo Albarado, and myself. From the start, we loved the project, as we had to study the plaza, maintain its essence and turn its weak points around. The plaza already had its own activity, but we identified the following needs: there were dark areas that made it dangerous; shady places were needed for the hottest hours of the day; facilities had to be included for sport and recreation for all ages, and there had to be a well for local residents.

Can you describe your project and the working process?

We conducted an analysis of the water, electricity, and sanitation networks to detect shortcomings and the necessary improvements. And we designed a plaza with different areas that would respond to the needs detected. In the end, it was not possible to carry out the project as we had designed it due to lack of funds, but some of the changes we had discussed with the direction of the ICEF were carried out, such as recycling benches, using car tyres to make flowerbeds, and painting the pond as planned. We hope that rehabilitation of the plaza will take place in the future, because it is very necessary and would further enhance it.

Source: Dominica Nchama Minang Ntang

Site plan for Plaza E'Waiso

São Tomé and Príncipe

Enerlid Franca, Saotomean architect, born in 1984 in Mé-Zóchi. Graduated from José Antonio Echeverría Higher Polytechnic Institute, Cuba. Opened an architectural practice in 2010 and Ké Design, an architectural company, in 2012; both on São Tomé.

Edwlne Neto, architect, entrepreneur, and ecologist, born 1981 in São Tomé. Graduate of the National Taiwan University of Science and Technology. Principal at Eneto Lda, focusing on ecological practices to replace wood buildings in São Tomé and Príncipe.

ST

The selection of colonial buildings was coordinated by Ana Tostões and
Daniela Arnaut with the team of the project Exchanging Worlds Visions:
Modern Architecture in Africa 'Lusófona' (1943–1974): Ana Tostões
(scientific coordination), Vicenzo Riso, João Vieira Caldas, Maria Manuel
Oliveira, Elisiário Miranda, Ana Magalhães, Maria João Teles Grilo,
Margarida Quintã, Jessica Bonito, Zara Ferreira, Francisco Seabra Ferreira,
Catarina Delgado, Ana Maria Braga, Paulo Silva, and Sandra Vaz Costa.
The publisher would like to extend special thanks to Coral Gillett
and Helder Pereira for their input into the selection of contemporary
architecture in this chapter.

Duarte Pape, Portuguese architect, born 1982
in Lisbon. Graduated from the Instituto Superior
Técnico, Lisbon, in 2006. Founded Paralelo Zero,
for which he studies Portuguese heritage in Africa.
His published works include *As Roças de São Tomé
e Príncipe* from 2013. *(dp)*

Cristina Udelsmann Rodrigues, Angolan-Portu-
guese social scientist, born 1970 in Luanda.
Graduated from the University Institute of Lisbon
in 2004. She has published on urban Africa and
related social issues. She is presently senior researcher at the Nordic Africa Institute, Sweden.

Introduction

Duarte Pape

Located in the Gulf of Guinea, the islands of São Tomé and Príncipe cover about 1,000 km² and are geographically part of an insular assembly comprising the Equatoguinean islands of Bioko to the north and Annobón to the south. The country includes islets such as Rôlas, Caroço, Pedras, and Tinhosas. São Tomé and Príncipe are part of the Macaronesian islands – archipelagos of volcanic origin in the North Atlantic: the Azores, the Canary Islands, Madeira, and Cabo Verde. In its genesis, the process of occupation and urban expansion on the archipelago of São Tomé and Príncipe does not have an innovative character when observed in the Portuguese expansion context. In fact, when analysing the occupation of the islands from their discovery in 1470 to the coffee and cocoa cycles, it is clear that the urban strategy resulted in a configuration that had already been realised in other Atlantic regions or South America, specifically Brazil.

The cities of Santo António (on Príncipe) and São Tomé have identical morphological characteristics to those of other maritime cities such as Ponta Delgada in the Azores; Ribeira Grande in Cabo Verde; and Rio de Janeiro in Brazil, which shows a certain specificity in the Portuguese urban settlements in these territories. All have sheltered bays that form a natural harbour. Watercourses supply the cities and they have favourable sun exposure. Each one has a framework in a hilly landscape, ensuring advantageous conditions for defence. In the settlement strategy of these Atlantic islands, it is possible to observe common elements, such as the investment in intensive farming of large areas; the sugar cane crops developed in the fifteenth and sixteenth centuries, with great commercial impact worldwide; the occupation of the islands as a resale platform of slaves and products; and the introduction of free people and slaves. In the cultural assimilation processes of these islands, it is possible

Source: iStock/Al-Travelpicture

Former hospital in the Roça São João dos Angolares on São Tomé

to verify numerous attempts to introduce Mediterranean food crops, which meant a profound change in the endemic landscape, and gave a Portuguese atmosphere to the territory.

The history of São Tomé and Príncipe was strongly defined by the permanent and cyclical change between production and development periods and ones of stagnation; these times correspond to phases of human and urban progress or inactivity. The first production cycle to be considered is the sugar cycle, which began in the fifteenth century with the islands' discovery,[1] and lasted until the late sixteenth century. This economic development led to the consolidation of cities such as São Tomé and Santo António, and to the occupation of low and coastal areas. From this production cycle, there are a few buildings of military and religious character that can still be seen, such as the fortresses of São Sebastião and São Jerónimo, and the churches of Bom Jesus and Nossa Senhora da Avé-Maria, which later São Tomé's main cathedral. In the late eighteenth century,

Source: Chuck Moravec

São Tomé and Príncipe's colonial inheritance is still present in its cities

the cocoa cycle originated the expansion and penetration into all of the islands' territory. The cocoa and coffee plantations – *roças* – were complex agrarian structures for the production of goods for export. They became one of the greatest examples of agro-industrial heritage in the African context. The structure of the *roças* consisted of several residential buildings such as a main house (*casa grande*) and *sanzalas* (lodgings for slaves); industrial buildings such as dryers, warehouses, and small factories; and also schools, hospitals, churches, and other buildings.[2] They became an attraction because of the variety and diversity of buildings within. However, while the *roças* are beautiful, they were ultimately an architecture of control and the spatial relationships reinforced the colonial power dynamics. The axial layout, with the *casa grande* in a prominent position

to oversee the rest of the site, flanked by the housing for white workers (which were differentiated by class), followed by the *sanzalas*, entrenched social conditions and relations that continued to reverberate after slavery ended in 1875.[3] After the cocoa cycle, it is possible to observe the process of expansion of cities and urban centres, which originated in areas like Trindade, Madalena, and Pantufo; Angolares on the south and Neves on the west of the island.[4] In the case of Trindade, expansion consolidates the higher and cooler areas that avoid the swamps that existed in the main city. Until the early twentieth century, the city of São Tomé had a reticulated grid along the coastline, already defining its main squares and functional areas. From the 1940s to the 1960s, the city developed according to the São Tomé Urbanisation Plan, published in 1956.

Source: David Stanley (left and right)

Igreja Nossa Senhora da Conceição in Santo Antonio, Príncipe Island (restored 1940)

Palacio do Governo Regional at Praça Marcelo da Veiga, Santo Antonio, Príncipe

Source: Enerlid Franca

Imposing colonial building in the city of São Tomé

It defines a zoning plan with structural axes, the construction of the canal and the embankment areas along the fortress. In this period some significant housing equipment and buildings were built to meet the needs of Portuguese workers in the archipelago: for instance, the Salazar Neighbourhood (now 3 de Fevereiro).

It was, however, with the obligations of urban plan for the city of São Tomé, studied in 1962 by the Overseas Urbanisation Office, that the most prominent buildings in the city were designed: public buildings such as the National Lyceum, the Império Cinema, and the post office. These are buildings in a modernist style and small scale when compared to other African contexts of Portuguese origin, which give a smaller scale and lower density to São Tomé. From the mid-twentieth century to the present day it is possible to observe stagnation and a low period within urban development, which occurs from the urban areas to the main road networks, with the widespread abandonment of previously occupied areas, such as *sanzalas*. The urban sprawl and the construction initiatives that are currently being developed in São Tomé and Príncipe do not obey any urbanisation plan or prior zoning. This lack of planning weakens valuable heritage and unparalleled architectural sets.

Notes

1 The islands were uninhabited by humans before the arrival of the Portuguese, and then were populated with slaves of predominantly Angolan and Mozambican origin. This was followed by a twentieth-century influx of Cabo Verdean contract workers.

2 The structure and organisation of São Tomé's *roças* were also influenced by the Brazilian model of plantations. This influence becomes more prominent in the period after Brazil's independence from Portugal (1822–1925), when a significant number of wealthy plantation owners/slave traders who were connected to the Portuguese crown left Brazil and moved into São Tomé – also affecting the cultivation methods utilised and the introduction of other crops.

3 Even though slavery ended in theory, by many accounts not much changed in practice. As the island was essentially a series of large parcels of private property, and the *roças* were a stand in for any other type of urban settlements, except the capital, and the movement of workers between *roças* was restricted, the now-freed slaves were left with little option but to continue working in the same *roças* that they were born in, and in conditions that did not markedly improve until much later, upon international scrutiny of the living conditions of cocoa workers under Portuguese rule in the early twentieth century.

4 The Angolar people (living in the area of São João dos Angolares) are a distinct group whose origin is disputed. Presumably they were living in settlements in the Angolares area (southeast coast of São Tomé Island) prior to the Portuguese moving that far south and developing that part of the island. Their language is known as Angolar, and is distinct from Forro, the Creole language spoken on the rest of the island. This is arguably one of the only types of settlements that exists outside of the city of São Tomé that was not created through the construction of a *roça*.

Source: Dário Pequeno Paraíso

Cubatas, **wooden houses on stilts, are typical in São Tomé's vernacular architecture**

View of Roça Porto Alegre on São Tomé Island

Source: Francisco Nogueira

São Tomé

Source: Chuck Moravec

Colonial-era residential building

São Tomé, located in the northeast of the island of the same name, is the capital city of the Democratic Republic of São Tomé and Príncipe. The small archipelago became an important colonial outpost of established sea routes and maritime trade. Uninhabited before the arrival of the Portuguese around 1470, the islands have a history characterised by sugar, cocoa, and coffee plantations and slave labour. The archipelago became one of the world's leaders in cocoa exportation by the twentieth century. The buildings are a direct reflection of these enterprises over time, which included the increasing destruction of vegetation, radical changes in land usage, implementation of major infrastructure projects, and the construction of *roças* (plantations), which shaped an environment that reflected, and responded to, the specific purposes of its colonial powers. Over time, however, production of cocoa declined. Its devaluation in international markets induced major economic difficulties for the small country and its capital city – resulting in increased poverty. The colonial inheritance of the city is still

Source: iStock/AL-Travelpicture

Modernist heritage from the 1960s: São Pedro Chapel in the city of São Tomé

Palácio dos Congressos, the seat of the National Assembly of
São Tomé and Príncipe, which was finished in 1975

Source: Enerlid Franca

São Tomé Presidential Palace, which was formerly the Governor's Residence

National Lyceum, one of the oldest secondary schools in São Tomé and Príncipe

Residential buldings dating from colonial times in the streets of São Tomé

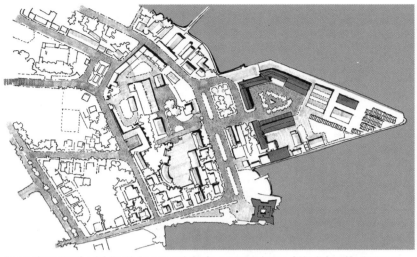

Coast of São Tomé, with Youth Square and the four-pronged star of São Sebastião Fortress

visible in its fabric, along with the monuments built following its independence in 1975. An axis parallel to the waterfront structures the older core of the city. Over the years, the city has expanded inwards organically. Urban growth over centuries was supported by expansion plans during the colonial period, but the provision of infrastructure was not able to keep up with increasing growth in recent times. Today the city is characterised by an increasing informal urbanity, with contrasts between planned and unplanned areas. Its extension along the coast and its ingoing roads form a widely spread yet continuous mass. *adp*

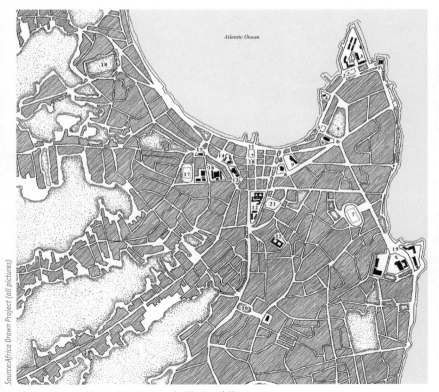

Source:Africa Drawn Project (all pictures)

Planned and unplanned areas meet in São Tomé City

Typical *cubata* in Bairro de Hospital, São Tomé city, with a
wooden extension on the ground floor serving as storage space

The Cubata: São Tomé's Vernacular Timber House

Edwlne Neto

São Tomé and Príncipe is home to a type of wooden house with very particular features: the *cubata*. This typology results from the successive urban transformations the county has gone through, its intense tropical climate, its fragile social context, and the lack of economic resources on the islands. Factors such as the various economic cycles, the geography of the archipelago, social stratification, different ethnicities, and the influences of different affiliations have also shaped the popular architecture.

Source: Dário Pequeno Paraíso (all pictures)

Cubata in Almeirim, São Tomé Island

Urban and Rural Areas

São Tomé's urban spaces were designed and built by the Portuguese colonial administration. They consisted largely of masonry administrative buildings, commercial establishments, and the residences for the former colonial administrators and civil servants, and were mainly built in a Salazarist style (also known as Luso-tropical). In the capital city and small towns, the buildings are arranged in a centralised pattern with a Catholic church, an administrative building, postal and telecommunications offices, and a commercial house that formerly belonged to the Portuguese companies overseas. In rural areas there are *roças* – plantations under the colonial administration – and single-family settlements known as *glebas* or *roças di forro*. In this context, some so-called classic forms of accommodation can be identified, such as chalets, villas, and *cubatas*.

Cubata Characteristics

Cubatas are elevated by stilts and feature a long staircase that leads to a veranda, while the ground floor is reserved as a store or for future extensions of the

house; their roofs are typically pitched or skillion. They are usually surrounded by small patches of garden, called *kintéh*. Footpaths follow the contours of the smallholdings to reach the main roads that connect to large and sprawling settlements. The houses are usually are inherited from a member of an extended family. Most people in urban or rural spaces live in these humble wooden houses. There is no coordinated plan other than the continual subdivision of plots as families grow and access to land decreases. A variety of shanties and shelters can be attached to these houses as households engage in informal commerce and services.

The suspension of the living space frees up the ground. Although this is not the only solution, it is frequently adopted in São Tomé and Príncipe because most of the early houses were put up in the low and marshy regions during the rainy season. Among the main reasons for suspending the building are the need for ventilation necessitated by the tropical

Cubatas in Almeirim, São Tomé Island, and the Bairro de Hospital Neighbourhood of São Tomé city (below) on sloping terrain. The stairways are always on the outside of the houses and face onto the main thoroughfare.

Source: Dário Pequeno Paraíso (all pictures)

Source: Dário Pequeno Paraíso (all pictures)

Unfinished *cubata* elevated from the ground by wooden pillars in Uba Cabra, São Tomé Island

climate, protection from wildlife (especially parasites), and the protection of the wood from harsh weather conditions. According to a 2001 housing survey, ca. 70 per cent of dwellings in São Tomé and Príncipe are *cubatas*. The lifespan can range from twenty to fifty years, depending on the quality of the wood, how well it has been preserved, and the climatic conditions – humidity is very high in São Tomé and Príncipe.

The Building Process

Construction of the houses is relatively straightforward. A client simply notifies a local carpenter, who sketches something within the stipulated budget. Once the quadrilateral form has been traced, the pillars – generally made from resistant wood Brazilian ironwood or wood from the jackfruit tree – are set up. The same wood is used for the skeleton, which is then locked properly by diagonally placed sticks (anchors). The walls are made of boards, leaving openings for windows and doors. The stairs are always located outside the house and face the main road. In the past, *cubatas* were constructed exclusively in wood, but depending on the economic status of the users, some now integrate concrete brick and stone into the construction. Despite these modifications, the *cubata* has become an icon of indigenous architecture in São Tomé and Príncipe.

Rituals during Construction

A ritual called *Agua Futado* is carried out during the construction of *cubatas*. This traditional process begins with choosing the right moon sign to start the construction. The belief is that, to start the house without knowing the moon sign one may start on an unfortunate

A *cubata*'s structure is typically made from jackfruit or Brazilian ironwood

The wooden construction does not provide good thermal and acoustic insulation

Incomplete *cubata* on reinforced concrete pillars in Conde, São Tomé Island

day, thereby negatively influencing the construction process and allowing accidents during the erection of the house or its lifespan. When implanting the first pillar, coins, cornmeal, beans, rice, palm oil, palm wine, and salt fish are put under each corner pillar and the middle pillar so good fortune will be always be within the house and will help its occupants to succeed in life. An old chamber-pot should be hung facing the main road during construction to inhibit evil eyes, or in some cases, a white and red bandana has been hung on two opposite sides of the house to bring peace and luck to the residents.

Once all of the structural elements (timbers) of the house are set in place, it is necessary to *Levantar Agua Futado,* which involves inviting the person who understands the positive moon sign to pray for good fortune. Afterwards the carpenter finishes the installation of the wooden trusses to complete the pitched roof and places on corrugated zinc to cover the house. On the same day, prayers are conducted and the owner offers food and wine to the carpenter and other workers.

Health and Safety

Cubatas in São Tomé and Príncipe are made either purely out of wood or from wood and masonry. Such houses do not meet health and safety conditions, and usually do not feature an adequate kitchen or bathroom. The latter rooms are usually installed in annexed structure, and many *cubatas* do not even have a latrine, constituting a threat to public health. The homes also have very poor sound insulation.

The growing demand for wood products for building and furniture continue to be a big factor in the deforestation process of the country. Furthermore, the poor fire resistance of *cubatas* has exacerbated the problems faced by families already living below the poverty line.

Rethinking the Cubata

As the result of the government's conservation and biodiversity policies, and the increasing need for housing, caused by the growth of the population, every aspect of the *cubata* is today being reconsidered. This has led professionals and academics to search for alternatives to wood by interpreting the *cubata* in a modern way. These fresh solutions can be built on a low budget, and are designed to mitigate risks while also improving living conditions for the inhabitants. Walls can be made of ecological bricks or stabilized earth blocks (a mixture of soil, sand, a stabiliser (often cement) and water, poured into a press and then compressed). This works out less costly than using wood, provides better thermal and acoustic insulation, and means the home is fire resistant.

São Sebastião Fortress/ National Museum

Avenida 12 Julho, São Tomé
Luís Benavente (restoration)
ca. 1575, ca. 1950

São Sebastião Fortress is located at the southern end of Ana Chaves Bay. Building work started in the mid-sixteenth century (1566). It was the first and most emblematic defensive military building in São Tomé and Príncipe. With a square-shaped star plan and four bastions built with European stone, the fort contains a central courtyard with a dense and unique architectural expression. Three of the fort's bastions are oriented to the line of the sea. It was constructed because of the need to defend against the constant attacks by French corsairs, which took place in the sixteenth century. The site was strategic point on the island, as well as the archipelago's location in the Gulf of Guinea. In the nearby square are statues of the three navigators who first discovered the islands: João de Santarém, João Paiva, and Pêro Escobar. They face the fortress and have their backs to the sea. Several restoration interventions have been made over time, particularly in the 1950s by Luís Benavente, an architect working at the Overseas Urbanisation Office in Portugal. In the 1960s Benavente was chosen to work in the Maritime Province Defense Command Headquarters. Currently the fortress integrates the National Museum, which can be can be visited along with the São Sebastião lighthouse, a beacon established in in the 1860s.   *dp*

São Tomé Cathedral

ST 02

Avenida Água Grande/
Avenida de Independência, São Tomé
1490s

Source: David Stanley

Located in São Tomé city centre, near to the president's palace, the main cathedral was one of the first churches that was built using stone and whitewash powder in the archipelago in the last decade of the 1400s. It was first named Nossa Senhora da Avé-Maria, and changed to Nossa Senhora da Graça when the status was raised to main cathedral. It was founded under the Portuguese king Manuel I, and successively rebuilt and transformed first under King Sebastião I in the sixteenth century, and then later in the twentieth century, between the 1940s and the 1960s, by the island's

governor. These interventions partially changed the main façade to what features these days. According to the postcards of 1907, during the Prince of Beira's visit to the city, an original façade showed a more modest setting, with a model of two towers church with only one floor on each side above the triangulated pediment. The elevation drawing had three triangular pediment portals on the ground floor, and five perfect arc spans the top floor. During the twentieth century the intervention has introduced significant changes, leading to a revival façade in a neo-Romanesque style, with a round arch portal and double and triple arches on the top floor. A small round stained-glass window was added to the pediment. A floor was added to each of the towers and they were finished with pinnacles. The external volumes of the main chapel and the other volumes built retained their modest, classic character. The interior also changed over time; initially it had only one nave and a lower height, but today it has three naves with round arches. The walls and chancel were covered with traditional Portuguese tiles in blue and white during the first half of the twentieth century. *dp*

Source: Enedid Franca

The Colonial and Contemporary Structure and Function of Roças in São Tomé and Príncipe

Cristina Udelsmann Rodrigues

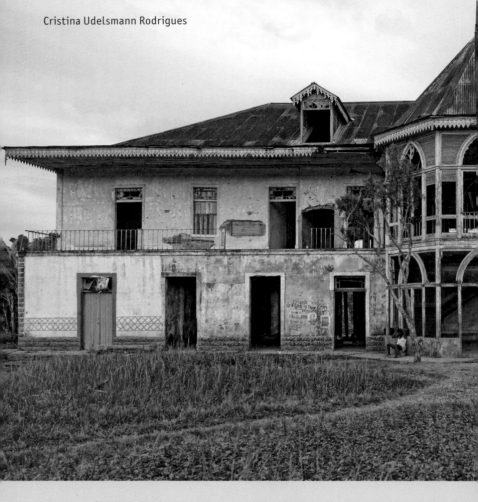

The *roças* of São Tomé and Príncipe display the colonial distribution of the plantation economy on the islands of the archipelago, and, at the same time, the social features associated with this system that dominated for centuries. Recently, they have either succumbed to the reorientation of the economy to other sectors and forms of organisation, or, in few cases, been revived as new projects in the sphere of tourism. Most *roças* were built between the late nineteenth century and the beginning of the twentieth to serve as the basis for the exploration of cocoa and coffee in the 'second' economic cycle on the islands that replaced the sugar, which was the main crop until the beginning of the eighteenth century.

They became the paradigm of the colonial action and the subject of praise from foreigners and Portuguese. The *roças* deeply marked the local urbanisation processes on the islands. The area of the two islands was almost entirely occupied by the *roças* at the height of the colonial cocoa and coffee production: of the estimated 150 *roças*, 103 are located in São Tomé Island. Each one had its own road, rail, and port systems, linked to the residential and production areas. The progressive settlement of *roças* in areas further away from the urban centres, which are disconnected from each other – except those that had interconnected smaller ones (*dependências*) – and in the majority of the cases difficult to access, served the

Boa Entrada Roça, on São Tomé Island, which is in a state of degradation
Source: Jorge Coelho Ferreira

purpose of isolating the workers for better control of both the population and the production, creating a closed self-sufficient settlement universe. The predominant and typical configuration of the roças involved a central vast open-air area (terreiro), surrounded by the buildings: the owner's house (casa grande), the hospital, the primary school and nursery, the aligned houses of the workers in the sanzala, the houses for the technical staff, the stables and the entrance portal. Some structural variations created different types of roças, like the 'avenue roça', aligned over a central pathway; at different heights or with more than one central terreiro, called 'city roça'; or quadrangular, with the buildings surrounding the terreiro, the roça terreiro. In a wider sense, the roças were more than mere production units. Constituting the basis for the social and economic development of the country for centuries, they are the foundational memory of the socioeconomic organisation, of the territorial organisation and of the national identity. Independence of the country in 1975 brought the coffee and cocoa productions almost to an end, with few exceptional initiatives afterwards, led by the state. The intentional isolation of the roças and the creation of conditions for autonomy and self-sufficiency in the colonial period left a legacy difficult to surpass after independence within the centralisation of the economy initiated by

Roça Saudade and the museum in the former home of Almada Negreiros, on São Tome

the newly established national government. The system rapidly lost its pertinence and functionality, while at the same time the population living in the *roças* had no economic or residential alternatives. The result was the rapid collapse of the production system and, consequently, the social and residential features tailored from the beginning to fit the plantation economic scheme. Over the years, an important portion of the former workers moved to the urban areas while the remaining had no capacity or authority to manage the common structures. The almost abandoned buildings of the *roças* initiated processes of

Hotel at the Roça Belo Monte, on Príncipe Island
Source: Jorge Coelho Ferreira (all pictures)

degradation, in most cases irreversible. Disintegration is the dominant trend all over the country. Today, the descendants of the workers from Angola, Mozambique, and Cabo Verde are left abandoned in the *roças*, where the buildings show the constant degradation they have been subject to since the end of the productive activities. The plots distributed after independence to these workers still provide food for the majority of the families but the communal production system no longer provides the ground for collective infrastructure and provision of services to the population. With the failure of a few post-independence initiatives to recover the productive capacity of the *roças*, rehabilitation today has increasingly been channelled to the touristic potential. While the recovery of agro-industrial activity faces several economic and structural obstacles, successful reconversions assume the form of touristic enterprises, in many cases concerned with the ecological sustainability of modern times. The few rehabilitation projects currently underway are reconverting the *roças* into touristic sites, absorbing some of the local population as workers. The

roças of São Tomé and of Príncipe now being rehabilitated or in the process of being bought and transformed are Belo Monte and Sundy in Príncipe, or Bombaim, São João dos Angolares, Saudade, and Monte Café in São Tomé. The projects usually transform the main house into the restaurant and central services, while the former schools and wards become bars or exclusive suites. The rooms for guests often occupy the former houses for the workers. In some plans, the former cocoa or coffee dryer is foreseen as a potential location for spas and jacuzzis. The exception so far is the Monte Café project, which involved the creation of the Coffee Museum in the machinery building and the opening of some local businesses related to coffee production. Also, the newly created museum in the home of of José Sobral de Almada Negreiros, a renowned Portuguese writer who lived in the Roça Saudade, reveals the varied possibilities open for the reconversion of the *roças*. Still, some of the largest and more emblematic *roças* of the country – like Agostinho Neto, Boa Entrada or Agua Izé – are visibly succumbing to abandonment, with no future plans known so far.

Interior of the main house

Roça Sundy

ST 03

Sundy, Pagué District,
Príncipe Island
1890, 1915–1921

Administration area

Located in the northwest of Príncipe Island, the *roça* (plantation) is divided into two spaces: the first corresponds to the entrance area near the main house and dryers; and the second is near the *sanzalas* (workers' quarters) and stables. All of the buildings come together to define the central yard, except for the large hospital and doctor's house, which are both out in the entrance area next to the access road. In Sundy Roça, the buildings' ages can be analysed through the lintels of the doors and windows. As there was a lack of large stones for lintels, round arch spans were designed. The main house, one of the newest buildings of the all complex, dates from 1921. From outside it seems to be single storey, but there is also a second storey. The interior houses rich textures and varieties of hydraulic mosaic tiles. From the late nineteenth century onwards the stables defined the top of the yard. Designed in a revivalist

Old hospital building

Source: Francisco Nogueira (all photos)

Exterior of the main house

style, they are defined by a medieval wall with arch spans and a crowned building with battlements and watchtowers. The complex of *sanzalas* dates from 1915 and is organised in a comb-like shape with two fronts. These complexes are placed perpendicular to the yard, with a curious window, similar to the openings of the foremen's houses, on top of the gable wall. The chapel, a very interesting building, is similar to a seventeenth-century chapel, but some interventions have altered the initial design slightly. From its original elements, it is possible to identify the porch and windows, the broken front, and the bell-ringer arc. Sundy Roca was the first place cocoa was planted in the archipelago, in 1822. It was also where, in May 1919, the British astrophysicist Arthur Stanley Eddington observed a solar eclipse; his findings in the experiment proved Einstein's theory of relativity. *dp*

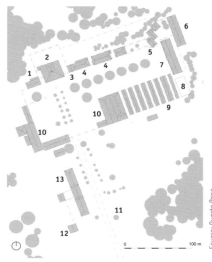

Source: Duarte Pape

Roça Sundy site plan:
1. Administration; 2. Main house; 3. Garage; 4. Foremen's houses; 5. Chapel; 6. Storage; 7. Stables; 8. Train building; 9. Workers' houses; 10. Warehouses; 11. Water store; 12. Doctor's house; 13. Hospital

Workers' housing

Roça Água Izé

ST 04

Água Izé, Cantagalo District,
São Tomé Island
1910–1920s

Workers' housing

Located on King's Beach Bay (Baía da Praia Rei), Roça Água Izé is famous for its owner, who was of African origin. João Maria de Sousa Almeida was very wealthy and a member of high society – exceptional for the son of a slave trader and a slave. The *roça* was the Água Izé company headquarters on Príncipe, and one of the most important agriculture units on the archipelago. The *roça* is developed as a city, in a slope area organised by small terraces, where a grid defines streets, neighbourhoods, gardens, and squares. The national road that crosses and connects the *roça* to the city of São Tomé and to Angolares village has no entrance or well-defined limits. The buildings blend with no apparent hierarchy of spaces. In the lower area are the administrative building, which is located next to the road without a central and dominant

Hospital nursery

Source: Francisco Nogueira (all photos)

Hospital exterior

position in the *roça*; the workshops; the metal workshops; the wood workshop and the warehouses. The extensive *sanzalas* (workers' housing) are placed along the slope, and the two hospitals are located in the higher area of the *roça* structure. Most of the existing buildings date from the 1910s to the 1920s, including the former hospital, built in 1914. It was not large enough to serve all of the *roça*'s inhabitants, so a new unit was erected in 1928. This action made the two hospital buildings into interesting areas to

see today. The plan of both was designed according to a radial layout with two floors and five distinct wings; this allowed the simultaneous monitoring of all the blocks from the central building. These two structures are the only examples on the archipelago, and followed imported models from England and France. Except for the hospitals and the main house, all the buildings follow a single design option; arched spans of jagged frames are found in both the *sanzalas* and the production units. *dp*

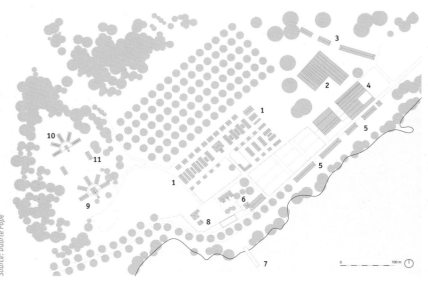

Source: Duarte Pape

Site plan of Roça Água Izé:
1. Workers' houses; 2. Production warehouse; 3. Stables; 4. Storage and factories; 5. Warehouses; 6. Main house; 7. Pier; 8. Chapel; 9. Hospital; 10. Old hospital; 11. Doctor's house

Source: iStock/AL-Travelpicture

Roça Agostinho Neto (Roça Rio do Ouro)

ST 05

Guadalupe, Lobata District,
São Tomé Island
1865, 1920–1960

The Roça Agostinho Neto, formerly the Roça Rio do Ouro, was founded in 1865 as the headquarters of the Valle Flôr Agricultural Society. The impressive structure is noteworthy for its size and architecturally monumental character. It integrated the most advanced rail system in the archipelago, establishing a link between its buildings and the port, located in Fernão Dias. The *roça* is organised along a central axis, which is marked by the imposing hospital, at the higher end, as well as the yards and terraces that follow the slope. The 'avenue' down the middle is flanked by all the *sanzalas* (workers' quarters) with their private terraces. At the opposite end are the museum and supporting buildings. The hospital, built in the 1920s under the influence of Art Deco, rises through two large wings, which are separated by the central body. Wards for European employees were on the top floor, and the pharmacy and the doctors' offices were next to the main entrance. A second floor was added to the main structure, emphasising the magnificence of the 100 m long façade. At the back, the hospital contained two buildings: a maternity ward and an area for the treatment of patients with contagious diseases. Closing the hospital complex were houses for doctors and nurses, the laundries, and the mortuary chapel. The main house, with its L-shape, marked the entrance to the complex. On the ground floor were the entrance hall, the office, and the dining room for employees. Upstairs, the rooms were situated along halls, and the bathrooms were covered by a large porch balcony. The museum, now in the location of the old main house, is organised in an U-shape, has views on to the botanical garden, which integrates a zoo and a small tea pavilion.   *dp*

Source: Francisco Nogueira (all photos)

Road to the hospital

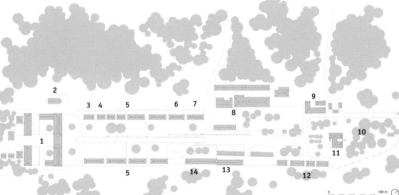

Source: Duarte Pape

Site plan of Roça Agostinho Neto (Rio do Ouro):
1. Hospital; 2. Church; 3. Doctor's house; 4. Social area; 5. Workers' houses; 6. School;
7. Day care centre; 8. Production area and workshops; 9. Main house; 10. Botanic garden;
11. Museum; 12. Foremen's houses; 13. Warehouses; 14. Offices

Workers' housing

Marcelo da Veiga Cinema ST 06
Praça dos Heróis da Liberdade/
Avenida da Independência, São Tomé
Overseas Urbanisation Office
ca. 1960

Situated in the northwest of the city of São Tomé, the old Império Cinema is within an urban expansion area from the first half of the twentieth century. In the same area, there are other attractions from the period, such as the city park, the Historic Overseas Archive, and the 3 de Fevereiro residential neighbourhood. The cinema was built between the 1950s and 1960s, and its monumental scale picks it out in Heróis da Liberdade Square. The modernist form was designed by the Overseas Urbanisation Office in an Art Deco style. Together with its monumental lines, which can be seen from outside, the building presents a symmetrical composition on its façade. This recessed façade, together with the exterior stairs, defines the entrance and establishes continuity between exterior and interior space. The interiors are of interest not only for their dynamics and the articulation of the stairs and foyer spaces which allow access to the screening rooms, but also for the decorated ceilings

and detailing such as the woodwork in the stairs and balconies. The cinema was restored at the beginning of the twenty-first century, and is currently named after Marcelo da Veiga, a local poet.   *dp*

Telecommunications Company ST 07
of São Tomé and Príncipe »
Avenida Marginal 12 Julho, São Tomé
José Pinto da Cunha, José Pereira da Costa
1965

Located near the coast, the Santo-mense Telecommunications Company (Companhia Santomense de Telecomunicações) building is prominent in the landscape of the Ana Chaves Bay. Opened in 1965, it was designed by two Portuguese architects, José Pinto da Cunha (1921–2007) and José Pereira da Costa (1923–1976), who were then based in Luanda, developing projects for the islands. The building was previously the headquarters of the Post and Tourism Information Office. It has a modernist design, and is clearly adapted to the tropical context. Reinforced concrete technology was adopted for the grid of brise-soleil on the façade. This emphasises the building's horizontality, despite its height, and performs the functions of shading

Source: Francisco Nogueira (all pictures)

and ventilation, while making a strong aesthetic impact. Originally the gridded façade was ochre in hue, but the building has been recently restored to move closer to Santomense's corporate colours. It is, however, one of the most innovative and significant works in São Tomé's modernist architecture. The interior remains mostly unchanged; it retains the structure's modernist image. *dp*

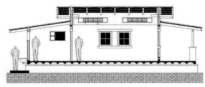

Cross section

Floor plan

**Ecobairro Muquinquim
Social Housing**

ST 08

Guadalupe, Lobata, São Tomé Island
*Baixo Impacto Arquitetura/
Márcio Holanda, Paulo Rodriguez*
2012

Priming for a bioclimatic comfort design and sustainable rural urbanism, the social and eco houses of Ecobairro Muquinquim are intended to demonstrate low cost and low impact technologies on São Tomé Island. The materials used include adobe walls; lightweight vaulted concrete slabs supported on simple stone walls; and bamboo used as a ceiling liner and thermal insulation for a zinc roof, something which is more economically viable. Local workers were professionally trained and the building materials were produced directly on the construction site. Such technologies have proved that it is feasible to use materials such as concrete and wood sparingly in home construction, and to avoid the excessive use of energy for air conditioning. *pa*

Source: Baixo Impacto Arquitetura (all pictures)

Jalé Ecolodge ⌃ ST 09

Praia Jalé, Porto Alegre,
São Tomé Island
Baixo Impacto Arquitetura/
Márcio Holanda, Paulo Rodriguez
2013

Following essentially the same methods as Ecobairro Muquinquim Social Housing, the Jalé Ecolodge went further and demonstrated more local development, bioclimatic comfort, and even reduced the environmental impact of the development. In the project, green roofs, landscaped with native species adapted to the local microclimate, were constructed with wood and bamboo lining and supported directly on structural adobe walls. The long roof eaves shield the walls from the wind and rain, and the high platform made from slabs guarantees structural security, protecting the constructions from the high tides that occasionally invade the site. The architects chose natural materials – locally extracted and supplied by the community of fishermen and farmers – to reduce the the development's environmental impact and to generate income for local residents. Local stone was used for foundations, earth for walls, and bamboo for cover. Wood and glass openings allow views of Jalé beach while also protecting from the strong coastal breeze. High openings covered with anti-mosquito screening give constant ventilation. The colourful stained glass windows were handmade using recycled glass bottles. *pa*

International Bank of São Tomé and Príncipe

ST 10

Praça da Independência, São Tomé,
Água Grande, São Tomé Island
Nuno Carrôlo & Álvaro Silva Arquitectos
2013

The International Bank of São Tomé and Príncipe (Banco Internacional de São Tomé e Príncipe) Headquarters, located directly at the seaside, across from the Central Bank of São Tomé and Príncipe, is one of the few recently constructed large

scale projects in the city of São Tomé. Like many of these projects, it was designed by a Portuguese firm; and it was built by Portugal's third biggest construction company, Soares da Costa. The complex consists of two parts: the older building and a new extension, towering above the original three-storey wing, which was also renovated. In an attempt to stylistically link and unify the two parts, the originally white bank building was painted grey, and the new tower's dark glass façade features horizontal

Source: Enerlid Franca

brise-soleils, which, though made from painted black metal, correspond with the old building's concrete shading elements. Both wings are traditional reinforced concrete frame constructions. The renovation and construction of the new four-storey structure with an area of 1,054 m² cost 2.1 million euros. The headquarters now speak a clean, international, and modern architectural language – interchangeable, yet undeniably elegant, and, thanks to the shading elements, adapted to the tropical climate.   *ed*

Source: Soares da Costa

Gabon

GA

Jean-Pierre Maïssa, Gabonese architect and urban planner, born 1965 in Moanda. Graduated from Genoa University in 1992, and obtained a PhD from Milano Polytechnic in 1999. He opened his architectural practice in 2002, and co-designed the Ministry of Water and Forests, Libreville. *(cc)*

René Boer, Dutch urban and architectural researcher in Amsterdam and Cairo. Works for the Failed Architecture foundation and the Cairo Institute of Liberal Arts and Sciences. He has worked with architecture think tank Archis/Volume and research collectives in Barcelona and Ramallah/Jerusalem.

Aerial view of Libreville, with Rue Ndende leading up to the Stade Omnisports Omar Bongo
Source: David Ignaszewski

Introduction

Jean-Pierre Maïssa

The name Gabon comes from *Gabão*, the Portuguese word for cloak, which was the rough shape of the Libreville estuary when Portuguese explorers first arrived. Since this so-called 'discovery' back in the fifteenth century, the country has been governed by the Portuguese, the English, and the French, who abolished the slave trade. The territory is covered by rainforest, is innervated by hundreds of rivers, and has a very diverse range of wildlife, which is attributed to the lower human population – an average of three inhabitants per square kilometre. The country has been a place for what the French geographer Laurent Pourtier termed 'the dialectics of void'. This was an attempt to conceptualise the dissolution of human settlement in the desert of uninhabitability, and the undernourished cultural and social relationships shaped by distance, time, and space, as a challenge to form a nation through new infrastructure and a brand new administration and governance.

Historically, Gabon has been a place for autonomous nomads and independent groups of Pygmy tribes, transiting freely, without restrictive barriers, over an immense land. Then the Bantu peoples came, emancipated from the bordering forest kingdoms, and a process of gradual absorption of the local population commenced, producing the now myriad peoples and cultures in the forest territory.

Independence from France dates to 1960. The economy has since been boosted by the abundance of natural resources, and the booming oil industry was a major provider in the mid-1970s, permitting prosperity and providing a good infrastructure within major cities (Libreville, Port-Gentil, and Franceville). Travelling through the country remains a problem as there is a lack of infrastructure and routes. To overcome the obstacles of climate, topography, and nature requires resources that are unavailable because of the sparse population and activities that still characterise the territory.

In the colonial era, with the fast pace of making the new nation, architecture was essentially created through missions being implanted within cities and evangelising new remote areas, which gave way to an early experimentation with modernism. A major example of that move is the case of the lesser-known Italian master, Marcello D'Olivo, a native of Friuli who graduated from the Higher Institute of Architecture of Venice in 1947. He was a contemporary of Carlo Scarpa and Angelo Masieri, and has been a prominent representative of the Italian modern architecture movement, under Bruno Zevi's theoretical lens. Late influences also relate to Le Corbusier's urban works in Algiers (Plan Obus), but mostly to Frank Lloyd Wright, who visited the renovated Venice School of Architecture, which was led by Giuseppe Samonà. Projects by Le Corbusier and Frank Lloyd Wright, even unbuilt, were a huge source of influence; for instance, Frank Lloyd Wright's never-built Masieri Foundation, designed to stand along Venice's Grand Canal. Marcello D'Olivo's projects spanned territories such as Africa, the Middle East, and the Americas, where attitudes to new buildings were less conservative than his native Italy and he could experiment with more avant-garde ideas.

Libreville became D'Olivo's major 'practice field' for around a decade, as he helped to shape the city through hundreds of sketches, between 1965 and 1977. The place later helped him to theorise his thoughts on the concept of an ecotown; these were later published in the book

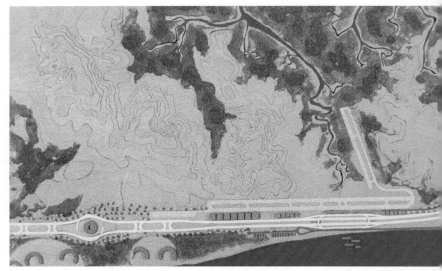

Master plan for Libreville: *Bande jaune* **study of the airport and highway along the seafront**

Ecotown Ecoway: Utopia ragionata in 1986. D'Olivo helped trace the linear city shape that best described the cities bordering the Atlantic Ocean estuary. The element driving the form remains the free curving highways, which expose the terrain according to topography, allowing natural drainage of the heavy tropical rainfall. As no comprehensive scheme leading to a certain state of the urban fabric was implemented, this master plan has been lost today. The city has become somewhat of an 'orphan' – speaking urbanistically. After D'Olivo left in the late 1970s, these highly speculative yet valuable premises for a decisive urban identity and directions to develop them were lost under poor urban development policies. In fact, slums emerged along the highways, covering the sloped terrain and encouraging floods while disturbing the natural drainage. Today, modern

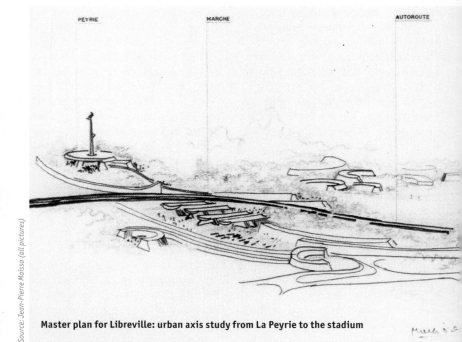

Master plan for Libreville: urban axis study from La Peyrie to the stadium

Source: Jean-Pierre Maissa (all pictures)

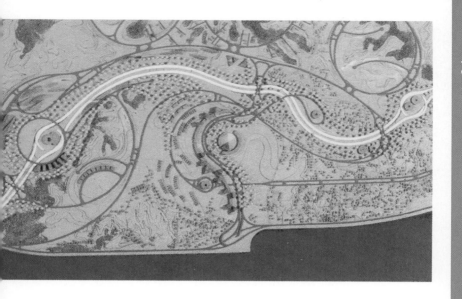

buildings are forced to cohabit with informal invasive housing along the central arteries around Boulevard Triomphal Omar Bongo, producing a well-known informal urban scene. Despite this, there is still much potential for sourcing from D'Olivo's vision to guide the future urban identity and development of Libreville. A comprehensive global architectural vision and tools still exist, but the operative guidelines and decision-makers required to understand that potential are lacking. Among the best tools for renewing the city are the management of rainfall drainage through topography; transport infrastructure design that connects integrated nodes; the creation of an economy of means by lowering ground works; the integration of nature in general; and the tempering of changes in the shape of the city through an organic approach to architecture.

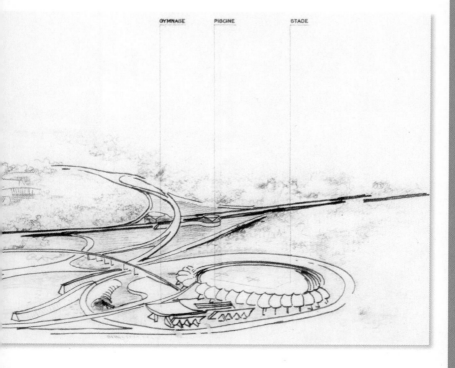

1. Port
2. City Hall
3. National Assembly

Libreville's Boulevard Triomphal Omar Bongo (above) and the Senate Building (below)

Source: Africa Drawn Project (top)
Source: iStock/Mtcurado

Libreville

Libreville, the capital city of Gabon, is situated on the tropical west coast of Africa. The port city, which is situated along the Komo River and on the north bank of the Gabon seashore, is a trade centre for the country and has a major railway station. Waterways play a significant role in its urban form and ability to expand, with the port dominating the urban fabric. National parks and dense natural forests surround the city to the east. This has impacted the expansion of Libreville, but also, through the logging industry, enabled its growth.

The initial settlement was located around the pier and current Boulevard Triomphal Omar Bongo. The latter is easily recognisable in the urban fabric as a result of the freestanding monuments to religious, political, and cultural powers along its boundaries. Various outlying villages were historically settled in the south, with an expansion to the north taking place during the 1940s. The coastal promenade was developed around 1955, when the main coastal road was upgraded. The area along the coast is the most densely populated today, in response to the energy and opportunities offered along the major road networks down the coastline. Rapid urbanisation followed independence during the 1960s, and was largely due to public infrastructure programmes, implemented

Source: iStock/Mtcurado

National Assembly on the Boulevard Triomphal Omar Bongo, Libreville

by the then-new government. The area bordering the Boulevard Triomphal Omar Bongo is taken up by commercial properties, with the industrial district, Oloumi, established around 1930, to the south, featuring warehouses to support the timber industries found there. To the north lie the only planned residential areas. Slums and an informal city fill everything in-between. The Cité de la Démocratie park and heritage district are easily discernable in the urban form, as they constitute large, undeveloped open spaces. The increasing pressure on available land has resulted in the informal occupation of areas such the Cité de la Démocratie park, though they are historically significant. Other landmarks that stand out in the city's low-rise, high-density sprawl are the Omar Bongo Stadium and the Presidential Palace. While Libreville is a reflection of a dynamic economy, the discontinuous, organic city form, with generous boulevards giving way to shantytowns, also reflects the increasing gap between rich and poor.   *adp*

Source: David Ignaszewski

Aerial view over Libreville, looking up Rue Ange M'ba from the waterfront

Source: iStock/Mtcurado

Presidential Palace on Libreville's waterfront avenue, the Boulevard de l'Indepéndance

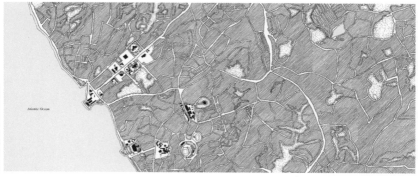

Source: Africa Drawn Project

Atlantic Ocean

Libreville streets: away from the coast, ordered boulevards turn to informal, unplanned areas

Source: iStock/Mtcurado

Former seat of the BEAC (Banque des États de l'Afrique Centrale) in Libreville

BEAC regional headquarters in Libreville, Gabon (ATAUB Architectes, 2010)
Source: Panoramio/Steephane

The Lonely Towers of African Capitals

René Boer on the BCEAO and BEAC buildings –
two banks shaping the African skyline

The skyline of almost every Western- or Central African capital is dominated by a single tower housing the local offices of the regional central banks of the Banque Centrale des États de l'Afrique de l'Ouest (BCEAO) and the Banque des États de l'Afrique Centrale (BEAC). These institutions were created at the onset of the decolonisation wave in the early 1960s and have been powerful economic and financial stakeholders in the region ever since. Since their establishment, the BCEAO and the BEAC have carried out an ambitious building programme, realising impressive office buildings and towers in the capital of every member country. Over the last few decades, this has resulted in a striking pattern of regional architecture, counting for the majority of this part of the continent's high-rises.

Currently, a total of eight Western African countries are grouped in the BCEAO and six Central African in the BEAC. These regional banks were set up to monitor the emission of the CFA franc, the shared currency named after the *Colonies Françaises d'Afrique* – an abbreviation quickly altered to *Communauté Financière Africaine* after the colonies' independence. Since

BCEAO building in Abidjan, Côte d'Ivoire

Source: Didier Mande

then, the BCEAO and the BEAC have managed the financial legislation of their member states to a large extent. France, the former coloniser of most of the participating countries, only slightly relinquished control and still has a remarkable influence on the institutions' policies today. An event that clearly shows the power of France over the BCEAO and the BEAC was Paris' unilateral decision in January 1994 to devaluate the CFA by half,

Source: iStock/Alarico

BEAC (Banque des États de l'Afrique Centrale) building in Bata, Equatorial Guinea

Source: Serigne Diagne

BCEAO tower in Dakar, Senegal

the urban landscapes of African capitals will, for many, continue to represent the neo-colonial relationship with France, known as the *Françafrique*.

Although the institutions' policies are characterised by influences from abroad, some of the BCEAO and the BEAC towers' architecture is characterised by various references to vernacular building styles. In particular the BCEAO towers in Bamako (Mali) and Ouagadougou (Burkina Faso) clearly echo the well known earthen architecture of Djenné and Timbuktu. Others are less extravagant and some are glass extravaganzas, such as BEAC's constructions in Libreville (Gabon) and Brazzaville (Congo). The main office in Bissau, capital of the newest BCEAO member country Guinea-Bissau, is clearly the least inspired, though this has a lot to do with the complexities related to sourcing building materials in the poorest of Western African nations.

arguing that a cheaper CFA would improve African exports. In reality it made imported goods from Europe, as well as debt repayment obligations, twice as expensive. Although the BCEAO and the BEAC have managed to avoid most of the financial volatility occurring in other African countries, both regional banks are often perceived by the population as being complicit in carrying out these policies. As a result, their inescapable towers in

BCEAO (Banque Centrale des États de l'Afrique de l'Ouest) building in Ouagadougou, Burkina Faso

Source: iStock/Mtcurado

Most BCEAO and BEAC offices are the only high-rises in town and are therefore defining the skyline of their respective cities. In particular the BCEAO tower in Bamako is dramatically situated next to the Niger River, but also the Niamey (Niger), N'Djamena (Chad), and Lomé (Togo) headquarters are towering over the otherwise low-rise African urban landscapes. Dakar (Senegal) and Abidjan (Côte d'Ivoire), both regional economic powerhouses, already have multiple high-rises, making these bank buildings less striking than elsewhere. A shared characteristic of all BCEAO and BEAC towers is that they are embedded in the urban fabric; none of them are directly located on a street. All are surrounded by a large garden or open (parking) space, closed off to the public by a high, well-protected wall. While the varied spaces of the rest of the city centre – full of

BEAC building in Yaoundé, Cameroon

Source: Albert Bergonzo

GA

covered shops, markets, food stalls, and public buildings – provide some shelter from the harsh climate, the architectural set-up of the regional banks create large, hostile 'urban islands' in the middle of African capitals.

As a consequence, the BCEAO and BEAC towers can be interpreted in various contrasting ways. One such is that they can be seen as isolated palaces which take up large swathes of urban space in city centres, housing the complicit officials implementing policies from the Global North. Seen another way, the advent of the high-rise in the African capital could also be perceived as a sign of progress and development, as the tallest construction is typically viewed in a similar way around the world. One thing is certain: building the BCEAO and BEAC towers has provided a remarkable opportunity to experiment with African architecture on a different scale than is usual on the continent. Economic progress, though not benefitting the majority of the population, might soon lead to the construction of more towers – company for those lonely towers standing in African capitals.

This article was first published at www.failedarchitecture.com.

Source: iStock/Mtcurado

BEAC edifice in Brazzaville, Republic of the Congo

Source: David Ignaszewski (all pictures)

Sainte-Anne Church GA 01

Omboué, Fernan Vaz Lagoon,
Ambroise, Nengue Sika,
Ogooué-Maritime Province
Ateliers Gustave Eiffel
1892

The Sainte-Anne Mission was founded by French missionaries in the late colonial period, during the late nineteenth century. In order to consolidate the colonial presence in the territory, missions were founded, the indigenous people were evangelised, and a brand new administrative map of the country was created. This intent led Fathers Béleon and Bichet to the heart of the Nkomi people, in southwest Gabon, where they built the Sainte-Anne Mission on the outskirts of the village of Omboué, near the Fernan Vaz Lagoon. Because of the difficulties with gathering building materials on site, and the lack of skilled artisans needed for a modern and durable building – local building techniques were adapted for temporary rainforest habitats – the missionaries decided to look for builders abroad. They opted for an elegant, avant-garde, prefabricated structure, that was built in France by the civil engineer and architect Gustave Eiffel. The church was then transported to Gabon and built on site, founding

Source: David Ignaszewski (all pictures)

the Sainte-Anne Mission. Construction finished in 1892. The church is a simple structure with metal vaults that span the interior cross section, avoiding intermediate columns. The entire structure resembles a reversed basket. The building measures 35 × 12 m, and its campanile is 27 m high.   *cc*

Albert Schweitzer Museum   GA 02
Lambaréné, Moyen-Ogooué Province
1924

In 1912, Albert Schweitzer, a German-French doctor, philosopher, and theologist, went to Gabon for humanitarian purposes, delivering medical care to the indigenous population. He settled in Lambaréné, a key village fourteen days upstream by raft from the mouth of the Ogooué River at Port-Gentil, around 350 km from Libreville, the capital of Gabon. The current Albert Schweitzer Museum initally served as a house for the doctor and his wife, and also hosted his library and his nurse's room. The wooden building, though not designed by a professional architect, could be seen as a prominent anticipation of some of the contemporary frontline topics in architecture: adaptation to

the site, the integration of infrastructure, and sustainability features that stem from preventing excessive heating caused by the tropical climate – the structure is a porous perforated wooden envelope, cross ventilated by shadowed openings. The cantilevered building has its main floor isolated from the ground, ensuring ventilated interiors. The house has a sloped pitched roof that allows for the efficient drainage of heavy rainfall. The cross-section wood structure – made of V-rafters – offers free interior spaces, while allowing for an enlarged front porch. The sophisticated wood trellis leads to diffuse screen walls inspired by local basket weaving techniques and the light in the rainforest habitat. The humanitarian spirit that permeates this design went beyond the building: the hospital compound is organised in a way that permits patients to recover among their relatives, keeping the hospitalisation period in tune with social and cultural norms. The building's qualities were probably enhanced by guidance from professional advisers, and the result demonstrates how famous architectural design often comes from adapting to circumstances on site and from client sensibilities.   *cc*

Source: Yvan Gabon Pictures (all pictures)

Saint-Michel de Nkembo Church

`GA 03`

Nkembo, Libreville
Gérard Morel, Zéphirin Lendogno Ko Tonda
1967

The Saint-Michel de Nkembo Church was built in the Fang suburb of Nkembo in Libreville, as part of the development of the greater Libreville Archdiocese, from 1949 to 1967. What best characterises the church is the fact that, for the first time, there was a deliberate effort to introduce local artwork and aesthetics within a Western architectural typology. While Father Morel intended to build one of the largest worship spaces in the town – even in the country – which

was capable of hosting 3,000 people, he also wanted to ensure that the place would be identified as being locally produced. The simple rectangular temple is covered with a traditional pitched roof made of corrugated aluminium sheets. The internal space has a double-height nave, reproducing a typical Roman scene. What makes the church remarkable is the mosaic on the high entrance porch. This also features twelve wooden columns, carved by the late Gabonese artist, Zéphirin Lendogno Ko Tonda, depicting biblical scenes. Thirty-two wooden columns were carved by the artist, who also carved the altar, which dramatically embodies the cosmology and the art of Gabonese rainforest tribes.   *cc*

Source: Yvan Gabon Pictures (all pictures)

Rois Mages d'Akébé Church ≈ ↲

GA 04

Akébé, Libreville
René Lefebvre
1964

The Rois Mages Church was built in the then village of Akébé, Libreville, in 1964. The village has since been transformed into one of the most populated neighbourhoods of Libreville, showing an entirely transformed environment, compared to the one that hosted this modernist piece of architecture. As with many churches built in Gabon, this one does not have a major recorded architecture signature and has been attributed to the Spiritan priest Father René Lefebvre.

The church scheme features a light, concrete free-plan, created through a folded vault, echoing the engineering of the concrete structures of mid-century modern architectural ideas. Large cantilevered concrete slabs provide the overhang for shade, jutting out over the large porch in front of the church entrance façade. Advanced concrete techniques are associated with metal to shape an ensemble that borrows its symbolism and aesthetics from nautical architecture. The expression of mid-century modern architecture is evident in numerous ways across the building, starting from the curved shape, the subtly coloured glazed openings that filter interior lights, and the large overhang. *CC*

GA

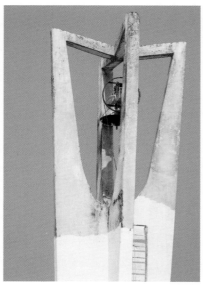

Source: Yvan Gabon Pictures (all pictures)

Immeuble du Pétrole ☆ ☆ GA 05
Boulevard Triomphal Omar Bongo,
Libreville
Paul-Émile Simon
1987

The Immeuble du Pétrole was one of the first new buildings intended to mark the new urban development along the Omar Bongo Triumphal Boulevard, in Libreville. The complex celebrates the oil industry, an industry that played crucial role in modernising Gabon, through the huge revenue it generated over two decades. It includes the headquarters of part of the government, and the offices of the ministers of the mining and oil industry. The architect, Paul-Émile Simon, was a Haitian national who graduated from the École des Beaux-Arts in Paris. The complex features two buildings, both covered with an array of thin concrete ridges that serve as brise-soleil, shielding the buildings from excessive heat. The biggest element is arc-shaped, gradually decreasing in height at its extremities. It stands directly behind the core of this building system, an ellipsoid profile building of nine storeys. Its external envelope is an array of thin concrete ridges with a foothill-shaped base, all connected to an internal, glazed curtain wall. The external concrete elements are fully clad with coloured glazed mosaic tiles; this is intended to protect the concrete against high humidity and excessive heat. Inside, the complex features Carrara marble flooring, along with wood panelling that shows off the diversity of local wood types through different marquetry wood work. For the time the complex was completed, the building techniques were advanced, as were the technical and mechanical components, which took the form of air conditioning, electrical fittings, and plumbing. The exterior is extensively landscaped with terrace gardens, and local granite is used to evoke the country's geological and mineral environment.   *cc*

Institut Français du Gabon GA 06
Boulevard Triomphal Omar Bongo,
Libreville
François Lombard
1991

The Institut Français du Gabon, or the Centre Culturel Français Saint Exupéry, is part of a French network of worldwide

Source: Yvan Gabon Pictures (all pictures)

cultural centres that aim to promote French culture. The project is part of the architectural development of the Boulevard Triomphal Omar Bongo and was clearly positioned to act as one of the city's main landmarks. The French government organised a design competition, which was won by the late architect François Lombard. He had a long-standing portfolio of public cultural projects, after playing a prominent role in setting up the French guidelines for public project programmes and organising competitions. For his project in Libreville – which is very similar to his Biarritz project – there is a tectonic expression through the brutalist use of concrete along the building's entire envelope. This is emphasised by the play between the concrete blocks – used for the centre's various functions – and the voids. François Lombard's Libreville project shows off textured exposed concrete, in which local artistic expressions and figures are inserted. These are even echoed in the geometry of the Y-shaped steel columns that support the monumental wave-shaped roof. A double-height lobby connects the entrance façade with the back-yards where a terraced garden acts as a continuation of the public space. The lobby occupies the centre of the façade and benefits from the natural light entering through two double-height glazed curtain walls. The building features an auditorium with a capacity of 400 spectators for music, theatre, or films; a public library; a multimedia library; a space to host exhibitions and conferences; and administrative offices. *cc*

Source: Yvan Gabon Pictures

Ministry of Water and Forests GA 07
Boulevard Triomphal Omar Bongo,
Libreville
Francis Meyer, Jean-Pierre Maïssa,
Karla Chacon
2002

Historically, Gabon's primary industry has been logging, as about 80 per cent of the country is covered by rainforests. These are innervated by hundreds of rivers and lakes which constitute a huge water resource. Before the oil and mining industries merged in the 1970s, it was expected that the country's major economic shift would come through the exploitation of the rainforest resources,

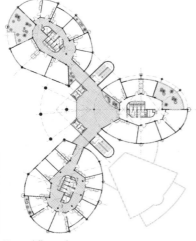

Source: Jean-Pierre Maïssa

Ground floor plan

accompanied by logging. In the early 2000s, the then-president, Omar Bongo, took the step of establishing thirteen national parks across the country, preserving about 12 per cent of the territory from excessive logging and making a decisive move for environmental concerns in the country's future politics. It was this context that lead to the project to house the Ministry of Water and Forests (Ministère des Eaux et Forêts), built on the city's main artery, Boulevard Triomphal Omar Bongo. The building plan features a composition of three ovals interconnected by horizontal circulations, each one representing one of the three main components of the ministry's responsibilities: water, forests, and the environment. On the ground level, a trapezoidal volume inserted between the second and third modules comprises an auditorium and part of the technical services. The building's vertical façade is meant to express a forest environment through cantilevered vertical gardens and wide painted walls. This expression provides a subtle solution to a common preoccupation in tropical architecture, with openings stepping back from the façade in order to temper the excessive heat and violent rain showers that challenge the best insulation methods. The building's interior features Gabon's main material – wood – in the wall cladding and flooring.   *cc*

Source: Yvan Gabon Pictures (all pictures)

Bord de Mer Building
| GA 08 |

Bord de Mer, Libreville
Aurore Cardot Architecture
2010

This office building was built in 2010 by Aurore Cardot Architecture and represents the current trends seen on the waterfront running along the Gabon Estuary. Libreville was born as a connection between villages on the Atlantic Ocean, a process that shaped the city and gave it its linear form. The road that connected the villages along the ocean shoreline has become the major city landscape – mainly because of its values which are borrowed from nature: namely the ocean, the beach, and the palm and acacias trees. The area is a welcoming place for leisure and open-air activities. The architectural language of the Bord de Mer Building is in line with the city's search for contemporaneity and a placeless spirit. This is illustrated in the modern structure's fully glazed façades; horizontal aluminium strip brise-soleil; metallic cladding side panels; and, spectacularly dominating the internal landscape, a generous double-height lobby with upper storeys and balconies supporting informal meeting places. Beyond these aesthetic elements, the building does not seem to explore the issue of sustainability. The glazed façades face the sea, but the full western exposure corresponds to the day's hottest moment, when the simple glazed curtain wall offers little protection against the heat of the tropical afternoon sun. *cc*

Onomo Hotel　　GA 09
La Sablière, Quartier Nouvelle
Ambassade US, Libreville
Koffi & Diabaté Architectes
2012

The Onomo Hotel is situated in an up-market neighbourhood of Libreville, near the new American Embassy and presidential residences. The hotel has a capacity of 115 rooms and was built when Gabon co-hosted the 2012 Africa Cup of Nations. The Ivorian architects Guillaume Koffi and Issa Diabaté conceived and built the hotel in time for the event. What best qualifies this architecture is the way it avoids revealing its true nature at first sight. From the car park, the hotel appears as if it is two separate blocks set side by side. To the left of the main entrance stands an elongated rectangular block that looks like a warehouse made of loosely woven wicker. This partially transparent façade changes according to the time of day – a palette of coloured light emanates from it at night. To the right of the entrance stands a slightly lower and fuchsia-coloured rectangular block, with limited opaque openings. The interior, however, quickly reveals the architects' conceptual choice to build a kind of secret garden. In fact, soon after passing through the double-height, spacious lobby – with its unusual central reception desk, surrounded by a bar and restaurant tables – guests discover two large enclosed courtyards, or forest gardens, towards which each of the hotel room balconies are oriented, responding to the programme's need to provide a view for each room. The architects intended the hotel to be seen as a self-contained world, suggesting a riad garden courtyard, typical of Moorish housing compounds in traditional northern and western African architecture. This building tackles both sustainability and function, delivering a contextual and culturally modern example of African contemporary architecture.　　*cc*

BEAC Regional Headquarters »　　GA 10
Avenue Jean Paul II, Libreville
ATAUB Architectes
2010

The Banque des États de l'Afrique Centrale (BEAC – Bank of Central African States) Regional Headquarters building is a landmark that was added to the Libreville

*Source: Koffi & Diabaté Architectes
(all pictures)*

Source: David Ignaszewski

skyline in 2010, when, with twenty-two storeys, it became the city's tallest building. The architects have often designed for the BEAC across the subregion. The building assumes a sculptural profile that alternates fully glazed curtain walls with vertical strips of ceramic tile. One side of the tower terminates with a sculptural cantilevered head that seems to be supported by two hands. There is an expressionistic will to sculpt the architectural form, in line with local culture of symbolism in traditional sculpture. The complex includes a detached volume on the basement level for the auditorium. At the top, there is a boardroom that offers a panoramic view of Libreville and the Gabon Estuary. Unfortunately, the building does not feature a particularly sustainable approach in both conceptual and mechanical ways. This underlines the BEAC's conservative stance when it comes to innovation through architecture, though the organisation is a major investor in public architecture across the Central African subregion.   cc

Source: Maïssa Architectures (all pictures)

E3MG Campus Moanda

GA 11

Route de Franceville, Moanda,
Haut-Ogooué Province
Maïssa Architectures
2016

Initially a village with a few hundred inhabitants, Moanda grew rapidly after the founding of a manganese mine in the late 1950s, expanding to become the second

Ground floor plan

largest city in the Haut-Ogooué Province. As part of its fiftieth anniversary celebrations, the Compagnie Minière de l'Ogooué (COMILOG) – a firm set up with French and Gabon capital and now owned by France's ERAMET Group – pledged to build a college to train mining engineers. The E3MG School of Mines and Metallurgy was set up in partnership with the Nancy School of Mines. Its 30 ha campus comprises thirteen buildings, including facilities such as housing for staff and students, a restaurant, a sports area, and a building that hosts both teaching and management spaces. The main school building houses teaching spaces, a library, laboratories, and administrative offices. As the campus is surrounded by forest, the architects wanted to design a place to contemplate the surrounding environment and allow for views over the trees and the mountains on the horizon. After various design iterations, they created

Source: WORKac

a series of H-shaped buildings with triangular pitched and cut-out roofs with high slopes, fully glazed reflective façades as the heart of the development. For the architects, these sharp volumes echo the pristine facets of manganese, revealing the raw material behind high-tech products – a raw material that comes from a natural environment. Though individual buildings on the campus are separate, the H-shape connects them visually. The continuous glazed façades provide not only natural light but also a panoramic view of the forest, enabling a sense of immersion in the woods while in any sector, be it the teaching rooms, the library, or the offices. In addition to the sharp slopes of the roof – convenient for draining off of the heavy rainfall that showers the region year round – the building's façade curtain walls have large mullions that act as brise-soleil to protect against the scorching equatorial sun.   *cc/ed*

Source: Mafissa Architectures

Assemblée Radieuse ⌃   GA 12
Cité de la Démocratie, Libreville
WORKac
2012 (design)

The Assemblée Radieuse was the winning entry in a competition to design a new 50,000 m² conference centre in Libreville. The design organises a vast programme of conference rooms, assembly halls, and dining facilities around three carved courtyards, each of which represents one of Gabon's rich and diverse ecosystems. Once it is finished, the centre will create a striking expression of President Ali Bongo Ondimba's vision for a *Gabon Vert* (Green Gabon). The Assemblée Radieuse will serve as an architectural landmark, with its dramatically sloped roof, which emerges from the lush hills of the surrounding diplomatic quarter, becoming one of the building's most prominent façades. Visible from the city below, it will reflect Gabon's emerging leadership in the region's political and environmental affairs, while celebrating the country's resources and potential to lead Africa into a new era. The building will harness elements of active and passive sustainable design: louvres made of African limestone to provide maximum shade and increased energy performance; courtyards to supply natural ventilation; light-coloured materials to reflect the sun's rays for thermal efficiency; a sloped roof to direct rainwater through a courtyard waterfall and into a treatment reservoir for reuse; and solar panels to provide energy for the building's hot water supply.   *cc*

Republic of the Congo (Brazzaville)

Ulrich Essimba, Congolese architect, born in Brazzaville. Holds a bachelor's in architecture and construction from the Fine Arts School of Brazzaville, where he worked on heritage issues. Since 2013, he has worked at the technical department of Bouygues Energies and Services. *(cc)*

Tristan Guilloux, French architect and engineer. He has spent time in Congo and the DRC on many occasions. He currently lives in Lyon and works for the French Ministry of Ecology. He also works with an artistic collective based in Lubumbashi, DRC, which deals with urban issues. *(cc)*

Philippe Guionie, French photographer. Historian by training. His work addresses ideas of memory and identity through documentary-style photography. Recipient of the 2008 Roger Pic prize. He is the artistic director of 1+2, a photographic residency programme in Toulouse, France.

Bernard Toulier, French architecture historian and honorary general curator for heritage at the French Ministry of Culture. He has led missions on the identification of architectural heritage in several African cities including Saint-Louis, Senegal; Kinshasa, DRC; and Brazzaville. *(cc)*

Assurance et Reassurance du Congo (ARC) Building in La Plaine, Brazzaville, which was inaugurated in 1980 and restored recently after the severe destruction caused by the 1997 civil war

Source: iStock/Mcurrado

Introduction

Ulrich Essimba, Tristan Guilloux, Bernard Toulier

Despite the evidence, architectural expression in Congo did not begin with the colonial era. The nature of buildings at these latitudes, which, in the past, were often made of perishable materials – raffia latticework huts, for example – makes displaying pre-colonial heritage problematic. This is illustrated by the difficulty of including on the World Heritage List the slave-trading port of Loango on the Atlantic Ocean and the Royal Domain of Mbé, a village located north of Brazzaville; both sites are still on the tentative list. The latter case is emblematic of this difficulty. Mbé was the capital of the last Téké king, Makoko, with whom Pierre Savorgnan de Brazza signed a treaty in 1880 to place the northern banks of the Congo River under French rule. Vestiges are scarce now, as, according to the Téké tradition, the capital has to be moved after every king's death. Another difficulty is drawing an architectural panorama that goes beyond the city of Brazzaville. As a colony and then an independent country, Congo has been characterised by the dominance of its capital. Only Pointe-Noire, a port and the country's second city, may have been adequate competition for Brazzaville.

During the early days of the colony, Brazzaville, on the Congo River, was an outpost that existed because of the need for trans-shipment: downstream from the city, the river becomes non-navigable, so goods had to be transferred to another mode of transportation there. The city was the starting point for the 'caravan route', where goods were carried on people's backs over 500 km to Loango. On return journeys, prefabricated elements were brought from Europe by boat for housing and transportation: dismantled steamers to travel up-river, metal tiles for the cathedral church, cast-iron pillars for the foundations of the colonial bungalows. Brickyards and surrounding forests supplied the building materials. The colonial settlement was organised around three cores. The administrative authorities were set up on the Plateau. The first Resident General, Charles de Chavannes, established a hut on a site dominating the River, which was transformed in 1903 into a palace that was designed in an imported yet poor Beaux-Arts style. The Catholic Mission settled on another hill facing the river, in a compound including a cathedral, a dwelling for religious people, a school and workshops, and a 'Christian village' to accommodate the newly baptised indigenous Africans. On the riverbanks, the colonial companies erected trading posts, wharfs, and shipyards. Most of the buildings were based on a type of colonial bungalow characterised by its surrounding veranda. The public facilities were drawn from architectural models designed by the colonial administration in France. As early as the 1900s, the indigenous population lived alongside the European neighbourhoods, with neighbourhoods separated by *non-aedificandi* (no-build) zones and arranged in a chequer-board pattern.

The construction of the Congo–Ocean Railway (from 1921 to 1934) radically transformed the precarious settlement by strengthening links with France. Trains replaced the caravan route and made it possible to transport cement and heavy construction materials such as ceramic tiles. During the 1930s, a local Public Works Department developed, hosting for the first time architects who attempted to break with the colonial bungalow model. New public premises, such as the central post office, were built in an Art Deco style, while the European villas borrowed a regionalist style from French vacation resorts: mock half-timbered façades of neo-Basque villas, and Flemish stepped gables. In Pointe-Noire, on the Atlantic Ocean, the styling

Source: Collection Bernard Toulier

Typical woven dwelling of the Téké (Bateke) people, around 1905

of the railway terminus was reminiscent of the neo-Norman railway station of Deauville in France. In Brazzaville, public gardens were landscaped, large driveways were lined with tree, and construction rules were enacted to transform the capital of the so-called 'Cinderella of the empire' into an attractive garden city, coined *Brazza la Verte* (Brazza the Green). In 1929, the governor general, Raphaël Antonetti, initiated the first town-planning scheme. This was later presented at the international conference on colonial urbanism during the International Colonial Exhibition in Paris in 1931. The plan sharply segregated the indigenous population into two main districts: Poto-Poto and Bacongo. Several premises such as schools or clinics were built by the Public Works Department, but most of the dwellings remained self-constructed – the experience of a *cité modèle* notwithstanding. The outbreak of World War II profoundly

altered the destiny of Brazzaville and the Congo. In October 1940 General Charles de Gaulle landed in Brazzaville to organise the political and military rule of Free France (France Libre) under the colonial empire. French Guianan-born Felix Éboué was appointed as governor. Despite the scarcity of resources, he launched a massive construction campaign to raise the city to the rank of other African capitals and bridge the gap with Léopoldville (now Kinshasa). A young architect, Roger Lelièvre, later known as Roger Erell, was appointed in 1941 by the Public Works Department to lead the construction of the main monuments of the period, including a new residence for de Gaulle, a military school, stadiums, and a shelter for Radio-Brazzaville, which aired Free France propaganda. In accordance with the new Indigenous Policy promoted by Éboué, Roger Erell built, at the entrance to Poto-Poto, a new civic centre, including a community house, Catholic

Governor General's House in Pointe-Noire (Société des Batignolles, ca. 1935)

Source: Bernard Toulier (left),

CFCO Train Station in Pointe-Noire (Jean Philippot, 1934)

Source: Collection Bernard Toulier

Palace of the Governor General in Brazzaville (ca. 1930)

basilica, Protestant church, and stadium. These were typified by the use of local materials such as mauve sandstone and fired bricks; reinforced concrete was reserved for structural elements, as cement was scarce. Erell was inspired by the 'classicising *moderne*' style, which was in fashion in France just before the war, such as in the Palais de Chaillot, built for the 1937 Paris International Fair. He also tried to define a regional style, borrowing forms from vernacular architecture and inviting local artists to do the decoration.

During the ten years following the war, Brazzaville underwent a major expansion. A new architect, Jean-Yves Normand, was commissioned to draw a new urban plan to modernise the city and bring it to European standards, at least in the white areas. A new airport was built to accommodate aircraft operating long-haul flights, and the obsolete public buildings were gradually replaced, including the courthouse, the hospital, city hall, and

several schools. Between 1947 and 1952, the European population grew six-fold, stirring the development of new buildings: a cinema, banks, and hotels, among others. Apartment blocks became more prevalent then villas. The architecture was largely influenced by modernism, and climatic issues were at the fore: orientation towards the prevailing winds to foster cross ventilation; mobile brise-soleil and egg-crate façades to prevent the penetration of the sun; piloti and roof-terraces as a renewed relationship with the tropical environment.

References to Le Corbusier's Cité Radieuse are frequent in the projects of the time. For the CGTA building, constructed in 1951, the architect Henri-Jean Calsat proposed a plan with semi-duplex apartments and defended it as the 'first example of Le Corbusier's style in Africa', though the kitchen was located on an intermediate level, betraying the presence of domestic staff, a clear indicator

Source: Bernard Toulier (left),
Tristan Guillaux (right)

Post Office in Pointe-Noire, featuring modernist lines

Vernacular house in the popular neighbourhood of Tié-Tié, Pointe-Noire (1995)

Source: iStock/Mtcurado

Ministry for Justice and Human Rights (Beijing Residential Construction Corporation, 2012)

of colonial conditions. The project most emblematic of the time was the Air France Housing Unit, which was built in 1952 and accommodated sixty-four flats furnished by the French designer Charlotte Perriand and the architect and engineer Jean Prouvé. Moreover, with the housing boom, the colony became a commercial outlet for companies producing prefabricated elements. Aluminium Français, a consortium of aluminium supply industries, settled in Brazzaville in two prototypes of the Maison Tropicale (Tropical House), a lightweight demountable building designed for the colonies by Jean Prouvé in 1951. In the 'Black Brazzavilles', as the sociologist Georges Balandier named the districts for indigenous Africans, the endeavours to reduce the development of slums were not

in proportion with growing needs, and the scarce examples of housing developments remained poor in comparison with the innovative solutions displayed in the European centre.

During the first decades of independence, new major buildings were not abundant, despite the authorities' wish to establish Brazzaville as an African capital by accommodating the first All-Africa Games in 1965 and the African headquarters of the World Health Organisation. The architecture of the post-independence period is characterised by two influences. The Marxist military regime (1968–1992) had recourse to Russian and Chinese cooperation to build facilities befitting a newly independent country – the Palais des Congrès conference centre in Brazzaville (1985), for instance – but the regime also relied on Western cooperation programmes. The discovery of important off-shore oil reserves at the beginning of the 1970s fostered a boom in office buildings for banks and ministries; these were mostly built by French architects already present during the colonial period such as Jean-Marie Legrand, Henri Chomette, or Jean-Yves Normand. With the increasing prevalence of air conditioning, the architects moved away from the climatic issues and attempted to combine international

Source: Direction Générale des Grands Travaux

Direction Générale des Grands Travaux Building (DGGT) in Brazzaville

standards with a reinterpretation of a supposedly organicity of pre-colonial architecture, using concrete and imported materials. The time's most representative building is the Nabemba Tower (1986–1990), which was competition for Kinshasa's skyscrapers.

Episodes of civil war between 1993 and 1999 led to destruction, particularly in the colonial centre, and effected a long-lasting period where the country was under construction – a period from which it only started to emerge less than a decade ago. Since the 1990s, the construction sector has been marked by the rise of a new generation of home-grown architects. They are mainly educated abroad, like their counterparts in Kinshasa, and face projects designed overseas through international cooperation and development programmes; China particularly has

Source: Direction Générale des Grands Travaux

Ministry of Foreign Affairs (Beijing Residential Construction Corporation, 2008)

become a major stakeholder. Architects in Brazzaville and Kinshasa – the 'mirror cities', as the historian Charles Didier Gondola called them in his 1996 book *Villes Miroirs* – experience difficulty setting new directions for these continually extending metropolises.

CG

Source: iStock/Mtcurado

National Petroleum Company (formerly Hydro-Congo) Building in Brazzaville (1987)

Brazzaville

Source: Tristan Guilloux

**National Bank of Congo in Brazzaville
(Charles Cazaban-Mazerolles, 1965)**

Brazzaville, one of the few African cities to have kept its colonial name, is the capital and largest city in the Republic of the Congo. It is set along the northern banks of the Congo River, across from the Democratic Republic of the Congo (DRC) on the other side of the river. Kinshasa, the capital of the DRC, is located directly south of Brazzaville. The result is that these two cities have one of the highest proximities of two capital cities in the world, which led, historically, to influence and exchange between them. The city core of Brazzaville is focused around the new port, near the railway station. Similarly to Kinshasa, Brazzaville was planned with a polynuclear layout, with the urban centres corresponding to political power. Several ravines divide the structure of the city and its operating systems, where small rivers unite with the main one. In the past, Europeans settled in the upper parts of the city, as these areas were

Source: Africa Drawn Project

Brazzaville's street grid between the Congo River and Maya-Maya International Airport

Source: Ministère du Tourisme et de l'Environnement

Aerial view of Congo's capital city (above) and skyline of Brazzaville (below)

considered healthier than along the river. On both sides of the Congo River, a segregationist system was operated. Traces of the colonial past are visible in the buildings of Brazzaville's central business district, which was not only an important commercial centre, but also the main colonial residential area. It is known today as Centre Ville.

The city appears to have expanded, without planning, in concentric semicircles over time. From 1960, the year of the Republic's independence, up until the mid-1980s, various attempts were made to plan urban development, but the demand far outreached the growth projections calculated in the master plans.

The Marxist-Leninist political discourse of the 1970s and 1980s was displayed in the erection of monuments and public works in the city. This was followed by widespread destruction and the exodus of a significant part of its population during sustained bouts of violent conflict in the 1990s. More recently, though, it has become a transformed city. The reopening of the railway between Brazzaville and Pointe-Noire symbolised the promise of a better quality of life for its residents. Today, the city centre is the site of activities related to international trade and information technology, and new services connected with finance and national administration. *adp*

The Maison Tropicale: An Elusive Heritage?

Tristan Guilloux

Paradoxically, one of the most notorious buildings designed for Africa is no longer on the continent. The Maison Tropicale, or Tropical House, laid out by the famous French engineer Jean Prouvé in the late 1940s was displayed for about fifty years in three prototypes, one in Niamey, Niger, and two others in Brazzaville, Congo. At the end of the 1990s, taking advantage of an upward market ranking for Prouvé's artefacts, the models were removed from Africa, restored in Europe, and raised in several cities in Europe and the USA. One prototype is now exhibited at the Centre Pompidou, Paris, whereas another was sold at auction for about five million US dollars in New York in 2007.

Prouvé's creations appeared at the threshold of the last decade of the colonial era. The prototype drew on a long tradition of prefabricated barracks for colonies,[1] under the pretext of a lack of material and appropriate skills to build in good conditions. Jean Prouvé, who was very much involved in rebuilding France after World War II, was called, during the summer of 1948, by the colonial authorities of French Western Africa, to present the results of his research on prefabrication. Paul Herbé, recently appointed as town planner for the Niger territory by the French authorities, ordered a survey for college buildings for Niamey, while underlining that 'all possible interest

should be shown, for a region so remote and deprived of means of transport, in the total contribution by metropolitan industry for pre-manufactured lightweight alloy materials'.[2] In April 1949, the administration cautiously signed a contract for the house of the college director. The 26 × 10 m plan of what would become the Maison Tropicale included two housing cells, one for during the daytime and another for during the night. The prototype was put up in October and displayed on the banks of the Seine River in Paris before being flat-packed and then shipped by air to Niamey.

In mid-1951, two other prototypes were sent to Brazzaville to accommodate the offices of the Aluminium Français consortium. This time, the project was supported by a private initiative, an industrial cartel that had taken shares in Jean Prouvé's workshop to boost its otherwise artisanal production. The urban construction boom experienced by Brazzaville in the late 1940s and the opening of an airport accommodating long-haul flights, in the 1950s, offered the opportunity to establish a commercial representation of a large material supplier like Aluminium Français. The first 10 × 14 m building was used as an information office, while the second 18 × 10 m building accommodated the director and short-stay guests.

Despite various projects ranging from houses to large public facilities, Prouvé's experiment did not extend beyond these three specimens. This failure can also be blamed on the slowdown in colonial investment with the perspective of decolonisation, as well as on willingness to 'progressively restrict the recourse to foreign specialised labour'[3] to reduce construction costs. Finally, in the colonies just as in the mother country, the concrete

Source: Archives départementales de Meurthe-et-Moselle

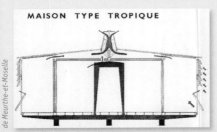

MAISON TYPE TROPIQUE

Section drawing of the Maison Tropicale

Source: Laurence Kimmel

Palm Pavilion (2006–2008) by Rirkrit Tiravanija, created for the São Paolo Biennale

plant took over the metal works: the age of metal demountable houses of the beginning of the twentieth century had indeed long passed. The prototype took the archetypal form of the colonial bungalow with its elongated shape and a peripheral gallery. And yet, this typology, which had pervaded in colonial construction almost exclusively until the 1930s, was then strongly rejected by the modern architects working in the tropical regions.

However, since its realisation, the Maison Tropicale has been embedded in the history of pioneering architectural movements that sought to turn overseas territories into laboratories of modernity, avant-garde outposts testing ideas that might find an application in the mother countries. One of the main reasons, besides the prefabrication, is the consideration given by Jean Prouvé to climatic issues. The whole conception is steered by the wish to offer a comfortable shelter. Aluminium is used for its lightness and also for its reflective properties. Swivelling

louvres are arranged all around the gallery to protect the walls from the sun's rays, and the double-skinned walls are equipped with small circular portholes of blue tinted glass to temper the sun's glare. The elongated form combined with sliding panels favours cross-ventilation. To limit the solar radiation coming from the ceiling, the roof is equipped with an axial lantern that drains off the overheated air by the ceiling even in the absence of wind. Mobile shutters allowed the lantern to be closed in case of torrential rain. Yet, despite the implementation of this sophisticated prototype, Jean Prouvé

Source: Bernard Renoux

Maison Tropicale in 1995

Source: Bernard Toulier

64. - Congo. - **BRAZZAVILLE**. - Maisons d'habitation

Cliché Vialle, Brazzaville - Phototypie Meyrignac et Puydebois, Brive (France)

Metal house in Brazzaville (ca. 1900)

reversed his position and finally agreed with the mainstream discourse of modern architects against the colonial bungalow. He drew some sketches, never carried out, for a Maison Équatoriale based on a newly developed shell structure, where the characteristics of the colonial house have disappeared. After independence, this endeavour sank into oblivion until the 1990s, when prices reached by Jean Prouvé's works in auctions shed new light on the prototypes that were said to be in danger, particularly in Brazzaville where the civil war broke out in the mid-1990s.

The future of these buildings was then aligned with their very nature as a prototype, minimising the context of their conception and their inclusion in an African urban landscape. As Robert Rubin, one of the main protagonists of their restoration, wrote, 'Before serving as a residence or even a building, the Tropical House was a "demonstrator" meant to promote its system of prefabricated elements as a means of constructing potentially thousands of houses, offices, factories, and public buildings in a variety of climatic conditions'.[4] Historically, there is no doubt that the very promoters of Prouvé's works in Africa put the nature of a demonstrator forward. But, at the same time, these prototypes settled in an urban landscape for several decades, as shown through the interviews of citizens of Brazzaville and Niamey in

a film shot by Manthia Diawara, a Malian scholar and writer. In the film, a former neighbour, a Tuareg woman, declares, 'I feel sad and often think of the house. Especially when it rains. When it was here, the house was my shelter. Now it's gone, I no longer have any shelter from the rain'.[5] The restoration was oriented to recover the dimension of an industrial object, as the prototype was when it was displayed on the banks of the River Seine before its departure for Africa. The only testimony of the 'African' history of these houses is a bullet hole preserved by the restoration as a memory of the Brazzaville civil war. Along with that, the narrative of an Indiana Jones-like 'rescue' emphasising the 'modernist trophy' and the performance of a very sophisticated restoration re-enacts the duality between an 'Enlightened North' and an Africa still considered as a 'Heart of Darkness'.

The removal of the Maison Tropicale, qualified by some as an uprooting and by others as a repatriation, has raised a debate about its place as an element of 'shared heritage' and addresses the ambiguous position of an architecture designed from the Western world for an African 'field'. The Cameroonian philosopher Achille Mbembe reveals this ambiguity when he assumes that 'as shape and figure, act and relation, the colonisation was in many respects, a coproduction of the colonists and the colonised. Together,

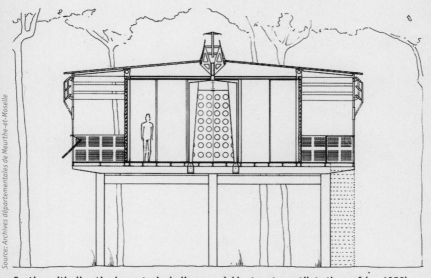

Source: Archives départementales de Meurthe-et-Moselle

Section with climatic elements, including an axial lantern to ventilate the roof (ca. 1950)

but in different positions, they forged a past. But to have a common past does not mean inevitably to share it'.[6] In this way, two artists committed to transcending this dialectic and shape the conditions of a 'common good': Ângela Ferreira, a Portuguese artist born in Mozambique, and Rirkrit Tiravanija, born in Argentina and working between New York and Thailand – two artists between worlds.

During the 2007 Venice Biennale, Ângela Ferreira displayed, in the Portuguese pavilion, an installation showing a kind of facsimile of the dismantled Maison Tropicale in transit between the worlds of the colonised and the colonisers. The installation is a 'passage' between two worlds, picturing Brazzaville and Niamey and highlighting the absence of the prototypes.

Source: Jean-Michel Gobet

One of Brazzaville's Maisons Tropicales in Paris in 2007

Maison Tropicale in London's Tate Modern Gallery in 2008
Source: Paul Simpson

Source: Richard Winchell

Maison Tropicale in New York in 2007, which was auctioned for ca. five million US dollars

Rirkrit Tiravanija has drawn from the prototype at several times for his installations: in Paris in 2006, when the restored house was displayed on the banks of the River Seine, and also in Mexico, and during the São Paulo Biennale in 2006. The artist picked up the formal vocabulary of Jean Prouvé, but translated it into materials stemming from the Thai countryside where he installed his workshop. He had the objects constructed by local artisans, whereas Prouvé envisioned prefabrication to avoid needing local hands to complete the work.

While Ângela Ferreira gives shape to colonial and post-colonial history, Rirkrit Tiravanija opens up a critique of a cynical present where everything is fake. In a so-called globalised world, the exchanges are unbalanced, since tropical countries are reduced to an exotic destination for Western travellers, symbolised by, for instance, artificial palm trees, while those countries are beyond the reach of migrants, as shown in the Paris installation. There, in a small outhouse that appears to have stepped from Prouvé's imagination, one can find copies of Schengen visas used as toilet paper. Yet, in the same installation, the artist has settled a table under a shelter also inspired by Prouvé. On the table, lies a puzzle representing the famous painting *Liberty Leading the People* by Eugène Delacroix. Tiravanija invites us to gather in order to re-assemble the scattered parts of this collective emancipation. This metaphorical discourse, which looks for public participation to recompose a wrecked world is characteristic of what the French curator Nicolas Bourriaud has called relational aesthetics.[7] This detour by the plastic arts may permit a new understanding of colonial heritage in order to subsume the traditional dead-end opposition between here and there. To paraphrase Bourriaud, concerning colonial architecture, we could refer to the term 'shared heritage', which makes reference to property, membership, and somewhere exclusivity, the designation of relational heritage.

Notes
1 For more on the circulation for colonial models see Sylviane Leprun and Alain Sinou (eds), *Espaces coloniaux en Afrique noire* (Paris, 1984).
2 'Maison préfabriquée type tropique' *Techniques et Architecture* 5–6 (1952), p. 12.
3 Sophie Dulucq, *La France et les villes d'Afrique noire francophones* (Paris, 1997), p. 238.
4 Robert Rubin, 'Preserving and Presenting Prefab: Jean Prouvé's Tropical House', *Future Anterior*, 2/1 (Summer 2005), pp. 30–39.
5 Manthia Diawara, *Maison Tropicale*, documentary film, Lisbon, 2008, 58 mins.
6 Achille Mbembe, *Sortir de la grande nuit: Essai sur l'Afrique décolonisée* (Paris, 2010).
7 See Nicolas Bourriaud, *Relational Aesthetics* (Dijon, 2002).

Cathedral and Bishop's Compound

CG 01

Avenue Maréchal Foch,
Aiglon Quarter, Brazzaville
1892 (cathedral), 1893 (residence),
1904 (towers)

Source: Tristan Guilloux

In 1887 the Congregation of Fathers of Saint-Esprit established the Saint-Hippolyte Mission on a large lot provided by the French colonial authorities, running from the top of Aiglon hill down to the banks of the Congo River. The fathers constructed a port, as Brazzaville was considered an outpost for evangelising the populations living in the upper basin of the River Congo. The side of the hill was cleared, and the first bishop drew a garden with paths that spread from a courtyard on top of the hill. In 1910, the compound was made up of 110 huts. The first hard wall buildings were erected in 1892 in fired bricks: the bishop's palace, the cathedral, and, down the slope, the convent for the Sisters of Saint-Joseph de Cluny. Bricks were laid in a mortar made of sand and clay, because of the lack of lime. Verandas and upper galleries protect the base of the walls from rain, which erodes the mortar. The roofing consists of small metallic tiles imported from France. The bishop's palace is the oldest construction in Brazzaville in these materials. In 1903 the two towers were added; in 1913 the cathedral was expanded; and by 1916 the Catholic Mission had seventeen buildings. In 1963 Jean-Yves Normand drew the plans for a new bishop's palace. *CC*

Source: iStock/Micurado

Source: Tristan Guilloux (all pictures)

CG

Case des Messageries Fluviales   CG 02
Avenue Amilcar Cabral, Brazzaville
1908

In 1900, Alphonse Fondère, a former colonial administrator, established the Messageries Fluviales (or Congo River Couriers). The head office of the company and later the Compagnie Générale de Transports en Afrique (now the Société Congolaise de Transport Fluvial) were built from around 1905 to 1908, from an existing hut. The raised ground floor sits over storerooms for goods. The building is organised into two twin pavilions sheltered by tin roofs. Its linearity is emphasised by a wooden gallery that protects the core masonry walls from the sun. The plot also includes a shipyard and a boat graveyard. This evokes the choice of site to settle Brazzaville: transshipment is necessary as the river is no longer navigable downstream. Since 1886, the bank of the Congo River has undergone changes to serve as a port: the Flotille (1889), the jetty for the brickyard (1911), Port Léon (1886), Messageries Fluviales (1900), the river terminal to Kinshasa known as Le Beach, the cargo port (1937), the new port of M'Pila upstream (1949) with its oil wharf, the marina and the landing facilities for logs from the rainforest. This exceptional example of colonial bungalow architecture is testimony to on-going commercial activity for over a century.   *cc*

Regionalist Villa ≋   CG 03
Clairon Quarter, Plateau, Brazzaville
1951

The arrival of the Congo-Ocean Railway revolutionised architecture. During 1925 and after, the new coastal town of Pointe-Noire became covered with Basque-style regionalist houses. The style, advocated by the local administration of the Public Works Department during the international congress of town planning at the International Colonial Exhibition in Paris, 1931, was also applied to public facilities such as the Chemin de fer Congo-Océan station in the capital. In Brazzaville, this regionalist reference appeared later but lasted until 1955. This housing estate was built from 1945 to 1951 to accommodate officers and non-commissioned officers' families of the military airbase. The regionalist style, with its mock half-timbered façades and overhanging roof, was supposed to turn the colony into a kind of vacation resort.   *cc*

Stade Vélodrome `CG 04`
Felix Éboué
Avenue Orsi, Poto-Poto, Brazzaville
Roger Erell
1944

Before 1940, on both sides of the Congo River the construction of premises for sports practice was promoted and supervised by the political as well as religious authorities, in order to monitor the leisure activities of the indigenous communities. The Stade Vélodrome Felix Éboué was erected in this respect and is part of a global layout including the Sainte-Anne Basilica and its presbytery. Father Charles Lecomte, who excelled in sports, promoted the original programme and led the construction, which began in 1941 and ended in 1944, sooner than the work on the basilica. Roger Erell realised the impressive stadium (180 × 100 m) on the marshes in the no-build zone between the European and indigenous neighbourhoods. Ponds fed by drained waters are arranged on both sides of the staircase to the main tribune. Over these are gargoyles by the sculptor Benoît Konogo. The gallery of the tribune is exceptional, with nine spans made of fired bricks that frame concrete trellised screens featuring ornamental motifs made up of geometrical figures that stem from the square, the circle, and the triangle. In 1957, at the entrance to the stadium, in front of the main tribune, a statue was erected of Félix Éboué, a black governor general of Free France who played a key role in the colonial administration from 1940 to his death in 1944. *cc*

Case de Gaulle ⇗ `CG 05`
Avenue Savorgnan de Brazza,
Bacongo, Brazzaville
Roger Erell, Charles Cazaban-Mazerolles
1950s

Construction of the Case de Gaulle began in May 1941 to accommodate the 'passing guests' of the government of French Equatorial Africa, and to provide General Charles de Gaulle with a residence worthy of his rank of leader of Free France. The project was assigned to recent architecture graduate Roger Erell. The construction is on a wide plot of land, in front of the Congo River, at the entrance to the indigenous African district of Bacongo, a first for an official residence. The ceremonial room faces the river. Erell designed this modest African palace in reference to the Palais de Chaillot built in 1937 for the Paris International Exhibition, and the façades were influenced by Roger-Henri Expert, his professor at the École des Beaux-Arts in Paris. As building materials were scarce during wartime, Erell made the most of local resources, using mauve stone from Kuambo, a quarry in south Brazzaville, for the rough masonry, and reserving the use of concrete for trellis screens and the roof-terrace. In September 1942, the building work finished for de Gaulle's arrival. Between de Gaulle's brief stays, the government's secretary general took up residence there. Charles Cazaban-Mazerolles completed the building in the 1950s. After independence, the Case de Gaulle became the residence of the French ambassador. *cc*

Palais de Justice ☒ ↵ 　CG 06
Allée du Chaillu, Plateau
Quarter, Brazzaville
Jean-Yves Normand
1957

Brazzaville's post-World War II urban boom spurred on the improvement of the first law court, which was built in 1910 in Plateau, the administrative district. The new building, moved a few hundred metres away, was planned on a vast plot near the detention centre to house the court and the court of appeal. The project was established in 1951 by Jean-Yves Normand, a young architect who arrived in Brazzaville in 1945, commissioned by the French authorities to draw the city's urban master plan. The court buildings are arranged to take into account the prevailing winds and minimise the façades that are exposed to the sun. Elegant concrete porticoes create wide shaded zones around the courtrooms, which become waiting halls for the court on ground level and the court of appeal on the first floor. The offices are in two thin buildings fostering cross ventilation placed on both sides of the courtrooms. The galleries facing north and south are protected by brise-soleil in horizontal blades, while the western façade, exposed to almost horizontal beams at sunset, is equipped with vertical shading. The rooftop terrace is composed of two slabs which are naturally ventilated for cooling. The technical options and the first use of prefabrication (beams, floors, ceilings) strongly influence the aesthetics of this building.　*cc*

CG

Source: Tristan Guilloux (all pictures)

Sainte-Anne Basilica CG 07

Avenue Orsi, Brazzaville
Roger Erell
1949, 2011

At the request of Brazzaville's bishop, a new parish was founded at the beginning of World War II in the indigenous district of Poto-Poto. After an initial attempt in the location of the current market of Moungali, the governor general, Félix Éboué, decided to arrange, at the junction of the European and African districts, a civic centre including a large Catholic church, a Protestant church, a velodrome stadium and a public garden. The architect Roger Erell, who had just finished the Case de Gaulle, drew the basilica after a Latin cross plan. The shape of the construction was inspired by Mousgoum dwellings – the emblem of French Equatorial Africa during the International Colonial Exhibition that took place in Paris in 1931. He appointed engineers to calculate the concrete structures, in particular the bold cantilever slab of the church gallery. He combined reinforced concrete with local materials: bricks fired on site and stone from the Djoué River to clad the façade and the lancet arches supporting the vault. The nave, evoking the 'church of joined hands', is illuminated by zenithal lighting and buttressed by forty small lancet arches. The roof's metal framework is clad with green glazed scale-like tiles imported from the south of France. When the basilica was inaugurated in 1949, the building work that had started in 1943 and was managed by Father Nicolas Moysan and Charles Lecomte was not finished, despite the direct and indirect help of public authorities and the creation, in 1946, of a committee for the construction of the sanctuary. In 1984, a few years before his death, Erell presented a model for the bell tower, but it remained unfinished. The spire was eventually completed in 2011, when the church was restored after the damage caused by the civil wars of the 1990s. In spite of a lack of finances, Erell enlisted various artists to decorate the basilica: the sculptor Benoît Konogo for the statue of the Madonna and an unknown M'Beti ironsmith from northern Congo for the gallery guardrail, which is adorned with the shape of traditional throwing knives. The church is an outstanding example of attempts to fuse African and European influences during the colonial era.   CC

Source: iStock/Mtcurado (all pictures)

CG

Air France Housing Unit   CG 08
Allée du Chaillu, Plateau Quarter,
Brazzaville
Hébrard, Lefebvre, Létu, Bienvenu
1952

The Air France Housing Unit was designed
in November 1950 by four followers of
Le Corbusier – Hébrard, Lefebvre, Létu,
and Bienvenu – for European Air France
staff living in Brazzaville. Construction
finished in 1952. This 140 m long and
10 m wide African Cité Radieuse, which
rests on a system of pillars, is coated
with endemic red Djoué sandstone
(hence its common name of Immeuble
Rouge, or the Red Building). It is surrounded by a wooded park, situated in
a residential neighbourhood, and oriented according to prevailing winds for
cross-ventilation. The building comprises five staircases, four chimneys,
and sixty-three dwellings – twenty-two
studios, forty apartments, and a top-
floor apartment reserved for Air France's
director. The latter opens onto a famous
rooftop garden, with fountains, a play-
ground, and a reception space. A *boyerie* –
accommodation for the African domes-
tics – included a toilet. Other references to Le Corbusier can be found on the
roof terrace: the same ocean liner-type
ventilation shaft as on Marseille's Cité
Radieuse, and an African Modulor figure
featuring a locally manufactured ceramic
mask. Charlotte Perriand designed the
interiors (cupboards, storage racks);
Ateliers Jean Prouvé made the furniture,
as well as the vertical and horizontal aluminium shades. The building was occupied by the military during the civil war
at the end of the 1990s and stripped of its
furniture, which was sold at high prices
to collectors worldwide. Today, the Air
France Housing Unit mainly rents to the
families of Congolese officials.   *cc*

Source: Philippe Guionie

Source: Archives nationales d'outre-mer

The rooftop terrace with its kidney-shaped pool
and ocean liner style ventilation chimney, typical for the 1950s.

The Air France Housing Unit: Africa's Cité Radieuse

Philippe Guionie

The Air France Housing Unit, Africa's Cité Radieuse (which is commonly called the Red Building – Immeuble Rouge), in Brazzaville, is a red and white building with six floors, situated in the Plateau Neighbourhood of Brazzaville. The European Air France personnel lived there, at the time when the imperial airport was an important connection for the long-haul flights between Paris and Johannesburg. Built in a residential area far from the centre of town, the Air France Housing Unit was considered to be 'the jewel of climatic tropical architecture' (Bernard Toulier) at the beginning of the 1950s.

This 140 m long building is a masterpiece by four French architects – Hébrard, Lefebvre, Létu, and Bienvenu, who were disciples of Le Corbusier – and refers to Le Corbusier's Cité Radieuse in Marseilles, as it articulates the Swiss-French architect's principles concerning sun, light, and space. The structure shows a desire to adapt the canons of modern architecture to the tropical climate: orientation according to the prevailing northeast winds, the choice of local coating materials (Djoué sandstone, for this specific project), and natural ventilation with mobile blinds and claustras. The building is set on pillars, has five staircases, and, in the past, comprised sixty-three lodgings: about 15 ground-floor studio apartments for single employees; 40 three-room apartments; and the whole top floor, with its magnificent rooftop terrace garden, was reserved for the director of the local Air France travel agency; there one can find the 'African Modulor' engraving. The designers, Jean Prouvé and Charlotte Perriand, brought a formidable aesthetic supplement to the interior décor, entering the Air France Housing Unit into avant-garde modernity. Charlotte Perriand designed the interiors: wall-mounted foldable tables, wall-furniture with an integrated serving hatch, bathroom cupboards, a 'Brazza' closet with sliding doors, and so forth.

This flagship vessel – with its futuristic lines – still stands today. Unfortunately, the passing years and the country's political upheavals have left their mark. The Red Building was abandoned by Air France a few years after the country's independence in 1960, in the context of nationalisation put in place by the Marxist regime. During the civil war at the end of the 1990s, the building was used by the military. Although property of the State, the housing unit is barely maintained and its general condition is now quite run-down: there has been no running water for years, the lift is out of order, electrical wire hangs loosely, rain water seeps though the cracked walls, the four chimneys designed for natural ventilation are obstructed by bee hives, the rooftop terrace of international renown has patches of cassava plants growing on it, and the wading pools are filled with garbage. The former underground car park is full of all sorts of accumulated junk. A burnt apartment on the first floor has been left in ruins.

The Air France Housing Unit presently houses a few hundred tenants – essentially Congolese officials and their families – for very low rent (a three-room apartment, at a monthly fee of 10,000 Central African CFA francs). They live in cramped, dark spaces and know very little of the building's prestigious

past. As usual, the public authorities' negligence motivates private initiatives: one of the tennants works every day, delivering a meagre 25 litre canister of more or less drinkable water to the other residents. There are also shopkeepers who have set up in the ground-floor studio apartments or at the foot of the building, mostly selling food (crêpes, waffles, cassava, tomatoes, okra, chillies, etc.).
According to Bernard Toulier, the precious interior furniture was the object of a complicit, cleverly orchestrated legitimised looting, a few years ago, with the complicity of authorities, both local and French, and was sold and scattered amongst private collections in France and abroad. The people living in the now stripped apartments improvise repairs: one family hung a simple plywood board on the wall in order to replace the old serving hatch. 'It's like in our countryside in the 1950s, when the farmers

would exchange their old furniture for Formica: the instigators played on the lack of knowledge regarding the monetary value of the furniture,' specifies Tristan Guilloux. Thus, a Tropique 506 dining table, designed by Jean Prouvé in 1952 for the Air France Housing Unit, was sold at Christie's Paris on 21 November 2012, for 217,000 euros.
The Air France Housing Unit is a masterpiece in peril. If measures are not taken rapidly, this jewel of modern architecture will soon be nothing more than a ruin. Like a shipwrecked ocean liner, the Red Building poses the question of the future of colonial or post-colonial architectures and their appropriation by the local populations and elites. Certain groups are campaigning to enter Brazzaville's historical monuments and architectural heritage into UNESCO's classifications. One can only hope that the Air France Housing Unit will be part of it.

CG

Source: Philippe Guionie (all pictures)

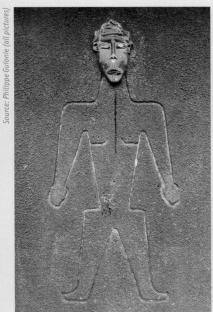

The 'African Modulor' engraved in concrete with a locally made ceramic mask

West side of the Air France Housing Unit

The staircase is ventilated and illuminated by claustra walls

Living conditions in the Air France Housing Unit
Source: Philippe Guionie (all pictures)

CGTA Building ⩔

CG 09

Avenue Amilcar Cabral,
Plaine Quarter, Brazzaville
Henri-Jean Calsat, Charles Berthelot
1951

In 1951, the shipping company CGTA (Compagnie Générale de Transports en Afrique) entrusted the construction of a building to accommodate its employees to the French architects Henri-Jean Calsat and Charles Berthelot who were designing the new General Hospital of Brazzaville (1953–1957). The three-storey CGTA Building is made up of six large apartments and three single ones. A corridor at the intermediate level allows access to the flats, which are alternately located at the upper and lower levels, endorsing the typology designed by Le Corbusier for the Cité Radieuse, built the same year in Marseilles, France. But unlike in the Cité Radieuse, each kitchen is not located in an extension of the living room but at an intermediate level, which is separated by a flight of stairs – a reminder that that the expatriates had domestic servants. Every apartment also had its own *boyerie* on the ground level to accommodate its staff. *cc*

Source: Bernard Renoux (left),

Source: iStock/Mtcurado

CG

Garage Barnier ↰   CG 10
Avenue Amilcar Cabral,
Plaine Quarter, Brazzaville
Roger Erell
1953

Brazzaville City Hall ≈   CG 11
Avenue Amilcar Cabral,
Plaine Quarter, Brazzaville
Jean-Yves Normand
1963

The architectural modernity of the 1950s also celebrated the automobile, a means of transport that drastically increased after World War II. All the major European and American companies had their car dealerships in Brazzaville. Since 1935 Georges Barnier Establishments had been representatives of tractors, trucks, automobiles, or motorcycles; they also specialised in the trade of accessories. In 1953 they opened their own petrol station in the city centre. The architect, Roger Erell, used the symbolic reference of an ocean liner, creating a prominent concrete canopy to shelter the fuel pumps and putting the offices, which are accommodated in a kind of captain's cabin, on top. The roof terrace, designed as an upper deck, is separated from the building structure to prevent overheating from the sun with its layer of air cooling.   *cc*

Brazzaville's original city hall was inaugurated in 1912. It was later found to be too cramped, so the municipality launched a competition for a replacement, which was won by two main architects of the moment: Roger Erell and Jean-Yves Normand. The start of the construction was postponed several times, so Normand presented a second project alone. The new city hall was inaugurated in 1963. Its plan is organised into two volumes, with one accommodating the reception rooms and the other the administrative offices. The façades are protected from the sun by brise-soleils – vertical for the reception room and a grid for the offices. A portico shelters the main entrance porch and a balcony, re-enacting the traditional image of the city hall in a modernist manner and underlining the monumentality of the building.   *cc*

Source: iStock/Mtcurado (all pictures)

Nabemba Tower `CG 12`
Rue Félix Éboué, Plaine Quarter,
Brazzaville
Jean-Marie Legrand
1990

Pierre Savorgnan de Brazza `CG 13`
Memorial ⩘
Avenue Amilcar Cabral, Plaine Quarter,
Brazzaville
Eugène Okoko
2006

To this day, the Nabemba Tower, at 106 m high, dominates the Brazzaville skyline. During the 1970s, the Republic of the Congo became an important oil producer in Africa. Different international companies operated offshore fields, and one, Elf Aquitaine, a French oil firm, decided, in the mid-1980s, to finance the construction of a monument representing of the economic success of the country, and construction began in 1986. The tower is set on the banks of the Congo River to compete with the Democratic Republic's building programme for Kinshasa at the time. Also known as Tour Elf, the tower is named after Mount Nabemba, the highest peak in the Republic (1,020 m). The tower is a hyperboloid shape and is built around a concrete core. The building is characteristic of the postmodern attempts to found an African architecture on an organic expression drawn from the equatorial rainforest. *cc*

On 3 October 2006, Brazzaville officially received the remains of its founder, Pierre Savorgnan de Brazza (1852–1905). This memorial is in striking contrast with the attitude of their neighbours in DRC. One year before, the statue of the Belgian colonial king Leopold II was taken down just a few hours after being re-erected on its former pedestal in the centre of Kinshasa. The site chosen for this memorial is closed to the ancient village Mfoa, one of the settlements upon which Brazza founded the city on 3 October 1880. Built by the Congolese architect Eugène Okoko, the memorial was inspired by the Pantheon in Rome. Under a dome of 12 m in diameter, made of steel and glass, the main room of the mausoleum is decorated with a mural by the painters from the Poto-Poto School of Art, which redraws the steps of the explorer. It also houses a library, a museum, a lecture hall, a café, and offices. *cc*

Source: ARPCE (all pictures)

ARPCE Building　　CG 14

Avenue de l'Amitié, Plateau
Quarter, Brazzaville
Kalilou Kaliste Kaba
2013

Since 2010, Brazzaville has undergone some important transformations, following almost two decades of stagnation. The economy is also experiencing change, with the liberalisation of the telecoms sector. When the old post administration turned into the Telecommunications Regulatory Agency (Agence de Régulation des Postes et des Communications Électroniques – ARPCE), a new head office had to be built. The seven-storey building by Ivorian architect Kalilou Kaliste Kaba is set on a granite-clad pedestal containing the hall, the public facilities, and a core housing the offices behind a glass curtain wall. A terrace surmounted by a 'cap roof' that emphasises the triangular form of the plot hosts receptions. Inside, an atrium opens to the full height of the building.　　*cc*

Maya-Maya Airport ⊿ ⊿　　CG 15

Avenue Denis Sassou Nguesso, Brazzaville
*Weihai International Economic and
Technical Cooperative*
2014

The new Maya-Maya Airport replaced the aerodrome built at the beginning of the 1950s to accommodate transcontinental flights. At that time it was a catalyst for economic development. When the civil wars of the 1990s came to an end, the Congolese government launched, in 2002, the New Hope programme to promote the reconstitution of destroyed or abandoned infrastructure. Maya-Maya Airport is part of this programme, and includes a new runway, a passenger terminal, a presidential pavilion, and a luxury hotel. Built between 2010 and 2014, the terminal covers 44,500 m², spans three levels to separate the various passenger flows, and services seven airbridges. The metallic roof has a wave form and is supported by a triangulated lattice of tubes on top of steel columns. Expansive glass walls allow light to penetrate the building. An access road viaduct serves the terminal. This project is characteristic of an enhanced Chinese presence in the public works market in Africa: the contractor is a Congolese branch of the Weihai International Economic and Technical Cooperative.　　*cc*

Complexe Sportif de la Concorde

CG 16

Kintélé, Brazzaville
*China State Construction and
Engineering Corporation, Zhengwei*
2015

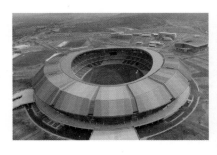

In 1965, Brazzaville hosted the first All-Africa Games. By 2015, the old Massamba-Débat Stadium, with its 33,000 seats, was inadequate for the eleventh games and their fiftieth anniversary, particularly because of the broadening of the Olympic disciplines. Constructed from 2013 to 2015 for the African Games (renamed that year), the Complexe Sportif de la Concorde stretches over almost 100 ha in Kintélé, 7 km north of Brazzaville, and is linked by a highway built on a viaduct structure that spans the marshland along the Congo River. The complex was built in the framework of the bilateral cooperation between the Republic of the Congo and China by the China State Construction and Engineering Corporation (CSCEC),

the main state-owned company in the construction field, and under the supervision of the DGGT (the directorate general for major projects). Over two tiers, the Olympic stadium accommodates 60,000 spectators, who are protected from the weather by a metallic roof of petal-like forms. The complex also includes a sports hall, an Olympic-size swimming pool, a conference centre, offices, and hotels. The Olympic Village, which can house up to 8,000 sportspeople, was built on a new polytechnic university campus, and after the games was transformed into student accommodation.   *cc*

Source: Délégation Générale aux Grands Travaux (top),
CongoKimia/Floyd Nzonzi (middle and bottom)

CG 12

Elbo Suites ⊼ `CG 17`
Avenue Amilcar Cabral, Brazzaville
Office 2K Architecture & Design/
Karelle Koubatika
2015

With its bold aesthetic, large scale, and downtown location next to the Congo River, the Elbo Suites residence is designed to stand out. The idea for it came from a group of Congolese women investors who wanted to contribute to the development of the Republic of the Congo through supporting innovative and characteristic projects, and it pays tribute to Édith Lucie Bongo Ondimba, the late wife of Gabonese president Ali Omar Bongo. Construction of the building, with a floor space of 11,080 m², began in February 2013 and finished in March 2015. The building by Karelle Koubatika was the first in sub-Saharan Africa to achieve HQE certification, a French award promoting sustainability and best practices in construction.   *ed*

New Sight Eye Hospital » `CG 18`
Ouésso, Sangha Region
Boogertman + Partners Architects,
Geyser Hahn Architects
2022

Residents of Ouésso, a small town deep in the Congolese jungle, fifteen hours by bus from Brazzaville, lack access to eye-care treatments. Planned for 2022, the New Sight Eye Hospital accommodates a surgery centre, staff and volunteer housing, and the supporting infrastructure. The length of the linear site will be used to create a series of privacy thresholds: offices in the east, theatres in the middle, and recovery wards in the western courtyard block. A series of inverted courtyards will foster comfort though indirect light and ventilated spaces. The architects focused on the users' experience, designing textured walls as wayfinding mechanisms and outdoor kitchens for patients' families. The construction plan relies on the local vernacular.   *pa/ed*

CG 17

Source: Harry Purwanto

Section drawing

Source: Boogertman and Partners Architects/Geyser Hahn Architects

Twiga Hotel   CG 19
Avenue Dr Jacques Bouity,
Lumumba, Pointe-Noire
Keldi Architectes
2016

The fast economic emergence of Africa has facilitated the realisation of ambitious, long-lasting real-estate and tourist programmes and high-return investments. The project to extend and restructure the Twiga Hotel was built around the desire to offer a qualitative image of architecture in Africa. Situated on the edge of a beach in Pointe-Noire, the Republic of the Congo's second largest city, the luxury hotel was designed to meet the needs of an increasingly demanding Congolese and international clientele. The architectural concept proposes a solution mixing urbanity, business, and relaxation. To preserve the spirit of the sea front and integrate the Twiga Hotel into its environment, the architectural volumes are organised

into 'bungalows' and 'big huts'. The three parts that include the lobbies, restaurants, and fitness area offer open spaces from the street to the shore, creating public spaces. Keldi Architectes' primary objective was to limit energy expenditure by taking advantage of the prevailing winds from the sea and by creating crossing spaces. The buildings' layout, the rooms, and, more specifically, the naves function as large areas that collect winds and generate draughts, thereby limiting the use of air conditioning, which is the source that consumes the most energy. Natural materials such as wood, stone, and thatch were employed to help the building blend into the landscape. While the architects included imported materials, they also made extensive use of local materials, and the employment of sustainably sourced wood helps reinforce the project's anchoring in the territory, since the Republic of the Congo is one of the largest tropical timber producing countries. The timber production is, however, usually intended for export, giving an image of little value to the population in general.   *pa/ed*

Source: Keldi Architectes (all pictures)

Rendering of the entire complex

Batéké family, Case Teke

Longitudinal section

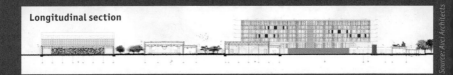

Source: Avci Architects

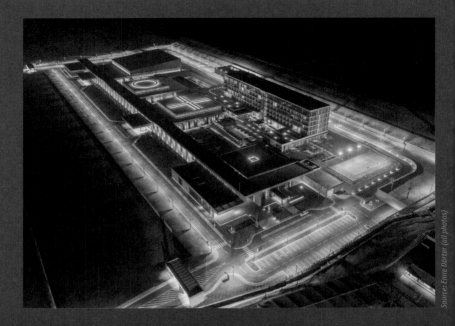

Source: Emre Dörter (all photos)

Kintélé Congress Centre and Resort Hotel

Kintélé, Djiri, Brazzaville
Avci Architects
2017

Kintélé Congress Centre is situated in a newly developing area of Brazzaville. The site has panoramic views of the Congo River to the south, and a forested unbuilt landscape to the north. The topography of the plot is a valley carved out by the Congo River and the buildings sit parallel to the contours of this valley sloping down to the river. The positioning of the buildings on the site was largely dictated by the concern of minimising the excavation and benefiting from the view. Large volumes such as the 1,500-seat congress hall, the 300-person presidential hall, the 1,000-seat banquet hall and the 1,000-person public piazza were placed in a linear sequence interrupted by courtyards. A sheltered colonnade links these masses and courtyards. The 350 m long colonnade also acts as a linear public space, sheltering people from the prevailing rains while allowing them to stay outdoors. It was crucial for Avci Architects to provide natural air flow in between the courtyards and semi-open spaces. The presence of water is also visually and audibly celebrated: it fills open pools by means of gargoyles and waterfalls. The high level of humidity in the region hinders the use of natural ventilation in large covered public spaces, so mechanical air conditioning was used in such areas. However, glazing is always deeply set into the north façade, and sunlight from the east and west is moderated by vertical shading elements and perforated metal screens to minimise the energy used. A 200-bedroom resort hotel – an adjunct to the congress centre – provides accommodation and leisure facilities. For privacy reasons, the spa, restaurant, bars, and pool are elevated 5 m above the level of the congress centre, which also helps these facilities to benefit from the panoramic views out over the Congo Valley. *ed/pa*

230

Call Me Here!

Sabine Müller, Andreas Quednau

Call Me Here! was developed as part of the research project Brakin – Visualising the Visible, which investigated the public spheres of Brazzaville and Kinshasa (Brakin), two neighbouring capitals separated by the Congo River. *Call Me Here!* looks at the cities through occurrences of the ever-present novelty of the mobile phone. Through mappings of the visible, such as antennas, advertisements, informal selling and calling points, or 'communication shops', and their impact on the colourscape of the city, the project reveals the logics of the infrastructural change taking place in Brakin. The revolution is based (on the part of the corporations) on portioning – combining the wide-reaching mobile technology with marketing adapted to the one-dollar-a-day economy – and (on the part of the ordinary merchant) on copying, distributing the supply and connectivity through individual acts that subscribe to successful corporate design. The project presents the territorial dimension of privately implemented utilities. Contrary to the modern paradigm of state-aided supply, this bottom-up transformation spreads the communication infrastructure with the speed of a chain reaction, but only where it is affordable.

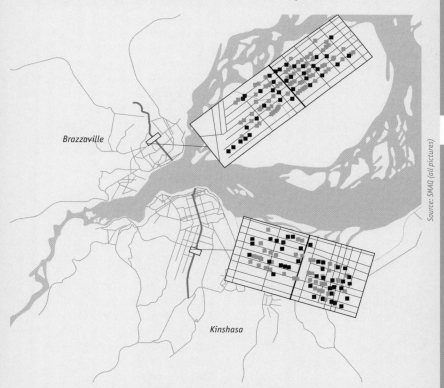

Source: SMAQ (all pictures)

CG

Left: Stores providing services related to telecommunication (*Maisons de communication*) are spread densely all over the neighbouring capital cities of Brazzaville and Kinshasa (Brakin). New colours (red and yellow) mark the predominance of one provider or another. Turquoise is the non-corporate colour that characterised the region before international companies came in.

Above: The maps of two random residential areas show the myriad of informal selling stalls for food and other daily commodities (blue), complemented by countless calling points (black). Almost every single household sells food and provisions, yet the number of *Maisons de communication* at street corners seem to equal the amount of selling points for food.

Democratic Republic of the Congo (Kinshasa)

Claudien Mulimilwa, Congolese architect, born 1969 in Bukavu. Master's from the Witwatersrand University, Johannesburg, 2003. He leads the architectural office Archplan International and represents the DRC in the International Union of Architects, among other organisations. *(cc)*

Johan Lagae, Belgian engineer and architect, born 1968 in Bruges. Graduated from Ghent University in 1991 and completed a PhD in 2002. Currently Full Professor in Architectural History at the same institute. He has co-curated several Congo-related exhibitions, both in Belgium and abroad. *(cc)*

Nicolas-Patience Basabose Rusangiza Gasigwa Tata Ande Bolongola Wa Badjoko, Congolese designer, born 1977 in Kinshasa. Runs Basabose Studio, a research-based design firm. Founded CongoHabitat, a collaborative urban think tank. He is a curator for CongoBiennale.

Andrew Brose, American architect. Graduated with a bachelor's in architecture from the University of Oregon in 2010, after which he joined MASS Design Group, where he oversaw the design and construction of the Ilima Primary School and housing for teachers in a remote region of the DRC.

Karine Guillevic, French architect. Graduated from the École d'Architecture de Bretagne in 1997. She moved to Burundi in 1999, where she founded her own architecture studio, ArchiNetwork. She has been focusing on the architectural and urban heritage of sub-Saharan African cities since 2009.

Stefan Krapp, German urban planner, born 1970. Graduated from RWTH Aachen University in 1998, where he now works as an assistant professor. Project collaborator in the partnership between RWTH Aachen University and the Université Notre-Dame du Kasayi, DRC, since 2001.

CD

Claudia Kruschwitz, German planner, born 1978. Graduated in 2003. Completed a PhD in 2011 at RWTH Aachen University, where she is a research assistant. She has been a project collaborator in the partnership between the RWTH and the Université Notre-Dame du Kasayi, DRC, since 2003.

Jean Molitor, German photographer, born 1960 in Berlin. Studied photography at the Academy of Visual Arts in Leipzig. Since graduating in 1993, he has become known worldwide as a photographer and is considered an ambassador of the Leipzig School of art.

Z. S. Strother, American art historian, with a PhD from Yale University. Extensive field research in the DRC, Nigeria, Ethiopia, and Senegal. She has published on art, architecture, photography, and iconoclasm and taught at UCLA and at Columbia University, where she is Riggio Professor of African Art.

Rolf Westerheide, German architect and urban planner, born 1952. Graduated from the RWTH Aachen University in 1980. Works there as Associate Professor. Project director of the partnership between RWTH Aachen University and the Université Notre-Dame du Kasayi, DRC, since 2001.

The Stade des Martyrs was built with Chinese aid and expertise
in the context of President Mobutu's 'nation-building' policy
Source: Bernard Toulier

Introduction

Claudien Mulimilwa, Johan Lagae

In writing the history of architecture of the Democratic Republic of the Congo (DRC), a Belgian colony from 1885 to 1960 and formerly known as Zaïre, we can no longer limit ourselves to start the narrative with the arrival of the first Europeans. For a long time, archaeologists have demonstrated human presence in various sites in Central Africa. Already during the 1920s and 1930s, important findings of prehistoric objects were made in the city of Kinshasa, and after more than two decades, historians have fully acknowledged the existence of urbanisation predating the colonial era in Central Africa. Sixteenth century writings mentioned the importance of M'banza Kongo, the capital city of the Kongo Kingdom, a territory situated in what is nowadays part of the DRC and Angola. Protourban settlements that also existed in the Kuba chiefdom – with Mushenge as its capital – have been documented through pioneering research in ethnography, linguistics, and oral history. Meanwhile, it has become clear that the spatial reorganisation of the territory that occurred during the colonisation that took place from the second half of the nineteenth century was fundamentally linked to the existing economic trade routes as well as sites where raw materials were to be found. The first colonial outposts often emerged in the vicinity of previous nodes of economic activity, in particular in the region near the Atlantic Ocean where the first encounters between European and African traders had taken place since the sixteenth century. In cities like Kinshasa or Matadi (the DRC's main seaport), one can still find traces of the pre-existing villages on top of which the colonial cities were constructed. The mining city of Lubumbashi, by contrast, demonstrates that colonial cities could also be erected *ex nihilo*, although the presence of water was crucial for transporting extracted materials and to keep the industrial facilities working.

Even though fundamental research on the topic remains rather scarce, some scholars have already investigated the great regional variety of traditional building forms in the DRC, ranging from the Azande homestead with its several types of circular huts, each used for a different purpose, to the houses on a rectangular plan with central posts supporting the ridge, typical of Bushongo villages. In many cases, houses, and palaces of important members of the community of particular ethnic groups were richly decorated with geometric motifs in contrasting colours. The architecture of the Mangbetu

Source: Antoine Moens de Hase

Stade des Martyrs (China Southwest Architectural Design and Research Institute, 1988)

238

Source: Johan Lagae (all pictures)

Two-storey house dating from the early twentieth century in a village near Vivi, in the former Bas-Congo Region. In early travel accounts it was noted on several occasions that customary chiefs built such imposing residences for themselves.

ethnic group made an especially strong impression on European explorers. In 1870, the German ethnographer Georg Schweinfurth described the meeting hall of the Nangazazi village of King Mbunza as one of the wonders of the world. Colonial architects, however, most often did not consider the vernacular building traditions in Central Africa as architecture in the strict sense of the word, as in their opinion these could not be defined along conventional Western categories such as durability, monumentality, or history. This does not mean, however, that colonial architecture was invented from scratch as traces of vernacular influence can be recognised in some, especially early building types.

At the Berlin Conference of 1884–1885, King Leopold II succeeded in obtaining the right to colonise and develop the territory of what is today the DRC. Given the challenging environment of Central Africa, death rates among the first explorers were high, leading doctors, engineers, and military officers to develop buildings that would help the white colonisers acclimatise to the tropical climate. Inspiration was taken

from British and Dutch experiences in Indonesia and tropical India, resulting in the widespread application of the typology of the so-called Tropical Bungalow. The metropolitan industry quickly seized the opportunity to enter the colonial building market by producing prefabricated constructions in wood or metal. In remote regions, where Catholic and Protestant missionaries often were the first to settle, constructions were most often erected with natural materials, before the local production of bricks started to take off around the turn of the century.

In the early 1920s, the Belgian government launched an important investment plan in infrastructure, building ports, railways, warehouses as well as vast workers' camps. Matadi, the main harbour city that connected the colony with the home country, for instance, witnessed a huge development in the interwar period. Within the colonial administration, the Department of Public Works gained in importance and architects started to be recruited in significant, albeit still limited numbers. Urbanisation evolved at a different pace throughout the territory. While Kinshasa remained

Houses designed by the Office des Cités Africaines (OCA) in the Lemba Neighbourhood of Kinshasa in the 1950s. Despite the substantial addition of informal constructions over time, the original pattern of settlement is still clearly visible when viewed from above.

somewhat of a village-like environment until the late 1930s, the mining cities of Lubumbashi, Likasi, and Kolwezi in the former province of Katanga thrived, with impressive public buildings starting to emerge, often designed in styles *en vogue* in the home country, such as modernism and Art Deco. New residential quarters were erected to accommodate the increasing number of Europeans in the colony, and the typology of the 'villa' gradually replaced that of the 'bungalow'. It was also during the interwar period, and especially from the late 1920s onwards, that colonial urban planners started to implement on a large scale the principle of spatial segregation along racial lines, constructing quarters for Africans, the so-called *cités*, which were separated from the European areas by a *zone neutre*, or sanitary corridor, as was the case in other sub-Saharan colonies.

Like other African colonies, Congo witnessed an important economic boom during the years immediately following World War II. In 1949, the colonial government launched a ten year plan for the economic and social development of the territory, which implied huge investments in

housing, education, health, and planning. The number of architects active in Congo increased considerably, with some of them working on an independent basis, while most were active in the building and planning departments of the colonial government or large enterprises. All over the territory, public buildings were constructed, often of remarkable architectural quality, even in secondary cities such as Mbandaka and Kalemie. To respond to the demographic pressure on large urban centres, the government installed the Office des Cités Africaines (OCA) in 1952, an architecture and planning office that built residential quarters for Africans on the periphery of major urban centres. These were conceived as satellite towns along the model of the neighbourhood unit and built in an explicit modernist architectural style, and the OCA quickly gained international recognition. Today, the OCA houses have often been transformed by their inhabitants. Kinshasa's urban landscape changed considerably in this period. On the one hand it was provided with an infrastructure of public buildings in line with its status of capital city, while on the other the real estate market boomed, resulting

Kinshasa's Main Post Office, on the Boulevard du 30 Juin, in the city's Gombe District
Source: Christian Stach (all pictures)

View over the harbour of the port city of Matadi, as seen from the balcony of a room in the Métropole Hotel, a 1930s Art Deco building. Apart from the port's infrastructure, one can see, in the background, a growing amount of informally constructed houses; these were mainly erected during the last decades on the steep slopes of the hills.
Source: Johan Lagae

in the construction of large scale high-rise buildings with mixed programmes along the city centre's main boulevards. Congo became independent on 30 June 1960 after a badly prepared transition, leading to a politically turbulent period that would only come to an end when Mobutu Sese Seko seized power in 1965. Little construction work occurred in the DRC during the early 1960s, but from 1966 onwards Mobutu's 'nation-building' project, labelled as a *recours à l'authenticité*, triggered a new dynamic in the field of architecture. French architects such as

Olivier-Clément Cacoub, Auguste Arsac, Anabel Bado, and Daniel Visart started to replace their Belgian colleagues and designed major public buildings. In 1965, a Mission Française d'Urbanisme (MFU) was launched in order to develop a new urban master plan for Congo's capital, Kinshasa. As Congo's economy thrived, real estate activity continued in the major urban centres, creating ample opportunities for foreign architects. Given the immense challenges in terms of education and healthcare, important initiatives were also taken in the domain of

development aid. From 1962 to 1969, the Sicilian architect Eugène Palumbo supervised the school-building programme in the DRC for UNESCO, building, among others, the Engineering Faculty of the University of Lubumbashi (1964–1966), while other designers authored projects financed by the World Bank or the European Development Fund. The Catholic Church remained an important agent in the country, providing the architect Paul Dequeker with numerous commissions for a variety of buildings, from churches to cloisters, educational facilities, and even residential projects. During this period, the first generation of Congolese architects also emerged, with figures such as Fernand Tala N'gai or Grégoire Magema as the main protagonists. Though they were trained abroad, a more sound formation of architects in Kinshasa was developed during this period, drawing largely on Paul Dequeker's approach to designing a climate-responsive architecture.

In 1973, President Mobutu launched his policy of 'zaïrianisation' in order to put an end to all foreign interests in Congo's economy. The effect of his decision was

Source: Christian Stach

Typical one-floor building near the Avenue d'Assossa in Kinshasa

disastrous, for it resulted in an economic downfall that would hinder the country's development for decades. European powers reduced their investments in development aid programmes in the DRC considerably but Mobutu skillfully repositioned himself within the changing geopolitical context by creating new alliances, looking in particular to China for support to sustain his official building programme. The monumental Palais du Peuple and the Stade des Martyrs, with its capacity of 80,000 spectators, are the only built fragments of a much more ambitious master plan to create a new administrative centre for Kinshasa, designed by Chinese planners. The formal building industry almost came to a complete standstill from 1975 onwards, with only some rare private commissions for the Congolese elite offering work for local architects. The economic networks of the Catholic Church remained operational, providing Paul Dequeker and his Congolese contractors with a constant workflow. In the field of urban planning, informality took over, despite the existence of the Bureau d'Etudes et

Source: iStock/Guenterguni

Our Lady of the Rosary Cathedral at the Congo River in Kisangani, the DRC's third largest city

Source: Johan Lagae

Engineering Faculty of the University of Lubumbashi (Eugène Palumbo, 1966)

Aménagement Urbain in Kinshasa. The immense growth of urban centres in the DRC indeed occurred in an ad hoc way, creating numerous problems in terms of urban hygiene, transportation, and services.

During the last two decades, the DRC has witnessed an important political shift. The Mobutu era came to an end, when, in 1997, Laurent Désiré Kabila seized power. After his assassination in 2001, he was succeeded by his son, Joseph Kabila, who was elected president in 2006. The relative political stability that the country has known since resulted in the return of large scale foreign investment in the DRC. The impact on the construction market has been significant. If the building industry slowed down during the worldwide economic recession of 2008–2009, the country is now witnessing a major building boom. This has produced some remarkable urban developments such as the Dubai-inspired project of the Cité du Fleuve in Kinshasa or the new town of Luano near the international airport of Lubumbashi; both of which testify to a growing interest among the elite in retreating to gated communities.

Corporate industries interested in developing activities in Central Africa, such as telephone and communication companies but also mining groups, are marking their presence via large scale building projects, in particular high-rise office towers in Kinshasa's city centre. After winning the presidential elections in 2006, President Joseph Kabila launched a national programme called *Les Cinq Chantiers*, proposing huge investments in infrastructure, public buildings, education, and healthcare. Today, the first results are becoming visible, including the upgrading of the international airport in Kinshasa. Churches belonging to various denominations (Protestant, Kimbanguist, Pentecostal, amongst others) are becoming major players in transforming the urban landscapes of various cities in the DRC, by appropriating and transforming old structures as well as erecting new, often grandiose temples. Even in smaller cities, one cannot help but be struck by the multitude of ongoing building sites, albeit that these most often remain limited to private commissions for single family houses.

The large scale projects that currently pop up in the major urban centres, however, are not necessarily commissioned to Congolese architects, since foreign investors often bring their own designers along. Nevertheless, a new generation of Congolese architects are now organising themselves to claim their rightful place in the DRC's building market.

PALACE ONATRA

Old terminal building of the passenger port of Kinshasa (above). The steamer would depart from here for Stanleyville (now Kisangani). Today, the building is called Palace ONATRA.

Typical fence in front of a middle-class mansion in Kinshasa

Source: Christian Stoch (all pictures)

House built with funding from the Fonds d'Avance in the 1950s, in the N'Djili Neighbourhood of Kinshasa. This situation is typical for the peri-urban areas of several cities in the DRC.

The fact that they have started to document and present their own work in exhibitions and conferences, is an important step in the process of writing a complete and inclusive history of architecture in the DRC.

Because of the new dynamic in the construction domain, the often dilapidated built infrastructure of the colonial era is increasingly under threat, in particular in the main urban centres. Often, several storeys have been added to existing buildings without too much concern for architectural aesthetics, urban coherence, or structural soundness. There are some notable examples, however, of colonial buildings having been successfully renovated. The Lycée Kiwele (a former Royal Atheneum) in Lubumbashi comes to mind, as well as the industrial complex of the textile factory in Kinshasa that is being turned into a luxury housing estate. In recent years, some initiatives have been taken to start a discussion on the importance of the architectural and urban heritage, but much work remains to be done before an effective heritage policy can be implemented.

Publicity panel for the Modern Titanic Office Building in 2010. The offices are promoted in the context of the *Cinq Chantiers* investment programme launched in 2006 by the president, Joseph Kabila. Several of these large-scale real-estate projects were never built.

The Memorial to Patrice Lumumba, and in the background, to the left, the Monument to National Heroes, which stands at the centre of an amusement park from the later Mobutu period and is now essentially used as a radio tower.
Source: Christian Stach

The Politics of Impermanence in the Kibulu of Eastern Pende Chiefs

Z. S. Strother

The Eastern Pende *kibulu* is the best documented example of a chief's house with sculpture, which was once a widespread architectural form in what is today the southwestern Democratic Republic of the Congo and Angola. Although paramount chiefs today prefer to build in adobe brick, they are required by law to make their official residence a small domed house built from reed, bark, or other vegetal materials. Curiously, all maintenance on the *kibulu* is strictly forbidden, with the consequence that few buildings survive for more than a decade. The history of the *kibulu* reveals that ephemerality is a choice with moral, aesthetic, and political ramifications.[1]

Drawings and photographs from 1884 to the present show that the shape of the *kibulu* and its site plan have remained conservative even while its sculptural adornment has changed continuously. In 1905, the German traveller Leo Frobenius observed that the Eastern Pende built their houses on a rectangular or square plan with a pitched roof. He was charmed by chiefs' houses, which looked strikingly different: 'The chiefly dwelling is apparently always built in square style. The old buildings of this structure were everywhere the same ... The roof of the house resembles a mighty bell.' He sketched the same baffled site plan in use in the 1980s and remarked on the 'snail's opening', which blocked a direct view of the door. Leo Frobenius also documented that he saw many *kibulu* in 'ruins,' the significance of which we will note below.[2]

Only a great chief (who owes no one else tribute) has the right to a *kibulu* and the dome over a square plan is rare in Africa, a fact of which chiefs are acutely conscious. The proportions are gauged by eye, based on the standard length of an oil palm branch, resulting in optically satisfying proportions of about 3 metres square and 3 metres high. The building materials have no symbolic justification. Only the geometry matters.

Ironically, the standardisation of form allows for a personalisation of the exterior decoration. For example, by varying the building materials, one chief invented a 'black' *kibulu* and another,

Chief Kindamba created a 'white' *kibulu* by layering husu palm leaves over bamboo cut from the oil palm (Kindamba, 1988). Domes over square plans are rare in sub-Saharan Africa.

Source: Z. S. Strother

Source: Léon de Sousberghe, n.n.n.n nnnnn, nnn tnbu in nnnnny aprie nnnnn/
National Museum of African Art, Smithsonian Institution

Chief Kombo-Kiboto's *kibulu* (ritual house) near Ndjindji, in 1953. Local law precludes all maintenance on houses of paramount chiefs, which must be built from reed or bark.

CD

a 'white' *kibulu*. However, the most notable distinction arises from the sculptures on the roof and surrounding the door. Certain chiefs invite famed sculptors knowing that the display of their work will draw (Pende) tourists from miles around.

Ritual specialists interpret the *kibulu* as first and foremost the 'house of the dead' (*inzo ya vumbi*). On the day of construction, the chief, his ministers, and a few trusted helpers rise before dawn, in the pitch dark, to plant the central post.

First they dig a hole, referred to as the 'belly' or 'womb' of the house. In June 1988, after depositing millet and other seeds crucial to Pende agriculture, Chief Nzambi offered the following prayer: 'You are the centre post of the house, you are the village with its people, fields, and forest. We have given you all these seeds for cultivation so that ... the seeds grow, so that the women may give birth ... so that there may be a lot of palm wine, so that the hunters may kill [their prey] with their guns.'

Source: Z. S. Strother

Constructing the *kibulu* of Chief Nzambi (Kibunda a Kilonda). The oil palm branch serves as a unit of measure to gauge optically satisfying proportions of around 3 m² and 3 m high.

Source: Henry Goertz

Eastern Pende chief's ritual house (*kibulu*). The *kishikishi* (rooftop statuette) was carved by Kaseya Tambwe Makumbi (near Nyanga, 1969), whose fame adds to the chief's reputation.

Although Nzambi addressed the post, his prayer was directed to his matrilineal ancestors. The act of burying representative seeds under the pole in the centre of the house places the life of the village under the protection of the dead. Because the door to the *kibulu* serves as a portal to the other world, people are discouraged from entering too easily (or staring inside) by an encircling palisade.

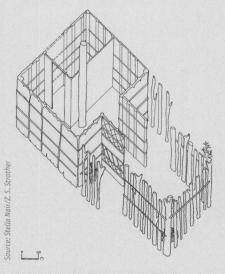

Source: Stella Nair/Z. S. Strother

Axonometric projection of the *kibulu* of Chief Nzambi (Ndjindji, 1988). Very few people are allowed to see the centre post, a conduit to the other world.

This palisade must incorporate living tree slips. The growth of at least a few of the slips demonstrates that the family has received a benediction from the dead. However, one tree in particular must be planted without exception, the 'giant' *Chlorophora excelsa*. Recognised instantly from a great distance, this 'ornament of the forest' serves no function other than memorialising the chief. In contrast to the beloved palm tree, it provides neither building materials nor comestibles. Its wood is too sappy when young, and too hard when mature, for all but the most rugged steel tools. In the village, it soon outgrows even the welcome capacity to provide shade. In form, it is unusually anthropomorphic because its trunk grows straight and smooth without lower branches. As such, it is an aestheticised object that represents named chiefs.

Although elected for life, the Eastern Pende chief is held to have a mystical relationship with his population that can affect his health. Every seven to ten years, the rebuilding of the *kibulu* constitutes a referendum on the chief's performance in office. If people dawdle, coming up with excuse after excuse not to build a new house, it communicates quite clearly their unhappiness and puts his life in danger. If they refuse, he knows he will die. However, even if the community rebuilds the house, they will require that the chief live next to the decaying wreck of his previous home (including statuary toppled from the roof) as a lesson on the limits of political power. The rotting *kibulu* serves as a *memento mori* stating, 'the chief should remember that one day he will die [like the rest of us].' The decaying wreck of the chief's house is orchestrated as an aesthetic experience that signifies fully as much as the new building, resplendent in its cherry-tinted sculpture and sprouting trees. Ironically, the impermanence of the chief's house is contrasted with the relative permanence of the long-lived trees planted in his honour in the courtyard. The chief lives with his funeral marker, as well as signs of his inevitable decay. The lofty *Chlorophora excelsa*, towering over the village, flatters him with the memory he will leave behind. However, the quality of trees that is most admired is their unstinting obedience – they grow where they are planted. The chief who does well models himself on a tree and accepts that his glory lies in subordinating his will to that of his people. The perpetual renewal of his house requires regular renegotiation of the social contract between the chief and his people and underscores their interdependence.

The ephemeral nature of the *kibulu* contrasts with the vigour and longevity of its landscaping. The last *kibulu* of Chief Kombo-Kiboto (Mukanzo Mbelenge) decays in the background, while the trees planted in the courtyard of an earlier house serve as his funerary monument (Ndjindji, 1987).

1   This essay draws on fieldwork conducted from January 1987 to September 1989 and a follow-up visit in 2007. For a full analysis, see Z. S. Strother, 'Architecture against the State: The Virtues of Impermanence in the Kibulu of Eastern Pende Chiefs in Central Africa', *Journal of the Society of Architectural Historians*, 63/2004, pp. 272–295.
2   Leo Frobenius, *Ethnographische Notizen aus den Jahren 1905 und 1906*, iii: *Luluwa, Süd-Kete, Bena Mai, Pende, Cokwe*, ed. Hildegard Klein (Stuttgart 1988), pp. 58, 59.

CD

Source: Z. S. Strother (all pictures)

The *kishikishi* (rooftop statuette) for the ritual house of Chief Mudinga (Kamusa Albert) by the artist Munganga Sh'a Libako (Nyanga, 2007). The sculptures associated with the *kibulu* may vary but the building's distinctive shape with a dome over a square plan does not.

'We should write our own history of Congo's architectural past'

Interview with Claudien Mulimilwa on the role of Congolese architects

Claudien Mulimilwa Byankubi is a Congolese architect who trained at the Institut des Bâtiments et Travaux Publics in Kinshasa and consequently followed a third cycle programme at the University of the Witwatersrand in Johannesburg, South Africa, where he graduated in 2003. He runs an architectural office in Kinshasa, Archplan International, which is involved in a variety of projects from private commissions such as villas and collective housing schemes for the upper and middle classes to (feasibility) studies on urban infrastructure and built heritage for a variety of stakeholders, including the World Bank. In May 2015 he won an international tender in partnership with GS3 Architectes, a Belgian firm, for the design development of the UNDP building in Kinshasa. Recently, his office was nominated as the Congolese partner of Junglim Architecture for the construction of a new National Museum, to be built in Kinshasa. Claudien Mulimilwa also plays a crucial part in promoting the role and position of the Congolese architect in the Demoratic Republic of the Congo (DRC). He was president of the Société des Architectes du Congo (SAC) from 2008 to 2018, and has represented the DRC in a number of international associations, among which are the International Union of Architects and the Africa Union of Architects, of which he was secretary general in the period from 2011 to 2015.

Claudien Mulimilwa at a construction site

During my recent visits to the DRC, I have been particularly struck by the building boom that is occurring in many of the country's cities. Not only in Kinshasa or the major mining city of Lubumbashi, but even in smaller cities, one encounters large numbers of construction sites, ranging from individual residences to large scale hotels, office towers, apartment buildings, and sometimes even complete gated community-like neighbourhoods, of which the Cité du Fleuve in Kinshasa is the most notorious. Is this situation creating new opportunities for the Congolese architects of today?

Our country is witnessing an important building boom, but Congolese architects are only partially involved in it, especially since large scale prestige projects tend to be initiated and developed by foreign investors. These not only provide the necessary funding, but also import technical expertise, including architectural design, and this, despite the fact that the current legislation prescribes that Congolese architects be involved in major building operations. It has taken, for instance, quite some effort to convince the government that the project team for a new National Museum in Kinshasa, which will be funded by the government of South Korea, should include architects from the DRC. The SAC, of which I was president, is playing a crucial role in the protection and promotion of the profession, by making sure that the legislation is followed. But it also aims to change the widespread perception that the training of architects in the DRC is not in tune with current international standards, in particular regarding technical aspects. Over the last years we have been developing partnerships with institutions abroad, in Belgium in particular, to address this situation and upgrade our architects' training.

Source: Claudien Mulimilwa

Source: Archplan International

Study for a collective housing project in Lubumbashi by Archplan International

Training architects in the DRC indeed poses a number of challenges; all the more so since there is only one architectural school in Kinshasa, which dates back to the late 1950s. Which steps are being taken to address the situation, both in terms of the training profile and the extension of the number of training centres?

It was precisely the lack of an advanced training in architecture that made me decide to go to Johannesburg, to follow a third cycle programme at the University of the Witwatersrand. Today, that situation has still not changed. However, the architectural school of La Cambre in Belgium, which now is part of the Free University of Brussels (ULB) and has a proven track record in architectural education in the Global South, has been a sparring partner for several years in helping us upgrade the training of architects in the DRC. In 2015, it succeeded in setting up an ARES-project, together with other partners, such as the University of Liège, which should, in the long term, result in founding architectural schools in Lubumbashi and Bukavu. But the project also has an immediate impact by having already granted PhD scholarships in various domains for four senior lecturers of the Architectural School in Kinshasa. Funded by the Francophone and Brussels' community in Belgium, this project furthermore aims to strengthen the professional capacities of Congolese architects, introducing them to contemporary building technologies as well as current

practices in building project management. The ARES-project thus targets both lecturers in architecture and already practising professionals, by providing grants to study in Belgium and by offering specific training in the DRC, the latter also being open to civil servants in the field of urban management.

Considering the influence of the 1992 book L'Architecture tropicale: Théorie et mise en pratique en Afrique tropicale humide, *co-authored by architect Paul Dequeker and Kanene Mudimubadu on architectural training in the DRC, one could argue that current architectural training already focuses, in a substantial way, on the technical aspects of architectural design. What about developing a historical and cultural sensitivity in the schooling of these future architects of the DRC?*

The historical consciousness within the milieu of practising Congolese architects is currently rather limited, as they are primarily occupied with the practicalities of the profession. In our curricula, History of Architecture is based almost exclusively on the canonical survey of Western architecture, while our own architectural past is not taught. I believe that a lot is to be learned from the built legacy in the DRC in terms of techniques and craftsmanship. And knowledge of the past is of course also crucial for developing a sound policy towards (post) colonial built heritage. In this respect, the ideas and practices forwarded by

CD

Source: Christophe Graz

Claudien Mulimilwa working with local stakeholders to document Kindu's architectural legacy

the École du Patrimoine in Porto-Novo, Benin, which stress the importance of built heritage, not only in terms of the cultural but also the economic development of African cities, form an interesting line of inquiry that we have recently discussed in a workshop within the ARES-project. While it is important for us at this stage to learn from foreign experts in the domain of architectural history and heritage, we should also write our own history of Congo's architectural past. This is why we have been starting to document and investigate the work of the first generation of Congolese architects such as Fernand Tala N'Gai and Grégoire Magema, who designed and built significant projects in the 1970s and 1980s.

Is this interest in the Congolese architects Fernand Tala N'gai and Grégoire Magema also related to contemporary practice? Because I recognise an outspoken attention for sculptural architectural form in their work, which seems to be linked with a keen interest in formal issues amongst contemporary Congolese architects. Would you agree that architects in the DRC are now mainly focusing on issues of formal language, while the current discourse on architecture in Africa, as it is emerging in the West, is emphasising the issues of sustainability, as in the research by design-work of RTWH Aachen for instance, and that of 'Building Social', as Andres Lepik is emphasising in his 2013 book and exhibition Afritecture?

Source: Claudien Mulimilwa

Archplan on-site team meeting

The current production of Congolese architects does tend towards a certain formal exhibitionism. There is an outspoken preference for complicated roof shapes in the design of individual houses. But you should not forget that this is also due to the clients we work for and whose taste is often informed by Nigerian TV series in which the story is often set in luxurious villas. These clients also often explicitly insist on integrating air conditioning, as it is considered a symbol of one's social status. I had the privilege of designing a villa for a rather open-minded professor of the University of Lubumbashi who held a prominent

Source: Archplan International (all pictures)

Villa Samba in Lubumbashi under construction (Archplan International, 2004)

position in society. He accepted our proposal to base the design of his house on ecological principles that draw upon architectonic solutions to create natural ventilation. But once the house was finished, he was vehemently criticised by some of his relatives and colleagues, as the project was not considered in line with his standing. After his death this house has been significantly transformed by his children. To assess the current production, you need to understand that Congolese architects tend to comply with the desires of their clients for whom the representation of their social status is crucial. Opportunities for architectural experiment are extremely limited, especially in the domain of housing for the poor,

where informality is still the rule and where the government could help create a framework to develop approaches for social construction. This is precisely why, as a president of SAC, I am trying not only to protect the profession of the architect in the DRC but also think it is crucial to start a dialogue with foreign experts and stakeholders on how to re-orient our students' training and strengthen the capacities of those already practising. But in a country that is often described as a 'failed state' by outside observers and in which foreign investment in the formal building sector remains dominant, this is, of course, a slow process.

Interview conducted by Johan Lagae (2015)

Study for a collective housing project in Lubumbashi by Archplan International

Kinshasa

Kinshasa, formerly Léopoldville, developed over a century from a handful of pre-colonial settlements into a vast and polycentric metropolis of almost 15 million people. Its origins are in two colonial posts that coincided with two pre-colonial villages. These were interconnected by a railway reaching various trading posts along the edge of the Congo River. The city has multiple links to Brazzaville, the capital of the Republic of the Congo, which is situated directly across the river. As the colonial capital of the Belgian Congo, Léopoldville was where urban and architectural projects were developed, though not all were realised. The main colonial boulevard, today the Boulevard du 30 Juin, is a major circulatory axis that tracks the original railway connection. Various features demonstrating the architecture of the city's past can be found on this impressive road. Spatial segregation along racial lines in former times resulted in a binary city structure. This is recognisable in the axial boulevard-like urban structure of the European section along the river, and the controlled grid of the African section to its south. Originally there was a neutral unoccupied zone between these two sections, which was gradually populated as the city expanded. Recreational facilities for Europeans were established in this 'neutral zone', including a zoo, the Parc De Bock and the Léo Golf Club. Together with education, medicine formed one of the spearheads of Belgian colonisation, and as a result, the city boasts several impressive health facilities. These were often situated on prime sites for Europeans along the Congo River, benefiting from the breeze and spectacular views.

The original public market was located in the European Quarter of the city – something that challenged the colonial separation of races. The presence of African traders around the public market was considered unhygienic and inappropriate

Kinshasa's skyline along the Congo River: large parts of the city on the river's edge, where some of the recent construction boom is evident, are not open to the public
Source: iStock/Mtcurado

Source: African Drawn Project

Kinshasa city streets: the long, straight Boulevard du 30 Juin runs parallel to the river bank

by many Europeans. As a result, another market was set up in the neutral zone in 1943, where in the early 1970s President Mobutu Sese Seko implemented a new, modernist structure. Today, Kinshasa's Central Market, designed as a group of several concrete pavilions, accommodates more than 30,000 merchants, making it one of Africa's largest marketplaces. The site is often mentioned in discussion over public space in Kinshasa and remains an important meeting point for exchange and encounters between cultures.

Since the 1990s, public services and administration have collapsed, resulting in the degradation of the city and problems such as traffic congestion. However, the city is also in the middle of a construction boom, which can be seen in the numerous riverside developments. *adp*

CD

Cool Places in a Hot Climate:
The Fate of Unpopular Public Spaces in Kinshasa

Nicolas-Patience Basabose

Kinshasa has a nine-month rainy season with a good deal of precipitation and a record high temperature of 36 °C, while its three month long dry season receives barely any rainfall and has a record low of 14 °C. The yearly average temperature of this tropical capital is around 25.5 °C.

In the Téké villages of the city's origins, traditional shared open spaces were graced by a branch or two: a manifestation of the desire for shade during verbal exchanges. From a holistic perspective, the hundreds of nations or ethnic groups forming the cultural texture of the country have their settlements built on similar principles. From north to south, east to west; and from the Bakongo to the Balega, and the Ba Lokele to the Baluba peoples. For example, the Lega village (*kyumo*) is traditionally built on a hill, in a more or less natural clearing (*kilungulabo*) of primary rain forest. It consists of two parallel rows (*mikeke*) of contiguous

huts, a plan that creates the impression of longhouses. The open space (*mulungu*) between the two rows of houses serves as Main Street, a celebration space, and a public square. In the Lunda settlement, the royal compound (*musumba*) had multiple courtyards, each with designated functions; straight roads, and shaded public squares.

In recent years, Africa has emerged from decades of political bewilderment into an era of lauded economic development. The so-called African Boom. Infrastructure has, disputably, been upgraded. Governments entrust grandiose projects to foreign companies, and tales of the quality of their work in many places leave a lot to be desired. In the DRC, roads are being aggressively enlarged, glazed buildings are being erected to non-conformist heights, and many public spaces are being tampered with. One such example is the new Place du 30 Juin,

Source: Nicolas-Patience Basabose (all other pictures)

Place du 30 Juin, Kinshasa: a tree-less open space flooded with sunlight

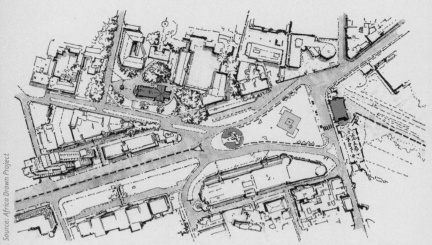

Source: Africa Drawn Project

Place du 30 Juin is on the Boulevard du 30 Juin, the home of various government ministries

in Kinshasa. The centrality of the space and its historic symbolism for the Congolese should make it a remarkable location. However, the imported design and realisation rationale leave it lifeless. Formerly a celebrated art market (*Wenze ya bikeko*) attracting locals and tourists, the now – supposedly – improved square is a tree-less, open space, copiously exposed to the blazing sun, a lifeless tiled arena. The square is a failed attempt at beautification.

The cause is the inability of many African governments to involve local experts in projects of national interest. Local knowhow is purposefully disregarded. The ferried exoticism of foreign architects or constructors is believed to flash gleams of 'modernity', which results in leaving lasting edifices to craftspeople who have no cultural references, and in proliferating unliveable slots and plots that are deprived of the spirit of the place, while gambling with usage longevity and relevance for the public. This leads one to wonder if this trend of tree-less open public spaces is meant to discourage public gathering in autocratic states where masses are expected not to gather, or if it is a simple desire to resemble distant places, completely disconnected from our social, cultural, and spiritual fibres.

This quest for modernity dismantles our cultural principles and references, while our contemporary existence should be evident in palettes that merge our cultural expressions from different times

across the centuries. Urban design, or the art of building cities, is the method by which humans create a built environment that fulfils their aspirations and represents their values and climatic requisites. As we migrate from rurality to urbanity, we can create liveable spaces that reflect us as a culture – with the evolution of spatial and historical relationships creating something unique. The lack of underlying logic or rationality in the creation of these spaces requires us to add our culture to the toolkit so we can return to our ancestral art of place-making.

Vast empty concrete: Place du 30 Juin today

Basabose Studio's proposal for the square, which adds green spaces and shaded seating to help increase the number of visitors

The Immo Kasai in Kananga city centre in 2002 (built 1950s)

Source: Institut für Städtebau und Landesplanung/RWTH Aachen (all pictures)

From Luluabourg to Kananga: The Changing Urban Structure of a Provincial Capital

Claudia Kruschwitz, Stefan Krapp, Rolf Westerheide

Kananga, once called Luluabourg, is an archdiocese, a university town, and the present capital of the province of Lulua. It dates from the site of a train station, Lulua(bourg)-Gare, which stood on a private train line between Lubumbashi and Ilebo (a riverside port city that was a connection point between Kasai Province and Kinshasa). Lulua-Gare's name originally came from the area's principal town, then called Luluabourg (now Malandji), founded by the German explorer Hermann von Wissmann in 1884 as the first station in the independent Kingdom of Kongo. The town was situated near Mukenge, which, as the capital of the Lulua tribe, was an important trade hub. With the Lulua-Gare station's grand opening by the Belgian monarch in 1928, the dynamic Lulua-Gare replaced Luluabourg as the main urban centre, inheriting its name in 1936. In the 1940s, the Belgian state planned a modern city, which was erected up until 1960. Fast-growing Luluabourg became the provincial capital in 1950, and, during the 1960 independence negotiations, Luluabourg's central location made it a potential candidate for the future Congolese capital. In 1966, the city was renamed Kananga, which derivatively means 'a place for peace'.

From the beginning, Kananga attracted many workers and trading companies, resulting, eventually, in the exodus of around one million inhabitants of various tribes from rural areas. Although the exodus continues today, the former commercial town has become a rural 'village of a million', with a colonial centre that has functioned, during the past few decades, as a self-supported structure without large regional or national exchanges of goods. The reasons are the continuing rural lifestyle and the missing or malfunctioning regional and national transport links. Only lately have improvements in the infrastructural sector reversed this development: the Ilebo to Lubumbashi railway line is still being used; inner city and regional roads have been (re)constructed; the capacity of the national airport has been increased; and the water and electricity supplies, as well as the sewage system, have been improved and introduced in the Congolese quarters. This has involved various levels of design and planning, making Kananga a model for many other Congolese cities. Because of Kananga's dynamic topography, the city's structure presents itself as a ramified linear settlement along various

Central Kananga shopping street with two-storey buildings and covered walkways in 2004

Kananga City Hall (1950s) on the central green of the Boulevard Lumumba, in 2007

ridges, parallel to the railway. Thereby, the railway line defines a green axis, along which a multitude of quarters and many solitary functions are beaded like pearls on a necklace. Starting with a small nucleus around the station and the Saint-Clément Mission and Cathedral, and with an additional residential estate for railway workers in the northeast and a military camp in the southeast, the Belgian master plan defined the basic outline of Kananga on plateaus on both sides of the tracks, with a length of around 11 km and a maximum width of 5 km. Today, through the integration of various villages on the outskirts and the unplanned settlements on the plateaus, which continue far down into the valleys' steep sections, Kananga has grown to a length of about 15 km and a width of 2–8 km.

The Belgian master plan integrates the train station and Saint-Clément Cathedral into the northern town centre as focal points, linking the two structures with a main street. Around the station, we find shops and services in two- to three-storey buildings, many with arcades on the ground floor. The cathedral stands at the beginning of a development that ends in a large hospital and a European

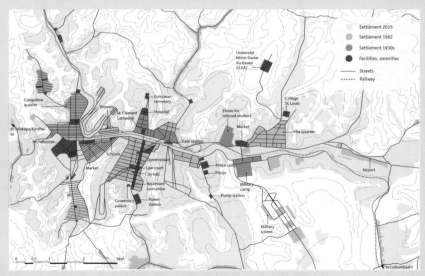

Urban growth and development of Kananga from the 1930s to the present

Source: François Vincent

Saint-Clément Cathedral (1920s), a focal point in the Belgian master plan for Kananga

cemetery in the north. Two major axes run across the train tracks to the southern town centre. While a diagonal axis used to align various banks, cinemas, and hotels between the Boulevard Lumumba and the station, the axis from the cathedral southwards accesses today's main shopping area, which also features two- to three-storey buildings with arcades.

The Boulevard Lumumba is shaped by a spacious central green, framed by impressive solitary, representative buildings (City Hall, Governorate, Court, Central Bank) of mostly three storeys in the centre, and by three- to five-storey hotels and commercial buildings with arcades to the north. It ends with the Governor's Palace in the south. The building styles mirror those of Portuguese modernist structures. The tropical trees with very high treetops give parts of the central green a park-like appearance. On the outskirts of the town centre, one- to two-storey villas are situated within spacious gardens on plots of about 1,600 to 2,400 m². These solitary houses defined the classical housing typology for the Europeans in Kananga. All of the colonial buildings there share a modern, climatically adapted architecture and brick or concrete construction.

Apart from the town centre – with its variety of functions and centrally located high-rise buildings – and an industrial quarter west of the northern centre, the other quarters are low-rise and residential with few solitary buildings. Among them are two Belgian villa quarters, east of the northern town centre. This is the old estate for railway workers, featuring mainly villa plots of about 400 m², and a large villa quarter similar to the villa areas of the town centre. The latter is home to one large solitary structure, the Collège Saint-Louis, and connects to the campus of the Université Notre-Dame de Kasayi, the country's first post-colonial university.

Western Kananga comprises several old Congolese residential quarters, which define the second large axis spanning the railway. They are based on a grid structure of plots of around 500 m², on which several small one-storey brick or clay buildings are grouped around a yard. The structure is divided with hedges or walls, which prevents interference with urban space. Small-livestock farming and the cultivation of crops takes place in these yards. In central locations, the homogenous structure is supplemented by spacious public squares with public buildings such as the domicile of the archdiocese, schools, colleges, and markets along the train tracks. In the east there are solitary functions: a police station, a prison, a military school, a market. Small shops run along the main road to the airport in the far east, currently Kananga's most dynamic zone.

The Transformation of Kananga's Colonial Villas

Claudia Kruschwitz, Stefan Krapp, Rolf Westerheide

Spanning styles: 1950s Belgian villas with varied roof shapes, in 2004
Source: Institut für Städtebau und Landesplanung/RWTH Aachen

The Belgian villa represents one of Kananga's essential urban elements, as it was the typical colonial housing for Europeans there, and, along with the Congolese urban housing plot, it still defines the rural settlement pattern of this city today. Yet, how relevant is the original concept of these impressive buildings for users now? Kananga's villas can be found on the outskirts of the town centre and in a residential quarter situated northeast of the centre. They were originally inhabited by Belgian colonial civil servants, entrepreneurs, merchants, and salesmen. Usually buildings of one storey (or in some cases two), the villas are placed within large, formerly lavish gardens on plots of ca. 1,600–2,400 m², measuring about 40 × 50 m. Because of these gardens, with their surrounding hedges or formerly low walls that run along broad unpaved roads, the clusters of villas contribute to Kananga's green settlement structure. The villas are plastered brick or concrete buildings. Their architecture is often well designed and encompasses a variety of styles: cottages with steep pitched roofs, cubic villas with hipped roofs, horizontally composed villas with slightly slanted shed roofs, cubist villas that hide all roof structures, and so forth. The façade

CD

styles range from International Style to designs inspired by Congolese ornament. Despite these differences, all of the villas share constructional elements that are adapted to Kananga's tropical climate. Among these are sloped roofs – often constructed with larger roof overhangs – several verandas, and, in every room, ventilation openings additional to the usual windows and veranda doors to ensure a constant, agreeable breeze. These openings are often of a prominent shape, generating a relationship to Congolese ornamentation. An additional link to the locality is crested by the use of local quarry stones.

The villas' layouts mirror the classical European house with common rooms and bedroom areas, offering spaces for an interior-oriented, European lifestyle. The example on the following page shows the floor plan of a villa that is entered through a veranda and entrance hall. To the right of this hall, the common rooms are accessed: the living room opens to the dining room, which connects to the kitchen and attached utility room. The living room and kitchen each open onto a veranda. To the left of the entrance hall is the bedroom wing. A central hallway accesses a servant's chamber and two bedrooms, with a centrally

Belgian villa exterior influenced by the International Style, in 2004 (built 1950s)

located bathroom on the left. The hallway ends at the master bedroom, which is equipped with a second bathroom. To the right, there is a toilet. The surrounding garden served representational purposes and could act as an addition to the spacious interior. The verandas probably played an important role as interfaces between interior and exterior, offering the most agreeable living space in the tropical climate.

Today, the still-intact villas are inhabited by wealthy Congolese or serve as polyclinics, kindergartens, offices, and so forth. While one small family inhabited the Belgian villa, today's inhabitants are manifold. It is still common to find only one residing family, but also for several families or one extended family to share one villa, resulting in new layout constellations. Sole officials live in some villas, and require additional security features such as high surrounding walls, guards, and additional adjoining buildings for staff or guests.

Irrespective of a villa's specific inhabitants, the Congolese lifestyle often reverses the European relation between interior and exterior and introduces rural elements. In extreme cases, the house itself only serves as a scarcely furnished location for sleeping and storage, with a certain infrastructure. Life happens on the verandas and in the garden.

In the floor plan example on the following page, only the bedrooms are used in the original sense. All common rooms mainly serve storage purposes. The dining room is relocated to the living room veranda; sojourn seats are placed in the walled yard. The kitchen is used for storage, while all cooking and washing activities are moved to the enhanced veranda. In practice, wood- or coal-fired hearths are used instead of gas or electric stoves. Water for washing the dishes comes from wells. This reflects both the traditional lifestyle and the current state of the technical infrastructure. The power network still functions and supplies the villa with electricity during certain hours. Additionally, a private generator is used. As the water distribution network does not function properly today, running water is not available, but has to be collected at a well. The sewage system consists of local absorbing wells.

The former garden has been transformed into a spacious walled yard. Its vegetation – ornamental shrubs and plants for food – is limited to the shaded spaces along the walls. Along the front, the garden is used as a common room, while at the back it serves as an area for crops, stockbreeding (mostly chickens), composting, and also infrastructural devices. In addition, new adjoining buildings (homes for staff, storage spaces, and

Source: Institut für Städtebau und Landesplanung/RWTH Aachen (all pictures)

Façade of a Belgian villa inspired by Congolese ornamentation, in 2004 (built 1950s)

guest rooms) are placed along parts of the side walls. The walled property is now accessed through a large gate from the street; this also obstructs the view in from the street.

On the urban scale, we therefore find two opposing developments. On the one hand, walls around the properties produce anonymous stony streets replacing green alleys. On the other hand, nature returns, adding to the rural character of the townscape: grass and other vegetation sprout through unpaved roads, turning them into tracks, and crops grow in areas within and between plots.

Thereby, a transformation has taken place using the model of the 'Congolese' urban housing plot, which itself introduced elements of the European villa to the rural settlement typology. The 'African' urban housing plot incorporated the clear differentiation between functional zones and the use of modern construction materials from European homes, while the layout of buildings around a yard, the cultivation of food in this yard, and the introverted character of the plot, generated through hedges or walls that prevent association with the urban space, correlates with traditional rural settlement typologies.

To conclude, the European villa offers creative elements for a contemporary Congolese housing typology, whereas the functional side, both indoors and outdoors, still has to be developed.

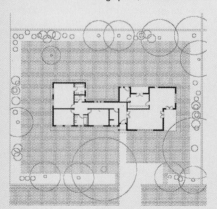
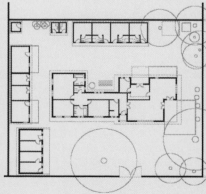

Comparison of everyday life in a colonial villa in the 1950s (left) and in 2010 (right); it was inhabited by a Belgian family in the 1950s and by a Congolese public figure in 2010.

Source: Hugues Sirault (all pictures)

Baptist Missionary Society Bungalows `CD 01`

Avenue Kalemie/Avenue Mbuji-Mayi,
Gombe, Kinshasa
ca. 1880

These two bungalows, located on the edge of the Congo River, illustrate the presence of Protestant missionaries in the DRC in the nineteenth century. They were built for the congregation of the Baptist Missionary Society (BMS), a group that arrived in Kinshasa in the early 1880s. In typological terms, these constructions adhere to the model of the tropical bungalow that was advocated by the British doctor John Murray as being the most suitable house for the tropics. Elevated from the ground for ventilation, and equipped with a ventilated roof as well as an all-round veranda to protect against sun and rain, this building type was an exercise in climate-responsive building. Constructed out of wooden elements posed on metallic piers, these bungalows, produced by Frodingham Iron and Steel Company, are also a reminder of the new market that opened in Central Africa for metropolitan construction firms. *cc*

Boma Church » `CD 02`

Plateau de Boma, Boma,
Kongo Central Province
1899

This small prefabricated metal church is one of the oldest colonial buildings left in the Democratic Republic of the Congo. Located in Boma, the capital of the colonial territory, it was part of a series of buildings that embodied the role of Belgium, and King Leopold II, as a colonial power. It was produced by the Belgian company Forges d'Aiseau that developed a special form of metal constructions, for export to hot climates, not only in Africa, but also, for instance, to Brazil. As it was immediately considered too small to accommodate the rapidly growing community of Christians in Boma, projects for an imposing cathedral were soon developed in 1904. In 1945, an initiative was undertaken to relocate the metal church to the African neighbourhood. After the dismantling had started and two parts had been extracted, the operation was halted, so only one third of the original structure remains in place today. *cc*

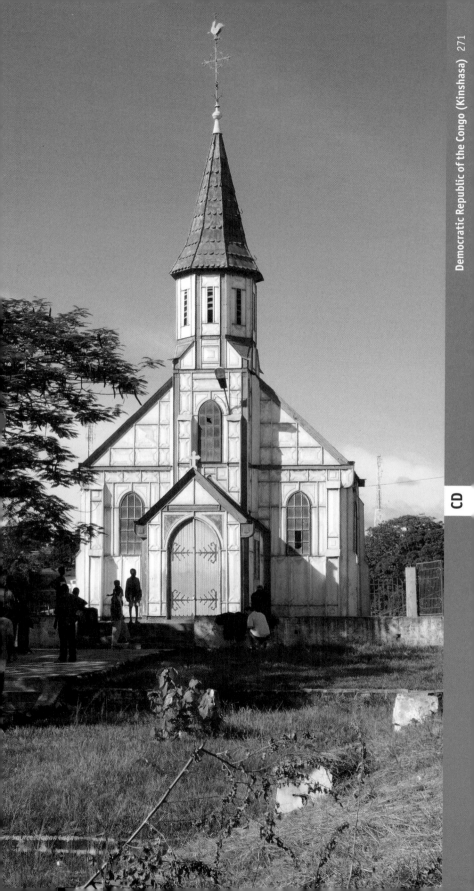

Source: Julian Legge

ONATRA Staff Housing   CD 03
Avenue Bosomi, Avenue Bolenge,
and Avenue Wenze, Mbandaka,
Équateur Province
OTRACO
1920s, 1950s

Because of the economic agenda of Belgian colonisation, railway and port infrastructures form a crucial element of the built environment in the DRC. In 1935, all of the firms involved in constructing such infrastructure were united in the Office d'Exploitation des Transports Congolais (OTRACO), today known as the Office National des Transports (ONATRA). Through OTRACO's architecture department, which developed a number of building types to be used all over the territory, the organisation had an impact on the urban landscapes of many Congolese cities. Mbandaka, a city on the Congo River, serving as an economic pole of regional importance, forms a case in point. In the 1920s important port infrastructure was already being constructed there, including docks and warehouses, and a number of modest houses for its European staff. The latter were later complemented by a series of large villas and two-storey houses during the 1950s. OTRACO also built a camp that provided accommodation for the African workers in the form of small, prefabricated dwellings.   *cc*

Source: John Lagae (all pictures)

Lubumbashi Synagogue | CD 04

Avenue Jean-Félix de Hemptinne/
Avenue du 30 Juin/Avenue Lumumba,
Lubumbashi, Haut-Katanga Province
Raymond Cloquet
1929

Raymond Cloquet played a crucial role as a spokesman for the architectural profession in official circles. He also advocated the introduction of a Modern architecture in Congo, in tune with contemporary currents in his home country, Belgium. As architect-in-chief of the 1931 Exposition Internationale d'Elisabethville (Élisabethville was Lubumbashi's colonial name), as well as in his own projects, he opted for an aesthetic reminiscent of Art Deco. As such, he was instrumental in shaping the modern image of the mining cities in the Katanga area, which pervaded in colonial propaganda of the interwar period. Among his most prestigious commissions was the design of the synagogue in Lubumbashi, a place to accommodate the liturgical services of the largest Jewish community in the country at the time. Cloquet conceived the building in tune with its prime location in the city centre, giving the front façade a classical feel, even though he chose to flank the temple-like portico with two domes, vaguely evoking Hindu architecture. The building's overall composition clearly demonstrates Cloquet's keen interest in the contemporary brick architecture of the Dutch architect Willem Marinus Dudok.   *cc*

Commercial Buildings ≫   CD 05

Avenue Mundji, Mbandaka,
Équateur Province
Youssuf Ismael Patel
1930s–1950s

Small traders of Portuguese, Italian, Greek, or even Asian descent have played a crucial role in the making and shaping of urban landscapes in the DRC since the 1920s. Developing commercial activities that targeted both a European and African clientele, these intermediate figures in colonial society most often occupied the

Source: Johan Lagae (all pictures)

zones between the European neighbourhood and the so-called 'native towns' for Africans, at times blurring the racial boundaries that were so fundamental to colonial urban planning practice. During the interwar period, their trade houses consisted of modest, one-storey buildings, generally with arcades at the front that gave the streetscape a certain coherence. In cities like Kinshasa and Matadi, some more wealthy traders, like the Portuguese Nogeira family, constructed remarkable edifices. The case of Youssuf Ismael Patel, a trader of Indian descent who arrived in the eastern city of Bunia in 1929, before finally settling in Mbandaka in 1934, demonstrates that this phenomenon also occurred in more remote cities. Developing important trade activities and constructing several commercial buildings along prominent avenues in Mbandaka's centre from the 1930s up until the 1950s, turned Ismael Youssuf Patel into a highly respected citizen. He is still remembered locally as the 'Builder of Mbandaka'.   cc

Métropole Hotel

Place du Commissariat, Matadi,
Kongo Central Province
Ernest Callebout
1930

Located in Matadi, the DRC's main harbour city, the Métropole Hotel formed an
important gateway to the colony. Built
according to a design by architect Ernest
Callebout, the five-storey structure was
considered the first significant multistorey edifice in the Democratic Republic of Congo. Callebout's design was innovative in tectonic terms. While the main
structure was made out of steel components, the façades were assembled out
of prefabricated concrete panels featuring an imprint that evoked natural stone.
As the building was conceived around a
patio, its climatic performance was exemplary. At the time, observers noted
how it was one of the rare buildings to
succeed in creating a fresh environment
in the notoriously harsh tropical climate
of Matadi, a city built on rock.   *cc*

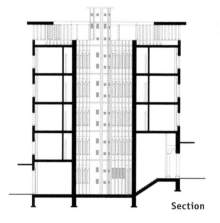

Section

Source: Luce Beeckmans

Source: Johan Lagae (all pictures)

Hospital for Europeans `CD 07`
Avenue du Clinique/
Avenue Cimetière/Avenue Salongo,
Mbandaka, Équateur Province
Etienne Popijn/Public Works Department
1930

The hospital for Europeans in Mbandaka, built from 1927 to 1930, is a feature in the urban landscape. As all the pavilions constituting the complex are oriented according to a north-south axis to respond to climatic constraints, the building of this large scale ensemble also resulted in the construction of a new avenue that cuts diagonally through the existing urban grid. The hospital was initially commissioned to the architect Etienne Popijn, who was active in Kinshasa at the time. But his grandiose project was modified for financial reasons, and to align it with the common guidelines for hospital buildings developed by the Department of Public Works of the Brussels' Ministry of Colonies. In terms of its general layout, architectural language, and tectonic features, this hospital resembles the Hôpital Reine-Elisabeth in Kinshasa (1929–1932) and the general hospital of Kisangani. All three constitute healthcare institutions that were planned to operate at a regional level. *CC*

Source: Johan Lagae

Boboto College (former Albert I College)

CD 08

Avenue du Père Boka/Avenue
Kisangani, Gombe, Kinshasa
Etienne Popijn
1947

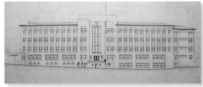

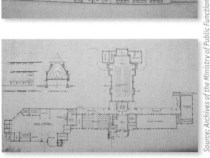

Source: Archives of the Ministry of Public Function

Preliminary design drawings

CD

During the rule of King Leopold II, Catholic missionaries were put in charge of educational affairs in the Belgian Congo. With the number of Europeans residing there increasing considerably over the 1920s, the education of their children became an important preoccupation and often the congregation of the Jesuit fathers was asked to take this matter to hand. In the 1930s, the congregation built impressive schools in some major urban centres, such as the Alfijiri College in Bukavu or the Boboto College, formerly known as the Albert I College in Kinshasa. Situated on a prominent site in the city centre, the latter was built from 1937 to 1947, and housed a number of facilities, including not only class rooms but also boarding rooms, a residence for the Jesuit fathers, a festivities hall, and a swimming pool that was used by the capital's white community. Paying close attention to climatic issues, the architect designed the complex in a style that was described in contemporary sources as Streamline Moderne.   cc

Source: Johan Lagae

Source: Johan Lagae

Lycée Kiwele `CD 09`
Avenue du 30 Juin/Avenue Ruwe,
Lubumbashi, Haut-Katanga Province
René Schoentjes, Albert Van Grunderbeek
1949

In the immediate post-war years, colonial authorities started to organise an official school network to break the Catholic educational monopoly in the DRC. The Lycée Kiwele, which was originally built from 1948 to 1949 as a Royal Atheneum, forms one of the first institutions demonstrating that shift in policy. Just like the contemporary projects of the Royal Athenea in Kinshasa and Bukavu, it was authored by the office of the engineer-architect René Schoentjes, who, during the 1930s, had occupied a prominent position in the Public Works Department of the Brussels, Ministry of Colonies. In formal terms, the Lycée Kiwele responded to the colonial authorities' preference for a monumental, yet modernising form of classicism that was characteristic for 1930s public architecture in Europe. Impressive in size, the vast complex is positioned somewhat awkwardly in its urban context, as its main axis runs diagonally in relation to the urban grid. In 2012, an extensive renovation of the dilapidated ensemble was initiated. With the addition of two swimming pools, one of Olympic dimensions, the fully restored Lycée Kiwele has regained its former grandeur.   *cc*

Bukavu Cathedral » `CD 10`
Avenue de la Cathédrale,
Bukavu, South Kivu Province
Georges Nef
1951

With such a distinctive silhouette, composed of two articulated, pointed arch-shaped roofs and a Streamline Moderne cupola perforated with slits for natural ventilation, Bukavu Cathedral counts among the most remarkable architectural projects of the interwar period. Radical in shape and materiality, its architecture deviates significantly from the typical brick religious buildings in the colony at the time. Commissioned by the congregation of White Fathers, and built from 1948 to 1951, the cathedral occupies a prominent position directly off Bukavu's main avenue. The architect Georges Nef, who made his career in the Department of Public Works during the interwar years, designed the cathedral as a landmark in the urban landscape. He also provided a local touch with the form of the conical cupola that bears a vague resemblance to an African hut. The white plastered interior is merely the counter-form of the outside, with pointed arches giving the space a clear rhythm, and a complex geometry. The Flemish artist Michel Martens was commissioned to design the rosary windows, which provide a bright and colourful interior accent.   *cc*

Source: Christophe Graz

Source: Christophe Graz

Conceived as a hospital and built by the Sankuru company in 1958, Bukavu's only high-rise is still unfinished. After independence, it was used as housing for the city's Catholic University.

Tropical Modernism in Bukavu

Jean Molitor, Karine Guillevic

Bukavu, a lakeside city in the east of the DRC, is home to a large number of modernist buildings constructed during the colonial era. In February 2014, the Berlin-based photographer Jean Molitor and the French architect Karine Guillevic requested permission from the town's mayor to photograph fifty buildings. Finally, in early March, after a long wait in the mayor's office, the deputy secretary handed over written permission. Copies were sent to nine different institutions in the city, including the offices of the province governor and the police commanders. Accompanied by two uniformed agents and a Bukavu resident, the expedition began on the platform of an old pickup truck, at a temperature of 40°C in the shade. Its path took them past the only high-rise building, the cathedral, and other constructions that survived the mercenary revolt of 1967 and the massive destruction during the Second Congo War (1998–2003). The resulting photo series, *Tropical Modernism in Bukavu*, emerged from conversations with locals, who reviewed the buildings' history over the past sixty years.

Official permission letter to take pictures of public buildings

Bukavu City Hall

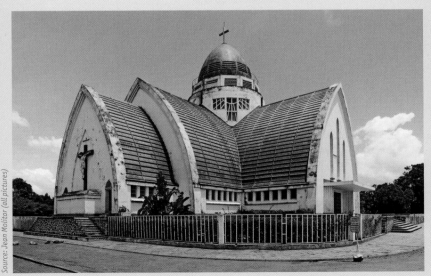

Source: Jean Molitor (all pictures)

Bukavu Cathedral was built from 1948 to 1951 by the architect Georges Nef. The conical cupola slightly resembles an African hut, giving the colonial building a local touch.

Modernist house in Bukavu (formerly Costermansville) that was built in 1945 and belonged to Maître Sharff Devitz, who also used his home for his law practice

Bukavu is a port on Lake Kivu, and a base for tourists going to Goma or Virunga National Park; the Hôtel La Riviera – currently abandoned – stands on the shoreline

Modern lines: La Maison Bleue (Blue House) stands across from the La Frégate Hotel on the Avenue Lumumba, and used to house a business owned by Monsieur Manbo

Source: Jean Molitor (all pictures)

Petrol station and apartments, situated at 84 Avenue de Tabora; the upper floor was once home to the Geerinckx family

Designed by the architect Pierre Van Der Oudera and built at the beginning of the 1950s, Bukavu Courthouse is situated on Place Royale, facing La Flamme Monument

Bukavu was once an administrative centre for the Kivu Region; its new post office was built around 1955 on Bukavu's former Stalingrad Plateau

The influence of Tropical Modernism is clear in Bukavu's streets,
including in this petrol station and the neighbouring houses

Garage on the Avenue Royale and Avenue de Tabora, Bukavu, South Kivu Province

Source: Jean Molitor (all pictures)

Bank building: one of the many modern structures that have survived conflict in eastern DRC

Source: Marc Gemoets

ONATRA Building

CD 11

Boulevard du 30 Juin,
Gombe, Kinshasa
A. Van Ackere
1955

Today, anyone driving along the main artery of Kinshasa's city centre, the Boulevard du 30 Juin, can only be struck by the imposing structure of the Office National du Transport's (ONATRA) main headquarters. It was erected from 1952 to 1955, and the main objective of the commission was to centralise the different services dealing with harbour and railway infrastructures in one building, in order to increase their efficiency. Monumental in scale, strictly symmetrical in composition, and somewhat reminiscent of post-war Eastern European public architecture, the building nevertheless displays some modern features – both in the architectonic solutions that make it climate responsive (the conception of the roof for instance), and in some of its interior design. The quality and detailing of the construction demonstrates the skill available in Kinshasa at the time, while the choice to clad the façades in simili stone, using local materials, speaks of a common practice in Kinshasa at the time.

cc

Source: Christian Stach

Sendwe Hospital ↵   CD 12

Avenue Likasi/Avenue Sendwe,
Lubumbashi, Haut-Katanga Province
Noel A. Van Malleghem
1955

This hospital complex constitutes one of the most intriguing pieces of architecture designed during the colonial era. Though still impressive today, the existing building in fact only forms a small part of the original project presented by the architect in response to the colonial authorities' request for a new healthcare infrastructure targeting Lubumbashi's rapidly growing African population. The ambitious design included several more multistorey wings, running parallel in a symmetrical composition. The hospital's design testifies of a typological shift, during which the former model of an *hôpital* *pavillonnaire* that was widely used during the interwar years was being replaced by that of an *hôpital en bloc*, as the latter was supposed to be more cost-effective and efficient in use. While the overall composition of the original project still reveals an adherence to Beaux-Arts design principles, the formal appearance of the façades testifies to the architect's effort to incorporate Tropical Modernism.   *cc*

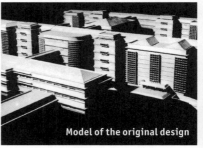

Model of the original design

Source: Noël Van Malleghem

CD 12 Sendwe Hospital

Source: Johan Lagae

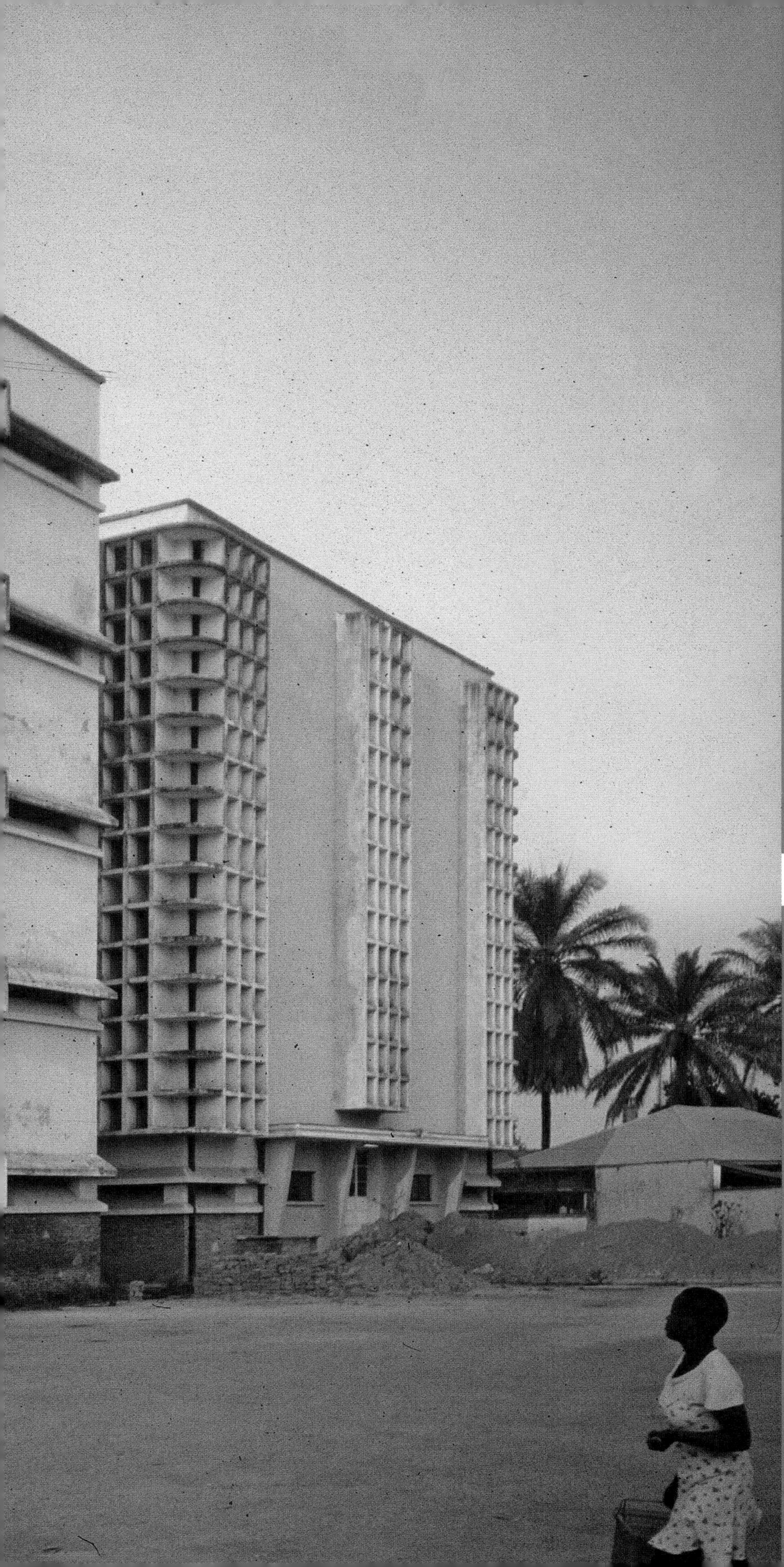

Boeskay Flats CD 13
Avenue Kashobwe, Lubumbashi,
Haut-Katanga Province
Julian Elliott, Philippe Charbonnier
1957

This collective housing project, built from 1956 to 1957, consists of eight individual units organised around a square-shaped inner courtyard. In his 1960s surveys of modern architecture in Africa, Udo Kultermann presented this project as exemplary for the way it responded to 'new tasks' and at the same time achieved 'a creative relationship to the African tradition'. Julian Elliott has often suggested that its spatial organisation was based on patterns found in the Great Zimbabwe ruins and the 'beehive villages in Ghana', but he also acknowledged that the design was informed by ideas encountered on a European trip, during which he worked in a British architectural office. As such, he was well acquainted with the ongoing debate in circles of modernist architects and the new ideas of Team X in particular. But the Boeskay Flats also bear echoes of the late work of Le Corbusier, in particular his Maisons Jaoul in Paris. *cc*

Source: Johan Lagae (all pictures)

Source: Sander Aelvoet

Lengema/SNEL Building ⌃ | CD 14
Avenue Lumumba, Kisangani,
Tshopo Province
Claude Laurens
1960

Claude Laurens is best known for the projects he designed in Kinshasa during the 1950s, such as the two high-rise residential towers built between 1952 and 1954 to accommodate the agents of Sabena, the Belgian national airline. Widely published in both colonial magazines and professional journals, his modernist buildings were immediately picked up by Udo Kultermann, who in his 1963 survey *Neues Bauen in Afrika* stated that the image of modern Kinshasa had been shaped first and foremost by this French-Belgian architect. Laurens also produced designs for other cities in the DRC. For instance, this building, currently known as the Immeuble Lengema. Originally commissioned by the Compagnie Immobilière de l'Équateur, the project, which was only partially realised, combines shops, offices, and flats. Presenting clear references to Le Corbusier's architecture and incorporating features of Tropical Modernism, the design has a progressive character which also resides in the split-level organisation of the flats.   *cc*

Cultural Complex | CD 15
Place Georges Arthur Forrest,
Lubumbashi, Haut-Katanga Province
Yenga/Claude Strebelle
1963

The architectural office Yenga – whose name means 'to build' in Swahili – produced an impressive oeuvre in Katanga, with projects ranging from commercial buildings, individual houses, schools, a variety of commercial edifices, and some religious buildings. At times, their approach to design reveals an attempt to steer away from the orthodoxy of a climate responsive Tropical Modernism, in order to root a specific project more deeply in the local context. Such is the case in this cultural complex, which encompasses a theatre, a museum, and a music school. The complex was built over a decade. Its theatre, built from 1953 to 1956, had an innovative concept as its stage was conceived with a double orientation, opening on one side to a room with a capacity of 658 seats, and, on the other side, to an open air patio behind the building with space for 2,000 spectators.   *cc*

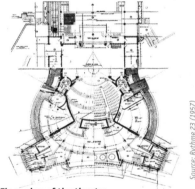

Source: Rythme 23 (1957)

Floor plan of the theatre

Source: Johan Lagae

Source: Marc Gemoets

Monument to National Heroes [CD 16]
Place de l'Échangeur, Kinshasa
Olivier-Clément Cacoub
1974

The French-Tunesian architect Olivier-Clément Cacoub is best known for his projects in Côte d'Ivoire and the work he did in the city of Monastir in Tunisia. Being well connected in political circles of the Francophonie, he also received important commissions in the context of President Mobutu's nation-building project, initiated in 1966, for which he produced a Presidential Palace on Ngaliema Hill and a large scale commercial centre – both in Kinshasa – as well as luxurious hotels in Inongo and Goma. Yet, his most remarkable commission in the DRC is the 210 m high tower he built on a major crossroads in the capital. The project was intended as a monument to the country's national heroes, with a belvedere on top and a museum devoted to the

independence struggle on the lower levels. The sculptural form of the tower, with some parts almost evoking an Art Nouveau aesthetic, was realised by making use of the most advanced concrete technology available. The project, which was started in 1970, was never finished and the museum never opened. In 2012, the exhibition spaces were refurbished and used for the first time to accommodate artistic events and concerts.   *cc*

Court of First Instance ❧ [CD 17]
Place de la Justice, Kinshasa
Eugène Palumbo, Fernand Tala N'gai
1971

This court is one of the many projects designed by the Italian architect Eugène Palumbo in association with the Congolese architect Fernand Tala N'gai. Before associating with Fernand Tala N'gai, who studied in Brussels, Palumbo had previously worked as a UNESCO expert in Congo, a position that gave him access to the country's political elite. The office, which remained active in the DRC until 2000, holds in its portfolio a large number of prestigious public edifices, such as the extension of the National Bank, as well as also luxury villas for officials, large scale commercial complexes, and so on. The Court of First Instance, constructed from 1969 to 1971, is exemplary of the free form architecture of the two architects, which, at times, seems inspired by Oscar Niemeyer's work in Brazil. The decorative programme, however, refers to Mobutu's policy of a *recours à l'authenticité*. Produced by Congolese artists from the Academy of Fine Arts, the mural mosaics evoke the traditional practices of law and justice on which the president claimed to build his rule.   *cc*

Source: Eugène Palumbo

Source: Courtesy Johan Lagae

Gécamines Tower

CD 18

Boulevard du 30 Juin, Kinshasa
Claude Strebelle, André Jacqmain
1977

This landmark tower speaks of President Mobutu's ambition to turn the capital of independent Congo into an international trade centre. Its construction began in 1969 along the main axis of Kinshasa's centre, which Mobutu wanted to turn into Congo's Wall Street. The commission given to the architects asked for a project that would be a 'symbol of New York-style modernity'. Claude Strebelle, who had been active in Lubumbashi in the 1950s, developed the design with the aim of creating an 'African skyscraper', together with André Jacqmain, a young architect from Brussels. With its sculptural mass, rounded forms, and façades clad with brown tiles, the Gécamines Tower breaks away from the slick design of International Style architecture. The roof's copper finishing refers to Congo's mining industry (Gécamines), of which the main offices were housed here. Luxurious apartments were located on the upper floors, providing a splendid view over the city. Constructed according to state-of-the-art building technology, the tower was provided with creative solutions to respond to the climatic constraints, and displays an exceptional level of detail and finishing.   *CC*

CD

Source: Marc Gemoets

Source: Marc Gemoets

OGEDEP Building ≪   `CD 19`

Avenue de la Justice, Kinshasa
Grégoire Magema
1980

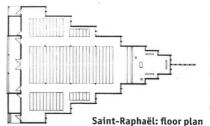

Saint-Raphaël: floor plan

Source: Archives Paul Dequeker/

During the second half of the 1970s, in order to implement his policy of 'Zaïrianisation', Mobutu proceeded with a substantial reform of the national services, related to the various aspects of the country's economy. In that context, the Office de Gestion de la Dette Publique (OGEDEP) was created in order to define a new way of financing policies at a national level. Its headquarters were situated in the heart of Kinshasa's administrative centre, adjacent to the Court of First Instance. Grégoire Magema, who received the commission, belonged to the first generation of Congolese architects active in the DRC. Accessed via a wide flight of stairs, the building is spatially organised around a circular entry hall, from which radiate a number of volumes housing different functions. With its overall sculptural composition, its strong tectonic expression, and its load-bearing concrete elements explicitly articulating the building's outer appearance, the OGEDEP Building is still highly favoured by the current generation of Congolese architects as an example of genuine Congolese architecture.   *CC*

Source: Hugues Sirault

Saint-Raphaël Church CD 20

Avenue Lumumba/Avenue de
l'Université, Camp Bakwanga, Kinshasa
Paul Dequeker
1986

Source: Johan Lagae

In 1958 the architect Paul Dequeker was sent to Congo by the Scheut missionary congregation. As head of the Bureau d'Architecture de l'Episcopat du Congo, which he would lead for over thirty years, he produced an impressive number of projects all over Congo: churches, educational edifices, seminaries, healthcare centres, and so on. Designing according to his training in Tropical Architecture at the Architectural Association School in London in 1957, Paul Dequeker put a strong focus on the climate responsiveness of his buildings, as well as on constructional solutions that were easy to realise with local manual labour. Yet some of his projects transcend the pragmatism that characterises a large part of his oeuvre. For the Saint-Raphaël Church, for example, he drew on the constraints of the triangular site to give the building a stepped pyramidal geometry, which not only serves functional needs but also turns the church into a striking landmark at a main crossroads in Kinshasa. *cc*

Dreaming of Housing, Creating Density

Nicolas-Patience Basabose, on the challenge of home ownership
in Kinshasa and the improvised density

It is difficult, and almost impossible, to spend a day in Kinshasa, the capital city of the Democratic Republic of the Congo (DRC), without being overwhelmed by the imagination of its inhabitants. The city is known for its miraculous and continuous survivalism, the unplanned, temporary arrangements that last many a lifetime. In 2020, Kinshasa should be, with Cairo and Lagos, the most populated metropolis in Africa with 14 million souls, stretching over 9,965 km², with around 600 km² of urban coverage. Today's estimation is 10 million inhabitants, with an urban density of 17,000 occupants per square kilometre.

High growth rates and rapid urban migration influences made Kinshasa the land of opportunities for Congolese from every corner of the country, and the city represents the challenges that face the majority of African cities today. On 30 June 1960, the country obtained its independence from Belgium, and during the decades since, the authorities have been overwhelmingly challenged. Continual sociopolitical instability never gave any government the time to fully articulate solutions to the increasing problems, to the point of virtually declaring defeat in the face of fateful incompetence. Life goes on: with

Source: Nicolas-Patience Basabose

95 per cent of the Kinois* left to fend for themselves, the people at their lowest have to draw inspiration from their ancestral ingenuity. They create services the state fails to provide, in order to sustain a minimum level of survival, in stunted slums shaded by palm and mango trees.

The biggest challenge is housing; and the prevalent rationale tends to favour urban progress. Looking for social status through the ownership of land, citizens go searching for plots in the peripheral areas. Developed on individual initiatives, *Nouvelles Cités* grew aggressively, resulting in the exponential explosion of Kinshasa between 1970 and today. In 2014 it was estimated that 75 per cent of households were living in these areas (Zone C on the following page). They are unplanned, chaotic, and chronically lacking basic infrastructure. Urban planners organise spaces and services; architects design and build houses; but in this chaotic sub-urbanity, the bulk of the built environment is constructed by the people themselves, unqualified but in need. The non-delivery of suitable housing and services challenges human development, predominantly among low-income urban households in non-industrialised nations. Time and again this deficit manifests in the spread of slums – Kinshasa is no exception. Affordable housing continues to be problematic as low-income households spend significant portions of their insufficient financial resources on securing a roof, leaving nothing for healthcare, education, or savings. Housing is fictitious to the population, just as governmental services are hypothetical.

Without a master plan to guide expansion and maintenance citizens wished to return to the city centre. The plots being sold were too expensive for ordinary

Kinois, popular term in French for Kinshasans, inhabitants of the province city of Kinshasa

Source: Nicolas-Patience Basabose (all pictures)

Multistorey residential building in Kinshasa; some have businesses on the ground floor

Kinois. With inherited ingenuity, the population bets on increasing density in already serviced areas. Spasmodic progress has characterised the way the city has occupied space. The city has always developed horizontally, apart from a few blocks in the centre, which are off limits for ordinary Kinois and mostly occupied by businesses and international NGOs with their expatriate manpower. The DRC is home to the largest UN peacekeeping force in the world; it is flooded with foreign troops, aid workers, and diplomats, many with substantial per diems. Combined with meagre infrastructures and a lack of production aptitude, this results in prices that match or outstrip those in most developed nations – the same ingredients that made Luanda, the capital city of neighbouring Angola, the most expensive city in the world. As the city is ill-prepared to claim its spot as one of the world's fastest-growing urban settlements, and has an ever increasing disparity between rich and poor that is influenced by traditional spatial expansion, housing takes the form of unplanned sprawls, with the infrastructure hardly maintained and services virtually non-existent. All of this implies that the city will need to make huge strides to bolster the weight of its expanding population.

As if by miracle, a new trend is materialising: Kinshasa is learning to expand vertically. We are now in the middle of a construction boom – unregulated for the most part, but directly responding to the urgent needs and pressing demands of the population. Plots in the city centre and surrounding planed areas are in high demand for vertical structures. The Kinois have autodidactically learnt the principles of population density when the provincial and national governments lamentably failed to promote it. Density is a subtle catalyst for local development, a tool to create a more sustainable city, while helping to stop the outrageous horizontal expansion Kinshasa has experienced in recent decades, and protecting the few remaining open public spaces from spoliation. Without government intervention, Kinois are finding temporary solutions to paving their own way back to the city that expelled them for lack of revenue. However, Kinshasa still needs the government to help it plan its more sustainable future. Housing remains the biggest test; supply is coming in small drops, while the purchasing power of the population cannot match the needs. Nevertheless, traditional ingenuity has preserved the spirit of the Kinois from its origins in a cluster of fishing villages to within this postcolonial metropolis in the making. Proven as a solution for many resilient cities across the planet, density strategically increases the number of families per square metre. Again, Kinshasa, even in its chaotic state, is no exception. This sudden intensification of density has made the housing market a little competitive and affordable, and offered many more prospects for previously excluded groups to flock back towards the centre, making Kinshasa a decent place to live again.

Map of Gombe (Zone A), Kinshasa City Centre

Map of Kasavubu Neighbourhood (in Zone B)

CD

Map of Masina Neighbourhood (in Zone C)

The population is divided into three zones in Kinshasa. Zone A is the city centre (Gombe),
which was exclusive to Europeans during colonial rule. It was well planned and executed
on the segregated urban planning principles. Today it is home to the wealthiest people.
Zone B represents the planned areas around the city centre – *Nouvelles Cités* – which were
formerly the 'indigenous quarters' and are reflective of traditional gridirons. Zone C represents the actual *Nouvelles Cités*: areas developed chaotically with no consideration for
urban planning guidelines.

Source: Constant Luzitu

Samba Kaputo Mausoleum ⌄ CD 21
Cimetière de la Gombe, Kinshasa
Archplan International
2008

Gombe Cemetery is a physical reminder of the policy of racial segregation that underlies colonial urban planning. Today, a large part of the cemetery is no longer maintained. However, a space has been prepared to install the tombs of prominent figures in Congolese society in future. In 2008, Archplan International designed the Mausoleum of Professor Samba Kaputo, who held a position in the field of political sciences at the University of Kinshasa and was a prominent politician. A sculptural concrete canopy provides shelter for the tomb; its design explicitly draws on the symbols of the feather and the hand to evoke the act of writing – features representative of the important role that Professor Kaputo played in the DRC's recent history.   *cc*

Source: Archplan International

Collective Housing CD 22
Avenue Kokolo, Kitambo, Kinshasa
Constant Luzitu
2009

Constant Luzitu is considered to be one of the leading architects in the DRC. His sculptural architectural work speaks of an ambition to develop a Congolese architecture, similar to that of the first generation of Congolese architects of the 1970s. Among his most well-known projects are a series of villas for the Congolese elite, La Conforta Festivities Hall, and La Française Office Tower in the city centre of Kinshasa. This collective housing scheme situated in the upper class neighbourhood of Binza was started in 2008 and it is a good example of the emergence of gated communities in the DRC. It consists of ten individual villa units that are grouped in pairs. Each villa has a habitable surface of 380 m^2 and a swimming pool of its own. The enclave also contains a number of collective facilities such as a sports room, a tennis court, and a festivities hall. Displaying a preference for a playful architectural form that complies with the desires of the target clientele, this project also demonstrates an outspoken effort to give the ensemble a formal unity via repetitive shapes and an almost continuous roof scape.   *cc*

Source: Arsène Ijambo Kambaza

Airtel Building ⌃ CD 23

Avenue du Cercle Sportif, Goma,
North Kivu Province
Arsène Ijambo Kambaza
2011

The city of Goma has witnessed turbulent times over the last two decades. Large parts of the city's built environment were wiped out by the eruption of the Nyiragongo Volcano in 2002, and its development fell victim, for a long time, to the extremely unstable political situation in the eastern part of the DRC, and the multiple border conflicts. However, investment returned for few years and Goma witnessed a building boom, largely financed through private investments. The Airtel Building, commissioned by one of the main mobile phone operators in the DRC and constructed over three years, is an early example of this revival. The design takes into account the site, situated at the crossroads of two important avenues in Goma.   *cc*

Immotex Site CD 24

Boulevard du 30 Juin,
Gombe, Kinshasa
JLP Concept
2016

Since 2006, Kinshasa has witnessed a growing demand for accommodation for the large expatriate community who are active in the DRC, as well as for the increasing Congolese middle and upper classes. While some gated-community-like environments were created at the periphery of the city, the Immotex Site has the advantage of its central location, just off one of the main axes of Kinshasa city centre. In a city struggling with major traffic congestion, such proximity is an important asset. JLP Concept, a practice founded by René Paquet, a Belgian architect with a long career in the DRC, was hired to transform the site, which was originally founded in the mid-1920s to house textile production, but had become redundant after the Chinese took over and relocated the industry within the DRC. Offering individual villas as well as spacious apartments in two-storey blocks, the project has been successful, due to the high construction standards, the elegance of its architecture, and the attention paid to the landscaping of the site, which is intended to form a green oasis at the heart of the city.   *cc*

CD

Source: Johan Lagae

Source: MASS Design Group (all pictures)

Ilima Primary School   CD 25

Ilima, Équateur Province
MASS Design Group
2015

In the Democratic Republic of the Congo (DRC), there is generally a sharp divide between the quality of schooling available to children, depending on whether they live in urban or rural areas. The Ilima Primary School, designed by MASS Design Group and the African Wildlife

Foundation, aims to provide education in the jungle of the Congo Basin. The facility has become a beacon school, attracting regional attention and helping retain the area's teachers to offer students opportunities beyond subsistence farming. The 800 m² school includes a library, teachers' spaces, and six classrooms for 350 students, from grades one to six. The site also serves as a community centre for interaction with local wildlife. Located six hours by motorcycle

from the nearest airstrip, the school was built entirely with materials and labour sourced on site, embodying the architects' 'locally fabricated' ethos. Timber trusses, roof framing, furniture, and architectural details were sawn, planed, and crafted by hand from local trees selected by conservationists. The local artisans and the architects experimented with modified earth mixes and regional trees to form the building's walls and roof shingles. Taking their cues from regional design practices, the school's steep roof, gutter system, and open clerestory respond to heavy rainfall and encourage natural ventilation and daylight. The architects used this project to further long-term local economic development, training local builders and two young Congolese architects in sustainable building techniques. They aim to set a precedent for what educational architecture can aspire to in resource-limited settings. *pa*

The state of disrepair of this bridge is not uncommon in the DRC. This limits access to rural areas to bicycles, motorbikes, walking, or (exceptionally rare and expensive) bush planes.
Source: Andrew Brose

Education Infrastructure in the DRC

Andrew Brose

Everyone deserves good design, no matter their location or economic and social status. This statement takes on special meaning in the education sector, where good design has the potential to greatly impact educational outcomes. In the Democratic Republic of the Congo (DRC), the universal right to good education is denied to millions. In the over fifty years since the country's independence, the Congolese have suffered at the hands of kleptocratic rule and the Second Congo War (the most deadly conflict since World War II), which have shattered infrastructure and crippled efforts at sustainable development. Low enrolment in schools, high dropout rates and gender inequality all contribute to low graduation rates for children living in poor parts of the country. Given the current relative peace in the region and a recovering GDP, the DRC has the opportunity to develop a more universal and sustainable education infrastructure than ever before.

In the DRC, there are between 15 and 30 per cent fewer children attending school in rural areas than in urban areas.

As the majority of the country's population – 57.5 per cent – is rural, this lag is particularly troubling. It is clear that the emphasis should first and foremost be on developing new school infrastructure and programming in rural areas. Historically, the isolation and resultant high cost of construction in much of the country has hindered this work. Building materials are often flown or carried in, due to terrible or non-existent transportation infrastructure, increasing cost, and limiting what materials can be used. Until transportation to these isolated communities becomes easier and cheaper, autonomous construction is the only financially or logistically feasible approach for architectural projects.

Gender inequality in education is a widespread problem, particularly in rural areas with lower household income. Literacy rates – at 78.1 per cent for men and only 50 per cent for women – tell a grave story; low school enrollment of girls is especially pronounced amongst low-income households and in rural areas, leaving girls living far from cities at

Source: Andrew Brose

A young man showing the raw earth brick mould (for making two at a time) used for the bricks behind him – the same type used for the building that stands in the background

the greatest disadvantage. Low income households give educational preference to the boys in the family, keeping girls at home to help families during times of financial insecurity or great need. An increase in household income will help balance enrollment rates, though this does not address the discrimination that lies at the root of the problem.

High primary school dropout rates, caused by both poor school implementation and by household financial insecurity, are another serious issue. The primary school dropout rate is between 3 and 8 per cent, with most students dropping out at the beginning or end of primary school. Many students repeat their first year of primary school, likely because they are not old enough to move on or because their first year of school proved harder than anticipated.

Design gives us the opportunity to improve education by creating atmospheres conducive to learning. School design should bring dignity and comfort to the learning process. Instead, current facilities (particularly in rural areas) often suffer from inadequate ventilation, overheating, or general disrepair if materials are inaccessible for maintenance. Yet good design can only do so much to combat dropout rates. Considerable evidence suggests these numbers are heavily dependent on families' economic well-being. Families with lower incomes have a higher need to send their children to work, rather than pursuing education's more distant promise of a higher quality of life. To effect real, systemic change, projects aimed at the education sector should strive to increase the economic well-being and independence of prospective students' families. The building process itself is an underutilised opportunity to train and develop local builders' skills, to generate economic opportunity and independence.

Developing educational infrastructure in the DRC requires a holistic approach. New projects should target rural areas, and must increase the quality of the school programming and facilities as well as contribute to the economic independence of the families that they serve. Utilising a 'local fabrication' approach – that prizes local labour, materials, and building processes – is a first step in combatting many systemic problems that face the country's crippled education infrastructure. In developing countries, one of the most under-leveraged opportunities to achieve impact through buildings lies in redesigning the construction process to increase the value of hiring of local labour through improved social engagement and training.

Rural road leading to Ilima Primary School, which was built by MASS Design Group in 2015. The site is situated six hours by motorcycle from the nearest airstrip and infrastructure is poor, meaning local materials, labour, and training were important.
Source: Andrew Brose

Such an approach can make these remote projects financially attainable as well as environmentally sustainable. With added skills, these trained craftspeople can continue to maintain their communities' schools and are able to better position themselves in the labour markets – with respect to the environment, but also and principally due to the community's ability to keep the school in working condition, thanks to newly gained construction skills. The employment and training inherent to this approach bring new economic opportunity and independence to households, lowering dropout rates among children and among girls in particular. Moreover, gender equity in hiring practices might more systematically disprove commonly held gender roles. Today, universal education developed through good design is an oft-repeated target; a local fabrication approach to infrastructure development in the DRC may begin to push the needle in that direction.

Source: Andrew Brose

Typical example: the state of Ilima Primary School before the construction of the new school is indicative of the educational infrastructures in most of the DRC.

Vernacular Strategies to Combat Urban Sprawl

Nicolas-Patience Basabose on how the expansion of the megacity
of Kinshasa might be contained

Kinshasa is the third largest city in Africa and home to an estimated 10 million people. The typologies of its buildings and the style of spatial occupation have helped the city contain millions in a rather moderate spatial configuration – all thanks to an inherited, yet passive vernacular architecture and ancestral settlement planning.

The primary city centre is still the main economic core of Kinshasa. While there are murmurs of a second urban hub to polycentrify Kinshasa, there needs to be an upgrade of its infrastructure to facilitate such a transition. Kinshasa's annual population growth rate of 9.2 per cent exposed the inability of various governments to match the capital's infrastructure to the population and to adapt to rising demand. Housing in the most populous parts of the city – the *Nouvelles*
Cités – is characterised by tin-roofed concrete-block structures in fenced villages with unpaved paths that are often inaccessible to vehicles.

In both the city and the countryside, a deep sense of community underpins peoples' lifestyles. This cultural element is expressed in many ways by the rural population who relocate to big cities across the country. Life in Kinshasa's *Nouvelles Cités* is reminiscent of fenced hamlets, or *villagettes*, grouped along precarious mud and gravel streets. Plots are seldom occupied by one single family. One way in which the vernacular architecture of Congolese villages is adapted to cities is in the internally shared, semi-private spaces where laundry, cooking, and other mundane activities are carried out under the watchful eyes of one's neighbours. This approach to community life in

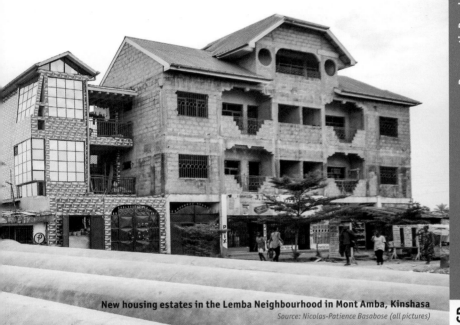

New housing estates in the Lemba Neighbourhood in Mont Amba, Kinshasa
Source: Nicolas-Patience Basabose (all pictures)

the city has saved Kinshasa from reaching extreme levels of spatial expansion. Horizontal extension being the common method, the grouping of households within parcels of land has, so far, maintained the city at a compact and manageable size. For the DRC to better absorb demographic growth, the secondary cities will have to play a key role in limiting the pressure on the capital. What is urgently needed is a strategic and comprehensive plan for the city that integrates the planning of mixed-use neighbourhoods and communities with a multimodal transport system that is adapted to local needs.

Although a significant number of trips are made on foot in developing cities, pedestrian infrastructure, amenities, and services are often neglected in municipal planning and budgets. The last workable

planning document for Kinshasa – a city of pedestrians with an immeasurable walkability index – dates from 1973. In 2013, though, the French planning firm Groupe Huit developed a plan for the provincial government, the *Schéma d'Orientation Stratégique de l'Agglomération Kinoise* (SOSAK), which covered a fifteen-year planning horizon up to 2030. In 2014,

Barumbu in the Lukunga District of Kinshasa

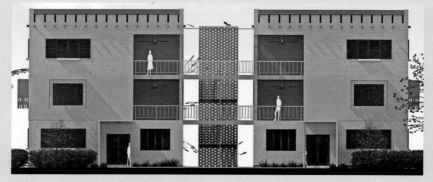

Northern elevation of Résidence Tombalbaye. Centred around a core of shared balconies, this housing complex is based on Congolese vernacular architecture.

a second planning firm, Surbana International Consultants, from Singapore, was appointed master planner for the city. The master plan aims to address the complex urban conditions of Kinshasa, owing to its size, population, and environmental sustainability concerns, as well as other socioeconomic aspects such as housing and employment.

The provincial government's sudden paradoxical quest for order shows that, regardless of which plan is implemented, Kinshasans are forging ahead to find solutions to improve their unbearable living conditions. Voluntary associations working to help the underprivileged in Kinshasa are also important for mutual aid, the pleasure of togetherness, and essential sociocultural links and exchanges. The inexorable logic of three or four families sharing the same plot is driven by both a sense of community and social economics. House owners with enough space invest in erecting one- or two-room houses for rental, creating density. This practice of urbanisation occurred in the absence of a strategic orientation framework.

The understanding of this paradigm in housing initiated a new movement from practitioners and investors in the property markets. Innovative forms are taking shape. A new architectural approach is apparent where the vernacular vocabulary informs contemporary needs, offering solutions we already had but did not know we had. With modern materials as facilitators, single and multifamily housing stocks are increasing, thereby showcasing urban growth. Informal housing built without any standards is slowly being replaced by well-planned and suitably executed living areas in the *Nouvelles Cités* closest to the city centre. The current social composition generates new prospects for young architects, and the dearth of opportunities for local architectural talent in major governmental projects drives many architects to find alternative sources of activity. Through direct references to vernacular architecture, newly developed housing stocks aim to solve a crisis that is beyond control. At the same time such references beautifully expose the fundamental association between cognitive practicality and

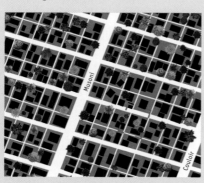

Surveyed plots in Bumbu, Kinshasa

Compound in Bumbu Municipality

North-south section of of Résidence Tombalbaye. A contemporary take on rural architecture in the DRC, the project extends three storeys upwards and uses locally sourced materials.

the prevention of squalor. New multilevel hamlets offer opportunities for growth in a city where living beyond the city centre's perimeter is very undesirable. Verticality is the new direction.

With this typology, Kinshasa finds a transitory solution for short-term sustainable urban growth, one which carries a decisive desirability and can achieve optimum land use – certainly in the short term, anyway. Plots and houses around the city centre are selling very well, with higher structures rising in new programmatic configurations.

The commercial side of Kinshasa streets, revealed by neo-vernacularism in architectural vocabulary, combines spaces for commerce, housing, and sometimes offices. When ideas, styles, and trends intertwine in our society, guided by current needs and aspirations, they formulate innovative concepts and forge new dynamics. We can hope that the master plans for Kinshasa will help provide clarity on the direction this future megacity will take, and allow it to assert its claim for a place among great cities.

Source: Nicolas-Patience Basabose (all pictures)

New high-density building in Gombe, Kinshasa, formerly a site of a single-family villa

CD

Angola

Filomena do Espírito Santo Carvalho, Angolan architect, born in Luanda. Graduated in 1985 from Agostinho Neto University, where she is now assistant professor. PhD student at Instituto Superior Técnico, Lisbon. She is coordinator of the Popular Architecture of Angola research project.

Maria Alice Mendes Correia, Angolan architect, born 1966 in Cacuso, Malanje Province. Graduated from Agostinho Neto University, Luanda. Holds a master's from the University of São Paulo, Brazil. Since 2009 she has worked at the Institute of Urban Planning and Management in Luanda.

Sylvia Croese, Dutch-Angolan urban and political sociologist, born 1984 in Kigali, Rwanda. Written and conducted extensive research in and on Angola as a researcher and consultant. Currently based at the University of Cape Town, South Africa, as a postdoctoral research fellow.

Joost De Raeymaeker, Belgian-born journalist, writer, photographer, and communication consultant, born 1968 in Leuven. Studied music at the Jazz Studio, Antwerp, and history at the UFSIA, Antwerp; the FLUP, Porto; and the University of Ghent. He has worked on projects in Angola, where he now lives.

Zara Ferreira, Portuguese architect, born 1988 in Lisbon. Graduated with a master's in architecture from the Instituto Superior Técnico, Lisbon in 2012. Researcher for the Exchanging Worlds Visions project. She is general secretary of the Docomomo International and co-editor of its journal.

Coral Gillett, born 1985 in Brisbane, Australia. Completed Bachelor of Built Environment at Queensland University of Technology in 2006, and Master of Design Futures at Griffith University in 2011. Co-founded Atelier Mulemba in 2012 in Luanda, where she currently lives and practises. *(cg)*

Ana Magalhães, Portuguese architect, born 1965 in Lisbon. Graduated in 1988 from the Technical University of Lisbon, and holds a master's and PhD from Lusíada University, Lisbon, where she has taught since 1990. Co-author of *Moderno Tropical*, which received a DAM Architectural Book Award. *(am)*

Paulo Moreira, Portuguese architect, born 1980 in Porto. Graduated from the Universidade do Porto in 2005. PhD student at the Cass School of Architecture, London Metropolitan University. Coordinator of the Chicala Observatory, a research project based at the Agostinho Neto University, Luanda.

Helder Pereira, born 1978 in Luanda, Angola. Graduated from Queensland University of Technology in 2007, and the Masters of Design Futures programme at Griffith University in 2010. Co-founded Atelier Mulemba in 2012 in Luanda, where he currently lives and practises. *(hp)*

Margarida Quintã, Portuguese architect, born 1961 in Porto. Graduated in 2007 from the University of Porto. PhD candidate at the EPF Lausanne. Holds a scholarship from the Foundation of Science and Technology, Portugal, to research Modern heritage re-use and designing with climate in Angola. *(mq)*

Nadine Siegert, German researcher of modern and contemporary African arts, born 1976 in Wiesbaden. Holds a PhD from the Bayreuth International Graduate School of African Studies. Curated exhibitions in Europe, Africa, and Latin America. Deputy director of Iwalewahaus at the University of Bayreuth.

Caren Melissa Santos da Silva, Brazilian architect, born 1979 in Curitiba. Graduated from Pontifícia Universidade Católica do Paraná in 2002. MBA from São Paulo University. Performed lectures on colonial architecture in Luanda in 2013. Currently works as a design manager in Luanda.

António Tomás, holds a PhD in anthropology from Columbia University, New York. Author of a study on the African nationalist Amílcar Cabral. He was Ray Pahl Fellow at the African Centre for Cities, at the University of Cape Town. Currently teaches at Stellenbosch University, South Africa.

Ana Tostões, architect and architecture historian, born 1959. President of Docomomo International and editor of its journal. Full professor at the Instituto Superior Técnico, Lisbon. Coordinator of the Exchanging Worlds Visions project on sub-Saharan African architecture during the Modern Movement. *(at)*

Fabio Vanin, Italian architect-urbanist, born 1977 in Treviso. Holds a PhD from IUAV University of Venice. Co-founder of the Brussels-based practice Latitude Platform. Completed research and design projects in Europe, Africa, and Latin America. Assistant professor at the Vrije Universiteit Brussel.

AO

The selection of colonial buildings was coordinated by Ana Tostões and Daniela Arnaut with the team of the project Exchanging Worlds Visions: Modern Architecture in Africa 'Lusófona' (1943–1974): Ana Tostões (scientific coordination), Vicenzo Riso, João Vieira Caldas, Maria Manuel Oliveira, Elisiário Miranda, Ana Magalhães, Maria João Teles Grilo, Margarida Quintã, Jessica Bonito, Zara Ferreira, Francisco Seabra Ferreira, Catarina Delgado, Ana Maria Braga, Paulo Silva, and Sandra Vaz Costa. The post-colonial selection was coordinated by Atelier Mulemba (Coral Gillett and Helder Pereira).

Luanda – a permanent construction site
Kostadin Luchansky

Bem-vindo a Angola

Helder Pereira, Coral Gillett

A visitor to Angola with an interest in architecture is likely to come away perplexed. In the capital, Luanda, the contrast of crumbling infrastructure and gleaming skyscrapers, of poverty and wealth startles travellers. The city centre has multiple personalities – slavery-era colonial *sobrado* houses with their rendered stone walls are overshadowed by modernist buildings with brise-soleil façades, their vision for a brave new world now somewhat dampened by verandas enclosed with concrete blocks and armies of satellite dishes standing to attention on every available surface. In amongst all this are both stalled construction sites and gleaming skyscrapers that land heavily on the edge of the footpath, scattering street vendors and trees in their quest to maximise floor areas.

As we leave the downtown, newer constructions of varying degrees of informality dominate – tantalising glimpses of palm trees along the coast are visible beyond the sprawl of neighbourhoods that pump their inhabitants out onto arterial roads that pulse with blue and white taxi vans. In Talatona, the clusters of gated communities and business compounds offer fleeting glances of the fantasy worlds within their walls as one drives past on the roads absent of pedestrians. On the way into Viana, street vendors and piles of rubbish line the edges of roads and the railway line, pedestrians thronging among light industrial buildings and commerce. On the highway, the large structures visible at a distance morph into the massive apartment buildings of Kilamba on approach, identical except for their different pastel shades of paint. As we continue further, more rudimentary structures made of concrete block and tin rooves appear – after a while the concrete gives way to *pau-a-pique* and adobe, and later the tin is replaced with thatch. The horizon opens up and large *imbondeiros* (baobabs) are now the dominant presence in the landscape. The open road stretches out ahead and the rest of Angola, very different to Luanda, beckons. To explain the logic of this rather confusing contemporary dynamic to our visitor, we have to look back at our history ...

Source: Flagrantes da Vida na Lunda, Lisbon 1958, p. 153

Ethnographic protographs of the Lunda/Cokwe people published in the 1950s by the Museum of Dundo and sponsored by the colonial-era company Diamond provide glimpses into pre-colonial customs and material culture

Source: José Redinha,
Campanha Etnográfica ao
Tchiboco, Lisbon 1953, p. 156

Fieldwork sketches by the Portuguese anthropologist José Redinha (1953) showing typical building typologies found in villages in the Lunda Region

Source: Flagrantes da Vida na Lunda,
Lisbon 1958, p. 127

Ethnographic photograph (1958) showing a master sculptor in front of a *jango*, the steep-roofed open-walled communal structure that is still common in most villages

The (Hi)Story of Angola and Architecture

That which existed in the territories that make up current-day Angola prior to the arrival of the Portuguese has not been static since a pre-historic era – rather, the various societies that inhabited these lands were always dynamic. The various Bantu-origin ethic groups that the Portuguese encountered (and who are the ancestors of the majority of the Angolan population today) arrived during the Bantu migrations between 2000 BCE and 1000 CE[1] and formed various societies and later kingdoms, whose power dynamics and strategic alliances were constantly shifting. Prior to this, the original inhabitants were semi-nomadic and pastoral peoples of Khoisan origin, who had an entirely different way of inhabiting the world.[2]

The discussion of architecture and urbanism in Angola typically begins with the arrival and settlement of the Portuguese. This is an issue that constantly rears its head: the (hi)story of Angola beginning with the colonial. While there is a truth here that often goes uninterrogated ('Angola' as a concept is

a European invention – one need only look at the clean right angles on the map to understand that these arbitrary lines could not reflect societal or geographic demarcations), this silence of the pre-colonial leads to an assumption that there was nothing of great value here prior to the arrival of European powers. There are two reasons for this – there is very little documentation of the non-European built structures, but also because much of the existing literature on the history of architecture in Angola deals with the dynamics of urban expansion viewed through the framework of a colonial administration with an almost complete exclusion of any alternate viewpoints that challenge what actually constitutes 'architecture'. Certainly architecture is by its nature a Eurocentric notion, and a relatively recent one at that, but it is worth considering how we actually define architecture, and whether this idea remains relevant when applied to a non-Eurocentric place, time, or society. The perceived lack of 'architecture' in non-European cultures, places, and eras is often pointed to as evidence of a lack of civilisation (one is reminded of the legal doctrine of *terra nullius* in Australia, for example), and infers that a society without 'architecture' can only ever be a rudimentary, primal society.

The lack of documentation of African or pre-colonial material cultures and their architectures does not mean that they did not exist, simply that they were not documented for one reason or another, or not deemed 'architecture'. One illustration of this is the significant body of work of Fernando Batalha, a Portuguese architect and architectural historian who lived and worked in Angola during the twentieth century – his work is limited almost exclusively to the documentation of the colonial (European) or the 'Creole' vernacular forms of architecture that emerged in Angola. Nowhere is this more apparent than in his survey of M'banza Kongo, the capital of the Kongo Kingdom, which in the height of its power covered an area four times that of France and apparently had nothing worth considering as architecture aside from the structures built by Europeans. Yet this was a large

Source: Instituto Nacional do Património Cultural (INPC) (all pictures)

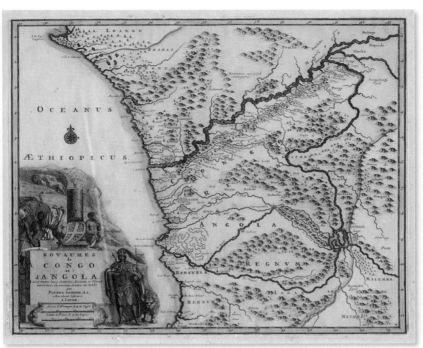

Map of the kingdoms of Angola (N'Gola) and Kongo (Pieter van der Aa, mid-18th century)

capital city of an empire that was thriving before the Portuguese even knew of its existence. More perverse than this type of blinkered vision is the seemingly deliberate suppression of evidence of pre-colonial societies – such as the archaeological remains of Feti, on the central plateau inland from Benguela. Feti was described as 'one of the largest known ancient sites anywhere in West Central Africa', and in 1893 was assumed to be 'at least as large as Lisbon'.[3] By the archaeological evidence available, it is hypothesised that Feti was occupied between the ninth and early sixteenth century, with its heyday during the fourteeth and fifteenth century, and it may have been the capital of a Royal Kingdom. The destruction of this archaeological site is attributed initially to a Portuguese fortune seeker and amateur archaeologist between 1945 and 1947, and later by the construction of a hydroelectric dam. Some photographic material in areas that encountered European expansion later than the coastal zones do provide us with glimpses into the material life of African societies. Looking beyond the stiff poses of the ethnographic 'subjects' in the foreground of these photographs,

we encounter in the background diverse and distinct typologies of buildings with different social functions in village life, steeply pitched thatch roofs with symbolic decorative embellishments, and richly decorative carved timber embellishment and furniture – all of which is still present in these same areas today, albeit with less consistent artistry, as the older generations, who would have witnessed these structures being built by their parents, pass away without fully transferring this knowledge.

The archive that we do have available to us today is a colonial archive, and while there is work being done in various fields

View of the capital of the Kongo Kingdom, M'banza Kongo, by Olfert Dapper (1686)

Source: Kostadin Luchansky

Nossa Senhora da Arrábida Church, Restinga do Lobito (Lobito Peninsula), Benguela Province

on piecing together knowledge of what existed outside this archive,[4] the fundamental problem of the nature of such an archive has been noted by Achille Mbembe: 'A Eurocentric canon is a canon that attributes truth only to the Western way of knowledge production. It is a canon that disregards other epistemic traditions. It is a canon that tries to portray colonialism as a normal form of social relations between human beings rather than a system of exploitation and oppression'.[5] We would go further to suggest that it not only 'normalises' but actually renders invisible the historic processes that have lead to the erasure of cultures and the dwindling of traditions, so that the contemporary perception that pre-colonial societies were 'lacking' (lacking 'culture', lacking a coherent 'traditional' societal structure, or more interesting to us, lacking an admirable

'traditional' architecture) is understood as being inherent to this place/people, rather than being understood as the result of the historical processes that have actively erased the practices that constitute exactly that which is now considered as 'lacking'.

Having made explicit what we consider to be the incomplete nature of the archive we do have at hand, let us review it. For simplicity, we will consider three rough phases in the (Eurocentric) architectural history of Angola: Early Colonial (from the arrival of the Portuguese through to the late nineteenth century), Late Colonial (twentieth century until independence), and Post-Independence (after 1975). Each of these eras presents different political, technological, and societal contexts, both locally and internationally, which determined what was built, where, and under which conditions.

Seventeenth century aristocratic house in Luanda (now National Anthropology Museum)

Source: David Stanley (left and right)

The *Português Suave* style Port of Luanda (1923–1945) with its new entrance (2014)

Source: Kostadin Luchansky

Catholic Mission in Cabinda, the capital of the exclave province of the same name

The Early Colonial Phase

The Portuguese navigator Diogo Cão led two expeditions to survey the West African coastline between 1482 and 1486, marking four strategic locations along the Angolan coast with the *padrão*, a large stone cross bearing the Portuguese coat of arms. One of these was located at the mouth of the Congo River and represents the first contact and beginnings of a strategic partnership between the Portuguese and the Kingdom of Kongo. Luanda exists on land that was ceded to the Portuguese by the Kongo Kingdom in exchange for military assistance against rivals.[6] While the Portuguese were the earliest European colonisers to settle in sub-Saharan Africa, their incursion was limited to the coastal areas and hinterland regions up to 200 km from the coast – for a significant part of

the early colonial period their knowledge of and influence on the interior of the territory was limited to the various kingdoms or groups who acted as the gatekeepers for trade with the territories and groups further east.[7] The Portuguese established a series of coastal centres at strategic ports along the coastline, many of which later became important cities or towns, connected via sea rather than land, and also to Europe and most importantly the Americas. The economic base of these settlements (and indeed the early colonial enterprise in Africa) was the slave trade, with these ports functioning as funnels for the extraction and sale of people who were sent to the other Portuguese territories such as São Tomé and Cabo Verde, and later to the Americas. Considerable wealth was generated in these port cities.[8] It has been argued that the colonial city is a research object

David Stanley (right)

City Hall of Benguela, the capital of the littoral province of the same name

Nossa Senhora do Populo Church (1748) in Benguela (Av. Combatentes da Grande Guerra)

Source: Kostadin Luchansky

What remains of the Totta Standard Bank in the centre of Tômbwa, Namibe Province

that allows us to understand not only the way that colonial societies were constituted (as shaped by a globalized economic logic), but also how the city reproduces or reorganises these principles in a post-colonial context.[9] This history can be 'read' in the architectural legacy that remains: large colonial *sobrado* houses still constitute the historic centre of major coastal cities, though they are under increasing threat from developers. These buildings are characterised by solid stone walls, lime rendering, timber shuttered windows, and typical Portuguese clay tiled roofs. The preservation of this architectural heritage is essential both for its architectonic value and for its social history – not only were the majority of the buildings from this era commissioned by the members of a colonial society whose wealth was generated through the slave trade, or buildings that held a function directly related to this trade, but many were built with slave labour, reminding us that slavery was not something that happened only once the enslaved arrived in the Americas.

This dynamic of a relatively independent coastal colonial centre with little incursion into the inland areas began to shift dramatically in the nineteenth century for various reasons: the independence of Brazil in 1824 (Portugal's most important colony at that time); the official end of the Portuguese transatlantic slave trade (1838, though it continued illicitly after this date) and outlawing of slavery in Portuguese territories (1869); and the European 'Scramble for Africa' (with the Berlin Conference in 1884). The loss of Brazil as a colony meant that the African territories effectively became the base of the Portuguese 'empire' – this, combined with the end of the slave

The Late Colonial Phase

The consolidation of control over the interior of the country and the impetus for development away from the coastal centres was furthered after the fall of the Portuguese monarchy and the creation of the First Republic in 1910, and then again with the *coup d'état* in 1926 and subsequent creation of the Estado Novo (New State) fascist dictatorship led by António de Oliveira Salazar, which lasted until 1974. It was during the early twentieth century that the production of coffee, cotton, wax, corn, and sisal became the base for a lucrative colonial enterprise. The notion of one Portuguese nation that encompasses the colonies as integral parts of Portugal itself was introduced, along with the push to populate the colonies with Portuguese settlers and to modernise, develop, and better control the territory through the creation of road networks, the construction of railways from coastal centres to the interior, and planned urban expansion. One notable example of such planned urban expansion is the development of the city of Nova Lisboa (today named Huambo).

After World War II, the price of coffee soared and Angola became one of the world's largest producers. This boom financed construction on a huge scale – both private (mainly in established cities) and public (a massive nation-building project undertaken to house increasing numbers of white settlers both in the cities and in important agricultural areas.) At the same time, a wave of independence movements swept across Africa and strong nationalist sentiments within the various Portuguese colonial spaces emerged. The Estado Novo regime employs the *Lusotropicalismo* narrative of a racially integrated society within a Portuguese nation that stretched from 'Minho to Timor'.[10] This nation-building project became, in part, a vehicle to justify the Portuguese retention of its colonies to the international community. It employed modernist architecture and urban planning not only because of the potential to rapidly construct the building stock required – something which new technologies such as reinforced concrete

trade, implied a massive rearrangement of the economics of the Portuguese colonial enterprise. The push to legitimise the economic and commercial interests in Angola away from the slave trade, combined with an increasingly hungry market in Europe led to extensive exploration of resource extraction and agricultural production in the fertile and resource rich hinterland. The formalisation of Angola's borders resulting from the contestation of colonial territories between European powers demanded an increased Portuguese presence at the land frontiers of the colony, leading to military and administrative campaigns to dominate and control the interior of the territory. All of these factors changed the perception of the territory as a whole; they demanded an expansion into the interior of the country and set the scene for the changes to come in the early twentieth century.

provided – but also as the social ideals embodied in the modernist project could be exploited to posit this large investment in the colonial spaces as a reason for their retention, communicating a political narrative of an egalitarian society with all races assimilated into a Portuguese way of life (however different the reality may have been). A generation of idealistic Portuguese architects who were heavily influenced by the International Style being practised across Europe, North America, and Brazil left the repressive environment of Portugal under Salazar and went to the colonies where they had both more employment opportunities and more freedom to innovate and practise this 'new' architecture, rather than being stifled by the more traditionalist (albeit Modern) *Português Suave* style of architecture that was being promoted by the dictatorship in Lisbon, many examples of which also exist in Angola, such as the Port of Luanda (1945–1953) and the National Bank (1956). At the same time as this massive national building

project was underway, nationalist and pro-independence sentiments were actively supressed, often brutally (such as the napalm bombing of communities in the Cassanje Region in 1961). The independence movements began the armed struggle and the colonial wars run from 1961 to 1974.

Much is made of the legacy of Tropical Modernism that is present in Angolan cities. While there is much to be celebrated (especially the responsiveness to climate, a trait missing from much of what is being built today), and certainly the current state of decay and neglect of this architectural legacy is painful to witness, the problematic aspects of this project need to be acknowledged. Firstly, the modernist project as it was implemented in Angola, was situated within (and was a tool of) the colonial project. Secondly, the notion of 'universalism' embodied within the modernist ideology was not in fact universal, but effectively meant the 'European', or at least the 'assimilated', excluded the vast majority

Informal constructions in the peripheral suburbs that emerged during the civil war continue to house the majority of Angola's population
Source: Kostadin Luchansky/Angola Image Bank

Chicala, a now-demolished informal settlement on Luanda's waterfront

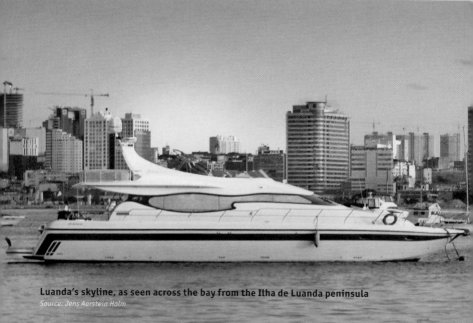

Source: Paulino Damiao

of the population. This ideology of 'universalism', as backed up by assimilationist policy that dictated the behaviour of those allowed to live in the modern centre, led to the further erasure of local African cultures. And thirdly, the Modern project was never fully implemented and its egalitarian ideals were never realised: the 'modern' city existed largely for the white, mixed race, and *assimilado* (assimilated) minority,[11] physically separated from the informal *musseques* (slums), located on the periphery and populated by the *indigena* (indigenous) majority. Ironically, it was during this period that the cities actually became more rather than less segregated. The influx of white settlers at the time of this modernist expansion and reorganisation of the cities through the various master plan projects created more legible divisions between the paved city centre and the sandy *musseques* on the periphery along racial lines, whereas previously the city was smaller and without these clear spatial, economic, and

Luanda's skyline, as seen across the bay from the Ilha de Luanda peninsula
Source: Jens Aarstein Holm

Source: Joost De Raeymaeker

New satellite town under construction on the outskirts of Dundo, Lunda Norte Province

racial divisions. This created a centre-periphery dynamic in which the modern centre relied heavily on the *musseques* for cheap labour to support the operations of a cosmopolitan society, a trait that continues and has expanded today. At the same time as this reorganisation of existing cities was being implemented, there were a number of greenfield *colonato* towns designed and built in strategic agricultural areas in the provinces that were intended for an entirely white population.[12]

Over the last fifteen years there has been a flurry of scholarship on the architecture in Portuguese colonies during this late colonial period, with a specific focus on modernism, largely supported by the immense archive (both institutional and that of individuals) that still exists in Europe today, contrasted with photographs of the same architectural heritage in its current, degraded state. While much of this recent scholarship is important, and given the precarious state of heritage architecture in Angola, there

are various aspects of much of this research that need to be addressed. As has been noted elsewhere,[13] in much of this recent scholarship architectural production in the colonial spaces during this era does not draw on a post-colonial critique or analysis. Much (not all) of this documentation and research conducted belies a tendency towards nostalgia, viewing the period as something of a golden era, and fails to contextualise what these particular architects, projects, policies, or built works actually meant in relation to the larger colonial project and the 'epistemological violence' this brings upon local peoples.

Post-independence

1974 saw a *coup d'état* in Portugal led by a military discontent with fighting an unending and unwinnable war in the African colonies. After a short and mishandled decolonisation process, Angola gained independence in 1975 and immediately entered into a long running and highly destructive civil war that took on an international dimension in the face of the Cold War. There was an immediate exodus of the white settler population along with the more gradual but even more massive migration of rural populations fleeing the war towards urban centres, especially Luanda. This put major pressure on limited building stock and urban infrastructure, (which was then inadequately maintained for three decades), and spurred massive uncontrolled growth at the peripheries of cities, the vast majority of which was informally built. What little was built formally during this era typically reflects the government's Marxist ideology and the influence of their international partners: the Cuban built housing blocks and the Soviet designed mausoleum are examples.

The civil war ended decisively in 2002, and it is hard to overstate the scale of change in the period since. It has involved a massive national reconstruction project – investment in the rebuilding of infrastructure and the restarting of industries that had ground to a halt during the war – an oil-fuelled construction boom, and also the embracing of capitalism, the establishment of an Angolan elite, and the emergence of middle class consumers. The post-war reality has been constituted of three main dynamics that are playing out in the built environment: informal construction and urbanism (the *musseques* which house the majority of the urban population: self-built and characterised by precarious land tenure); large scale state-led housing, industry, and infrastructure projects (typically projects that are highly centralised in their conception and implementation,

BAI Academy, a training institute for banking professionals in Talatona, Luanda (2013)

Source: Kostadin Luchansky

Source: Joost De Raeymaeker

Partial view of the new satellite town of Kilamba, which is around 30 km from Luanda

often implemented under joint ventures with foreign entities); and a new boom of speculative private sector real estate ventures (both local and foreign capital; also largely designed outside of Angola and built by foreign construction companies, squarely aimed at both international investors and the Angolan elite). Luanda notoriously has some of the most expensive real estate in the world – this speculation stems from the housing crisis that resulted from the astronomical increase of population in the city and its uncontrolled expansion, along with the skyrocketing oil prices that coincided with the end of the civil war, creating a boom in which multinational oil companies could pay whatever price was asked for the very limited housing stock available, effectively pricing out the majority of Angolans and condemning those without secure tenure (or political connections) to a precarious life in the *musseques*. Recently, many of these *musseques*, especially those located on valuable land, have become the sites of demolition to make way for large scale urban conversion projects (such as the Sambizanga-Cazenga project) or as yet unknown waterfront developments (such as the Chicala Neighbourhood). Another side effect of this speculative real estate market is the demolition of the significant architectural heritage that exists.

The 2008 demolition of the Kinaxixe Open-air Market took the academic and architectural community by surprise, and has become emblematic of the post-civil-war model of development underway in Luanda (and other Angolan cities, to a lesser extent). The market, along with other buildings and the large public square adjacent were demolished and absorbed into an enormous construction site, out of which is yet to emerge a commercial real estate venture composed of various twenty-five-storey buildings and a high-end shopping mall. The Kinaxixe Market has become a symbol (albeit absent) that highlights the precarious situation of this architectural heritage and spurred the creation of various organisations in Luanda with the objective of preserving historical architectural sites and preventing further demolitions, and led to a campaign to classify a number of buildings. However, there have been many other significant buildings of heritage value that have been demolished since the Kinaxixe Market, highlighting both the urgency of a more comprehensive classification of heritage buildings in Luanda, and the tensions that exist between different interests in a city where the price per square metre has surpassed that of New York.

No only did the civil war provoke uncontrolled growth in urban centres without

Source: Kostadin Luchansky/Angola Image Bank

New National Assembly Building in Luanda (Teixeira Duarte, Portugal, 2015)

the maintenance of basic infrastructure, but it also caused wide scale destruction in the smaller towns and rural areas, and of any nationwide infrastructure – roads and bridges fell into disrepair, or strategic connections were deliberately destroyed as two sides of the conflict gained and lost territory. This in addition to the fact that the national development project underway during the colonial administration was never actually finished: Angola has never had a national power grid, for example. This has meant that 2002 was in effect 'year zero', requiring the (re)building of an entire nation. It is not only the physical infrastructure that needs to be rebuilt, but also the human infrastructure. Communities and societies have been massively disrupted and displaced over the course of the civil war; education was interrupted for more than one generation; the economy effectively stopped (and though it was kick-started post-2002 with the oil boom, it remains largely dependant on that one commodity, as the 2014 to 2017 economic crisis has testified). A project of national reconstruction therefore should not only concern itself with the building of roads,

bridges, housing stock (though these are all of vital importance), but also the 're-construction' of communities. It demands the construction of an economy and a society that can integrate the majority of the Angolan population (who still live in poverty) in a manner that enables them to create livelihoods, not only as economic production units, but also with independence, self-determination, and agency. Whether this is the type of reconstruction underway is debatable – the priority has been the physical infrastructure first, with the social infrastructure to follow. However, the 2014 to 2017 economic crisis has exposed the fragility of many of the ventures that have been developed over the previous decade that were of extremely poor quality and/or entirely unsustainable from both a financial and political point of view, along with the mismanagement of funds inherent in many of these large scale construction projects. Similar to the massive nation-building project that was undertaken in the 1960s by the colonial regime, the recent reconstruction and development boom has also been deeply tied to a set of political ideologies, and the architecture(s)

Source: James Steinkamp

Campus of the Agostinho Neto University, Camama, Luanda (Perkins + Will Architects, 2011)

that have emerged during this period have been equally shaped by the political winds of the time. Architecture is never neutral, it is always available as a political tool. Angola is currently very centralised, in many senses. The economic and political power of the nation are concentrated in heavily populated coastal cities (especially Luanda) in contrast with an underdeveloped rural interior, which is sparsely populated due to two waves of depopulation – firstly slavery and secondly the 1975 to 2002 civil war. There are moves to decentralise both areas through the creation of local representative governments and elections across the country, as well as through the creation of *novas centralidades* (new centralities), which are essentially clusters of high density middle class housing being built in various locations both close to existing urban centres such as Luanda (Kilamba), but also on the periphery of most of the smaller regional towns such as Uíge and Dundo. While this approach represents a desire to counter the continued movement of populations from rural to urban areas (now for economic reasons) and attract a class of public servants to live in regional areas, it risks perpetuating the 'planning at distance' of modernist-era *colonatos*, equally disconnected from the contextual reality of a place (the local traditions and environment, the social and economic contexts of the local people).

Notes
1 Alberto Oliveira Pinto, *História de Angola: Da Pré-história ao Início do Século XXI* (Lisbon, 2015), p. 28.
2 Jan Vansina, *How Societies are Born: Governance in West Central Africa before 1600* (Charlottesville, VA, and London, 2004; citations from 2012 edn), pp. 29–33.
3 Ibid, p. 170.
4 Isabel Castro Henriques/Alfredo Margarido, *Percursos da Modernidade em Angola* (Lisbon, 1997), pp. 18–19.
5 Achille Mbembe, 'Decolonizing Knowledge and the Question of the Archive', WISER (2016).
6 John K. Thornton/Linda M. Heywood, *Central Africans, Atlantic Creoles, and the Foundation of the Americas, 1585–1660* (Cambridge/New York, 2007), pp. 85–86.
7 Henriques/Margarido 1997, p. 17.
8 Maria João Martins, 'No Sobrado Sobre a Baía: Retrato da Burguesia de Luanda no final do Século XIX', *Camões: Revista de Letras e Culturas Lusófonas*, 1 (April–June 1998), pp. 46–53.
9 Nuno Domingos/Elsa Peralta, A Cidade e o Império, in: id. (eds), *Cidade e Império: Dinâmicas Coloniais e Reconfigurações Pós-Coloniais* (Lisbon, 2013), pp. IX–L.
10 Cláudia Castelo, 'O Luso-Tropicalismo e o Colonialismo Português Tardio', Buala (5 March 2013).
11 José Maria Nunes Pereira, 'Mário de Andrade e o Lusotropicalismo', Rio de Janeiro 2000, bibliotecavirtual.clacso.org.ar/ar/libros/aladaa/nunes.rtf.
12 Maria Manuela Alfonso da Monte, 'Urbanismo e Arquitectura em Angola: De Norton de Matos à Revolução', PhD thesis (rev.), UTL, 2013, p. 227.
13 Isabel Castro Henriques/Miguel Pais Vieira, 'África – Visões do Gabinete de Urbanização Colonial (1944–1974): Uma Leitura Crítica', Buala (17 March 2014).

334

View from São Miguel Fortress: downtown Luanda and the new Marginal, a promenade that runs from the main harbour to the Ilha de Luanda peninsula
Source: Kostadin Luchansky

Source: Museu de Roeynaeker

The Tale of an Intangible City: M'banza Kongo

Joost De Raeymaeker

Reading about 'African history' in global mainstream media, it's easy to come away with the impression that there isn't much of it. Before Europeans arrived, anyway. In lusophone countries, this is evident in the way that even today terms such as *os descobrimentos* ('the Discoveries') are still widely used. This casual linguistic position has two basic results: We are led to believe that there wasn't anything (worthwhile) present before Europeans showed up; and it conveys the idea that they were 'discovering' places merely for the noble act of finding them. Wrong on both counts. M'banza Kongo, the capital of the powerful Kongo Kingdom, is a useful point of study in considering the pre-existing structures (be they physical or not) and how they have changed over the course of the last five centuries.

The founding story of the town goes back to the thirteenth century, and the figure of Nimi a Lukeni, who came from Bungu, close to the present day town of Boma in the Democratic Republic of the Congo. With his entourage, he crossed the Zaïre River (Congo River) southwards into an area populated by the Ambundu and Ambwela peoples. After establishing matrimonial bonds with the local communities, Nimi a Lukeni founded the capital of the kingdom on the M'banza Kongo Plateau, surrounded by twelve water sources and an ideal topography for its defence, since the top was only approachable from a northeasterly direction.

M'banza Kongo was not the geographical centre of the Kongo Kingdom, but its political and religious umbilical cord. The kingdom's borders were not based on military conquest, but on recognition of the king's authority and power. Access to the throne was purely through matrilineal order, but not automatic. Power

Detail of the Kulumbimbi stone church

shifted from one social group to another through a process of elections. Only after going through the sacred rite and settling into the kingdom's capital, M'banza Kongo, could the king gain his full powers and divine attributes.

On the northern end of the plateau were the 'Sacred Woods', a traditional place of rituals where the Royal Cemetery (*Kulumbimbi*) was located. South of this area was the town, which was encircled by a staked fence, adding further defensive measures to the strategic location. Inside this was the Royal Palace (*Lumbu*), with a circumference of around 1,000 m. And inside the palace was a smaller enclosed area with the house of the king in the centre. Certainly this defensive radial planning is reminiscent of many medieval European cities, and early Portuguese navigators compared M'banza Kongo to the town of Évora in Portugal, which at the time was a thriving place in its golden age.

By the end of the fifteenth century, when the Portuguese explorer Diogo Cão dropped anchor at the mound of the Zaïre River and 'discovered' the place, the Kongo Kingdom, with its six provinces and four vassal states, was some

Depiction of the Battle of Mbwila in a tiled mural is on the wall of the Nossa Senhora de Nazaré Church in Luanda, portraying the beheading of the King of Kongo in 1665

Source: Joost De Raeymaeker

Kulumbimbi, a former cathedral and sub-Saharan Africa's oldest Christian church (1548)

2.5 million km² in size, about twice the size of modern day Angola, or four times the size of France. After an initial period of mutual exchange of ambassadors, scholars, artisans, and (of course) relatively peaceful Christianisation (including the king, Nzinga a Nkuwu, sending a mission to Lisbon to learn the language, religion, agricultural, and culinary techniques of the Portuguese), we see a gradual change in structure. Africa's oldest sub-Saharan Christian church was built in stone in the sacred area of the Royal Cemetery by the Portuguese in 1548, and is currently referred to as Kulumbimbi (the name of the Royal Cemetery). Further churches were built in stone – the ruins of some of these surviving to this day, where many of the original buildings (built of less resistant materials, such as adobe and timber) have disappeared.

From this point of initial contact with Europeans in the late fifteenth century, through to the seventeenth century, M'banza Kongo continued to be ruled by Kongo kings. Interaction with the Portuguese was mainly commercial, religious, and cultural. The Europeans were after gold, copper, and, most importantly, slaves. What seemed initially like a way for the king to get rid of some pesky opponents or prisoners soon turned into a lucrative trade. From this time through to 1836, when the Portuguese stopped

the deportation of slaves, more than five million slaves were shipped from this area, being hastily baptised before being hauled on board slave ships. To put this number in perspective, it is equivalent to a little under one quarter of the current-day population of the whole of Angola, and represents well over 40 per cent of the total of slaves that left Africa during the transatlantic slave trade.

While the Kongo rulers initially participated in this trade, it soon became a major problem and had a significant impact on the Kongo Kingdom with the depopulation of the majority of the fit and healthy; however, numerous official complaints to the Portuguese king went without effect. A number of conflicts and changing alliances (including one with the Dutch), had little impact, and after the major blow of losing the Battle of Mbwila against the Portuguese in 1665, things went downhill for the Kongo Kingdom. By the time the Berlin conference came around in 1884–1885, the Portuguese had officially colonised the entire territory that is now present-day Angola, signifying the end of any real political power held by the Kongo kings.

The slave trade had a major effect, not only in the Kongo Kingdom, but also in the areas to which slaves were deported. One of those effects is the cultural influence of these people and their traditions,

The Sacred Woods and the Royal Cemetery, on top of the M'banza Kongo Plateau

which has been passed down through generations. The word 'Kongo' is today used in rites, the naming of places, and in other collective cultural expressions by Afro-descendants throughout the world. We have the Congo drum (Haiti, Colombia, Dominican Republic, Mexico, Venezuela, Argentina, Suriname, Barbados, Cuba, Uruguay, Peru, Paraguay), the Congo dance (Brasil, Cuba, Colombia), Congo Square (USA), *congadas* parades (Brasil), and Kongo nation (Jamaica). Apart from this, numerous Kikongo terms are present in popular language, pharmacopoeia, culinary vernacular, and in almost all cultural activities of Afro-descendants. (If you live in the southern USA, you might be eating a 'goober' or two while reading this. *Nguba* means 'peanuts' in Kikongo.) In every place that received Kongo slaves lives, mostly unconsciously, a part of the Kongo culture. M'banza Kongo survives far outside its original borders. The inclusion of M'banza Kongo in the World Heritage List will, hopefully, help to spread Kongo culture even further.

AO

Production of traditional fired earth bricks on the side of the M'banza Kongo Plateau

Headquarters of the BPC Bank in Luanda, designed by Januário Godinho in 1967, is currently being remodelled

Introduction to Angola's Colonial Modernity

Ana Tostões

The Portuguese colonisation of what is today Angola began along the country's Atlantic coast in the fifteenth century. São Paulo da Assunção de Loanda (now Luanda) and Benguela were the first cities established by the Portuguese on the Angolan coast in 1575 and 1617 respectively, and they were founded according to a typical Portuguese colonial urban matrix reflecting both trade and commercial interests and the spontaneous occupation. The fortresses located in strategic high points evidence the defensive character of these early cities. Urban areas grew, supported by the various commercial trades (initially the slave trade, later various agricultural and mineral trades) and the development of ports in sheltered coastal places like recesses or the calm waters of bays that were protected by sand ridges – for instance, the Bay of Luanda or the sandbank where the city of Lobito was founded in 1842.

This colonisation of the coast was consolidated during the nineteenth century by inland penetration campaigns carried out along rivers. Following the

National Bank of Angola, in central Luanda

definition of political boundaries at the Berlin Conference (1884–1885) and the 1890 British Ultimatum (where Portugal capitulated with regard to applying its Pink Map), this drive was reinforced by the building of a railway network from

National Union of Angolan Workers (UNTA) Building, in the Mutamba District of Luanda

Source: Hans Engels

Interior of the National Union of Angolan Workers (UNTA), in Mutamba, Luanda

west to east, perpendicular to the coast, and later, in the twentieth century, the construction of a road system, which, until 1961, took the form of a number of unpaved roads, with the only paved sections linking Carmona (now Uíge), Salazar (now N'dalatando), and Luanda.

During the early days of colonisation, Brazil, Portugal's largest territory, was the first destination for Angolan goods and slaves, fulfilling the role of trade intermediary between Portugal and Angola. From 1856, though, Angola's ports were directly connected to Lisbon. The independence of Brazil in 1822 and the abolition of slavery from 1869 to 1879 marked a new phase in the Angolan economy, one that was based on a broad colonisation strategy for the entire territory. With

the abolition of Portugal's monarchy and the establishment of its First Republic in 1910, this colonial occupation policy was implemented by the governor general of Angola, José Norton de Matos, who founded a city that was intended as the dream capital of Angola: Nova Lisboa (now Huambo), which was established in the centre of the country, on the fertile plateau of Huambo, in 1912.

The 1920s saw an increase in the Portuguese development of Angola, in particular with regard to the production of coffee and sisal in the highlands of Benguela, and cotton in the province of Malanje, with the Companhia Geral dos Algodões de Angola (General Cotton Company of Angola – also known as Cotonang) created in 1926. That same year, a military revolution put an end to the First Portuguese Republic and led to a military dictatorship that was followed by the establishment of the Estado Novo (New State) autocracy, whose constitution was adopted in 1933. In 1930, its leader, António de Oliveira Salazar, identified the colonies as a strategic objective of the centralisation of the state. From a nationalist and centralist ideology, colonialism was understood as a vocation and the Portuguese nation's historical right. The 1938 Exhibition-Fair of Angola, designed by Vasco Vieira da Costa, expressed a vision for the entrepreneurial capacity of the colony.

From the 1940s onwards, and continuing through the post-World War II era, there was a significant increase in urban populations, driven by exports of various agricultural and mineral products. This spurred the installation of industries and hydroelectric projects, and the application of capital in the development of works through the launch of the *Planos de Fomento* (Development Plans) in 1953. Part of a policy based on a strategy of accelerated growth in the various Portuguese colonies in Africa, these plans advocated significant investment in various infrastructures and the development of modern architecture and urbanism.

Cities attracted both the white urban population and the indigenous population of Angola's rural interior, so new *colonatos* (settler towns) were created. Cities were planned by the Office of Colonial Urbanisation (GUC). Founded in 1944 to promote the development and systematisation of colonial urban planning through the centralisation of all of the metropole's projects, the GUC designed the Lobito Urbanisation Plans (1949), Nova Lisboa (now Huambo; 1947–1948), and Luanda (1949). This development cycle took place in the context of a colonial policy that was increasingly challenged at an international level after the creation of the United Nations in 1945. In a process that started in the early 1950s with the independence of Libya, Africa's colonies began to become independent. In 1960, the 'Year of Africa', many countries gained independence, including Côte d'Ivoire, the Central African Republic, Nigeria, Congo, Gabon, Mauritania, and Senegal. The Portuguese Colonial War broke out in Angola in 1961, when the colonial power tried to combat uprisings and growing demands for independence. Occurring the context of Cold War allegiances, this war (fought in separate theatres in Angola, Guinea, and Mozambique) extended over thirteen years, with the Estado Novo regime gradually losing control. The Carnation Revolution in Lisbon in April 1974 led to Portugal's withdrawal from Africa.

Angola's architecture was, of course, affected by all of these political changes. In Portugal's constitutional revisions

Source: Joost De Raeymaeker

Atlântico Open-air Cinema, in Luanda (António Ribeiro dos Santos, Eduardo Paulino, 1964)

Iconic book-shaped building: Prédio do Livro, in Maculusso, Luanda
Source: Hans Engels

Source: Hans Engels (all pictures)

Luanda's modernist heritage on Rua Major Kanyangulo in the city's Ingombota District

of 1951, terms such as 'empire' and 'colonies' were replaced by 'overseas territories and provinces', and the Office of Colonial Urbanisation (GUC, 1944–1951) was designated the Office of Overseas Urbanisation (GUU, 1951–1957), while the Minister of Colonies was renamed the Overseas Minister. Led by João António de Aguiar, the GUC brought together several renowned architects, among them Francisco Castro Rodrigues and Fernão Simões de Carvalho. In the context of the exponential increase of the population in the late 1950s, and the local autonomy process, Fernão Simões de Carvalho developed the Luanda Master Plan (1961–1962), which defined a strategy for the reorganisation of the road system and the functional zoning of the city. He also developed partial plans, including for the Futungo de Belas (1960–1962) and the Prenda Neighbourhood Unit #1 (1963–1965). Paradoxically, it was during the period of the Colonial War (1961–1974) that the Portuguese invested most in infrastructure – although this was expressed mainly in the formal city, which was populated by settlers, and came at the expense of the informal settlements, which had a predominantly indigenous population.

Understanding the need to work locally, some of this group of architects choose to live permanently in Angola. As a result, the architectural landscape gradually changed, developing away from the references of an authoritarian and conservative political regime. Thus, from the late 1940s onwards, the formal, technological, and ideological principles of Modern Movement architecture began to prove significant in built works. The African colonies were geographically distant from the repressive control of the regime, and they also constituted a new world, where the scale and the need for development were promoted within a wide field of experimentation and innovation in planning actions and construction during the Colonial War. The place and climate proved to be sources of inspiration for the creation of devices of control, constituting stimulating reasons for the development of an original language, full of plasticity in volumes, expression, and light and shadow research.

Local architectural production increased after 1957, when the GUU was abolished and several local institutions were created. A number of urban plans began to be developed by 'local' architects who possessed knowledge and awareness of the specific problems, characteristics, and expansion needs of each city. In 1959, Fernão Simões de Carvalho, an Angolan-born architect, returned to Luanda after joining Le Corbusier's studio between 1956 and 1959, and created the Urbanisation Office of the City of Luanda, for which he developed a set of master plans. The Portuguese-born architect Vasco Vieira da Costa, who also worked with Le Corbusier, returned to Luanda in 1949, where he integrated the technical services of the municipality and developed several projects. Using a modernist lexicon, Vasco Vieira da Costa expressed Luanda's climate through the combination of passive climate control systems, leaving a clear stamp on the city's landscape.

Between 1957 and 1960, Francisco Silva Dias and Antoineta Jacinto – the director of the Public Works and Transportation Services of Luanda and the only publically employed woman in a leadership position in Angola at that time – generated works where each individual project was an investigation task in order to adapt their architecture to the tropical climate and its site and users.

In Lobito, Francisco Castro Rodrigues worked extensively as an urban planner and architect for the city, designing the Universal Building (1957–1961), the Flamingo Open-air Cinema (1963), the Comandante Saydi Mingas School (1967), and drawing the Urbanisation Plan of Lobito (1969–1972), and the Nossa Senhora da Conceição Church in Sumbe (1966). He explored the principles of modernist architecture, together with economic, social, and climate concerns.

The open-air cinema, both as programme and architectural solution, represents a (colonial) philosophy of leisure and constitutes an Angolan typology: the Miramar (1964) and Atlântico (1964)

Oliva Housing Block, in the Largo Amílcar Cabral, central Luanda

Source: Atelier Mulembo

Prenda Neighbourhood Unit #1, in Luanda (Fernão Lopes Simões de Carvalho, 1965)

open-air cinemas were symbols of Luanda, as was the Kalunga of Benguela, and the Flamingo of Lobito. Modernism was expressed in religious architecture in Angola from the 1960s onwards – in the new neighbourhoods in the northern expansion area of Luanda through the Sagrada Família Church; in Sumbe through the Nossa Senhora da Conceição Church, and also in Benguela through the Nossa Senhora de Fátima Cathedral.

Angolan independence was declared in 1975, following the Carnation Revolution, which took place in Portugal in 1974. A civil war began soon after, and slowed the development of the country, leaving marks of destruction on cities, infrastructure networks, and the population. Lasting peace finally came in 2002, accompanied by rapid development of the country. During peacetime, the reconstruction of the territory has, in Luanda, an epicentre of accelerated growth and transformation. Today it constitutes a huge metropolis of approximately 6.5 million people. This growth necessitates solutions for the demands made by urban development and territorial planning; solutions are required for basic infrastructural problems, and in particular for mobility issues

and the road system. On the one hand, the infrastructure of the informal city is urgently in need; on the other hand, it is also vital to maintain and update the formal city and the historic centre, which contains the architectural heritage of the modernist movement. Two demolitions – Kinaxixe Market (Vasco Vieira da Costa, 1958) in 2008 and the Cuca Building (Luís Taquelim da Silva, 1950) in 2011 – highlighted the debate on modernist architecture in Lusophone Africa, according to which this modernist inheritance can be understood as a cultural asset that integrates sustainable solutions to climate issues. Today, some iconic buildings have been protected with heritage classification as a result of this debate. This has prevented demolitions and replacements with glass façade buildings, as in the case of Luanda's Hotel Presidente Meridien (António Nunes e Silva Campino, 1974). Works such as these are a small example of the potential realised by modernist architectural production in Angola and reflect the iconic, tectonic, and programmatic qualities of this unique legacy – one that organisations such as Docomomo International are working to preserve.

AO

Hotel Katekero, in the Largo Amílcar Cabral, Luanda
Source: Hans Engels

Science Faculty of the Agostinho Neto University,
on the Avenida 4 de Fevereiro, Luanda
Source: Hans Engels

AO

Luanda: Taking the Musseque Out of the People

António Tomás

Informal housing is a major problem today. It is estimated that in the cities of the Global South over one billion people live in substandard homes. The problem of informal housing in Luanda is a contemporary issue, but has its own history. Understanding this is necessary in order to arrive at appropriate solutions.

Modern Luanda is a city that has been shaped and structured on the basis of the race and class of its inhabitants. When the slave trade ended in 1849, Luanda lost both its main economy and its wealthiest inhabitants, plunging the city into a lethargy from which it only awoke after World War II with the coffee boom.

This flow of capital provoked the migration of a large white population, predominantly from Portugal, driving the expansion of the urban grid. But this movement also attracted a large native African population, the majority of whom worked as inexpensive manual labour. They inhabited the edges of the city, in the areas that later would become known as *musseques* (dwellings in sandy areas): large informal clusters at the periphery of the (asphalted) city.

The Modern city which began to take shape in Luanda in the late 1950s was deeply marked by the social division of labour under the colonial system. Up until

Kostadin Luchansky / Angola Image Bank (photo)

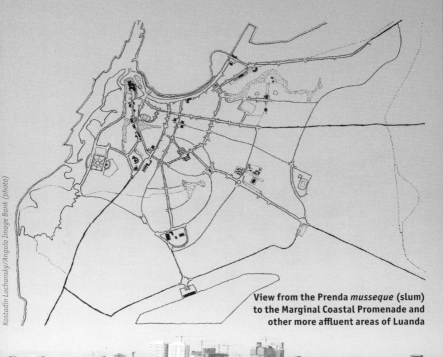

View from the Prenda *musseque* (slum) to the Marginal Coastal Promenade and other more affluent areas of Luanda

AO

Source: Africa Drawn Project

Luanda's (colonial) centre contrasts with the informal *musseques* on the city's periphery

this point, formal and informal clusters had peacefully co-existed in the city, and did not necessarily constitute separate identities. In certain privileged areas, such as Coqueiros, it was common to find informal housing. Modernist planning attempted to put an end to this: thousands of shacks were destroyed and their populations pushed beyond the edge of the consolidated city. Geographers and social scientists of the era argued that the formation of the *musseques* was the result of a mismatch between the delay in industrialisation and the rapid urbanisation of African populations. Economists, however, had a different opinion – they highlighted colonial laws that prohibited or hindered the creation of industrial

Source: Kostadin Luchansky/Angola Image Bank

Circulation is a major issue for the capital

parks in Angola and the lack of training of an indigenous labour force; instead the colonial power on relied on the arrival of more settlers to fill even the positions of unskilled labourers. The result of this division of labour was reflected in the fabric of the city: the centre was consolidated for an almost exclusively white population who controlled the upper and middle sectors of the economy; while the *musseques* housed an overwhelmingly African population, whose main source of income were the services they rendered to the affluent.

With the end of the colonial order in 1975, the upper strata and especially the middle class abandoned the city. The former residents of the *musseques* on the perimeter occupied the urban centre but had neither the consumption patterns nor the financial means nor the urban culture to take care of these spaces. To make things worse, the civil war which began in 1975 intensified and rural populations flocked to the city. Luanda grew, and more than anything else, the *musseques* expanded dramatically.

During the socialist era, Angola's housing stock became nationalised, only to be privatised in the early 1990s after the first economic reforms were undertaken. As there was no official real estate market, most transactions involving property were informal. When large

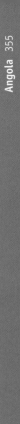

Remnants of Luanda's modernist architecture; this is still the most distinctive architectural style in the city centre
Source: Kostadin Luchansky/ Angola Image Bank

Musseques – large clusters of informal housing with substandard living conditions – remain a pressing issue in contemporary Luanda
Source: Kostadin Luchansky/Angola Image Bank

companies moved into Angola (oil companies and other sectors) seeking office spaces and residences, they rented them at exorbitant prices. In this manner, Luanda won the reputation as 'the most expensive city in the world'.

Thus followed the housing crisis that we speak about today. The way to solve this issue has concerned the central government since the end of civil war in 2002. The solution was seen as quantitative: the housing crisis was simply a mismatch between supply and demand, and investment in the expansion of the housing stock would solve everything. This thinking is the basis for the expansion of housing stock in Luanda. The government has both promised and built a great deal, but housing insecurity has not disappeared.

The problem is that the government's initiatives in this area do not attack the root of the problem. Firstly, because of the nature of the typologies that are being built – concrete high-rise buildings, as seen in the Nova Vida (New Life), Kilamba, and Sequele housing projects. These models are conceptually repeating the premises of architectural modernism seen in much of the centre of Luanda. Secondly, it appears that the primary concern of these initiatives is to remove poor people from certain valuable areas of the city such as Chicala or Roque Santeiro, and build high-end urban developments on these sites.

But this approach does not in any way solve the housing problem associated with such poverty – to do this, economic

considerations must be taken into account. Many of the city dwellers living in informal areas depend on the informal sector for their livelihood, and are not adapted to formal dwellings. Here lies the link between the economy and housing. The colonial geographers understood this with a certain degree of perceptiveness. They had hoped that one day the slums would be urbanised, but not before there was industrialisation and job creation. In the Luanda of today, urban expansion is not accompanied by the formalisation of the economy.

What impoverishes the debate on housing in Luanda is the absence of a broader understanding of the relationship between urban planning and the economy. High-rise construction, which is a post-colonial emulation of colonial architecture, suffers from a serious problem: it is simply continuing to repeat the same approach today in a context that is now different. The large urban housing developments that have emerged recently do not answer many uncertainties – questions about the inclusion of these new inhabitants in the labour market, or the relationship between these new developments and sources of employment, which are still in the (colonial) centre of the city. The risk here is not that the government fails on its promise to remove millions of Luandans from informality (here understood simply as housing). But precisely the opposite – that it removes people from informality, but does not prevent the degeneration of the city.

The newly redeveloped Marginal Promenade (2012) and the *Português Suave* style National Bank (1956) stand in front of the International Style BPC Bank Building (1967) and the new Sonangol Headquarters (2008)
Source: Kostadin Luchansky

A New World-class City:
The Redevelopment of the Bay of Luanda

Sylvia Croese

Ten years after the end of a twenty-seven year civil war, in 2012, the then president of Angola, José Eduardo dos Santos, inaugurated the first phase of the redevelopment of the Bay of Luanda. With a total investment of 376 million US dollars, the waterfront of Luanda has been transformed from a degraded, polluted, and congested place into a revitalised public space with over 2,000 newly planted palm trees, 147,000 m² of pedestrian space, around 3 km of cycle lanes, three playgrounds, three sport fields, five basketball courts, and five spaces for cultural events, plus a new waste water system, a six lane road, a fuel station and a flyover connecting the Marginal or waterfront road to the Island of Luanda and the new Marginal or Praia do Bispo road.

Hailed internationally as a successful waterfront redevelopment project and widely promoted as the 'new face' of the city, the redevelopment of the Bay of Luanda represents the epitome of efforts in the post-civil war era to position

Angola's capital as a modern 'world-class' city in the image of places such as Dubai. More than simply rebuilding infrastructures and services, such as roads, schools, hospitals, and water and energy networks, these efforts have involved the planning and implementation of megaprojects such as the 3.5 billion US dollar construction of the new city of Kilamba, a new port and international airport, and a special economic zone, as well as major private real estate, office, and commercial developments – turning the city into a permanent construction site.

As in other aspiring world-class cities, world-class city making in Luanda has also been accompanied by its fair share of urban boosterism, including extensive media campaigns and hosting huge sports events and political summits, all aimed at rebranding and promoting the country, and in particular its capital. These campaigns and events have been implemented against the backdrop of the adoption of a number of development

Source: Joost De Raeymaeker

Luanda's 'new face': the redeveloped bay provides spaces to walk and play

Panorama of the Bay of Luanda, with a new shopping centre under construction
Source: Kostadin Luchansky

plans which position Luanda as a future regional and global hub that is 'open for business'. In line with these plans, the new master plan for Luanda, launched in December 2015 to be implemented over the next fifteen years, foresees the establishment of Luanda as 'a future economic, touristic, and service pole in Southern Africa' by 'keeping its international profile' and 'creating world standard infrastructure'.

Yet, while these practices of world-class city making appear to replicate world-class city making elsewhere, projects such as the redevelopment of the Bay reveal important internal, political, and historical rationales that drive the re-making of the city of Luanda.

Unlike cities such as Dubai, where the development of world-class infrastructures primarily serves to cater to international visitors and investors, the redevelopment of the Bay of Luanda forms part of a wider project that serves to convey an important message to an international as well as a domestic audience: that of the return of the state and political power in the city after years of virtual absence and neglect. More than anywhere else, the projection of the state's power onto the

city's landscape is illustrated by the rehabilitation of the politico-administrative centre in the Cidade Alta, or High City, of Luanda, also implemented following the end of the war. The new politico-administrative precinct now houses a restored Presidential Palace, a new High Court and National Assembly, and a massive rocket-shaped mausoleum which holds the remains of the first president of the country, Agostinho Neto. This memorial overlooks the Bay and extends to the Ilha de Luanda, tying the new politico-administrative centre not only symbolically but also physically to the redeveloped waterfront area.

Moreover, whilst the aesthetics that underpin world-class city-making generally are associated with futuristic glass buildings, the redevelopment of the Bay of Luanda instead reveals a penchant for the revival of modernist colonial architecture. Hence, the first phase of the redevelopment as currently completed represents a modern version of the waterfront as it was designed under the urbanisation plan for the waterfront of Luanda of 1943 and subsequent construction works under the Office of Colonial Urbanisation, an institution created

in 1944 for the design and execution of architecture and urbanisation projects in the Portuguese colonies.

Similar efforts to restore or rebuild heritage in line with modernist architecture include the construction of the new building of the National Assembly (2015). Part of the new politico-administrative precinct, the building is modelled after the National Bank of Angola, a symbol of the Estado Novo's neoclassical architecture that was completed in 1956. At the same time, such efforts go hand in hand with the demolition of icons of colonial modernist architecture – for instance, the Kinaxixe Market – and their replacement with new and shiny shopping centres.

The redevelopment of the Bay of Luanda therefore illustrates the different and seemingly contradictory rationales that are at play in the remaking of the city, through which the past and present, the economic and the political, and utopia and nostalgia intersect. Indeed, while the first phase of the redevelopment of the Bay focused on the development of public infrastructures, the second phase is aimed at the development of high-end private residential and commercial real estate. This recently completed second phase included the installation of kiosks at strategic points along the promenade. These will function as restaurants, snack bars, and shops, introducing the concept of 'open-air shopping', and the construction of a new shopping centre at the foot of the city's sixteenth century São Miguel Fortress is already underway.

While the open nature of the Bay so far has allowed for the wide appropriation of the space by residents who use the waterfront on a daily basis to walk and play, in future these developments may turn the waterfront into an increasingly exclusive and privatised space. Currently the space has a permanent presence of both police and private security guards.

The interrogation of the tensions, continuities, and discontinuities that underpin the remaking of Luanda is therefore not just a necessary exercise for practitioners or academics, but also a civic duty for all of those who inhabit the city.

Research on the redevelopment of the Bay of Luanda was conducted with financial support from the United Kingdom government's Department for International Development as part of the research project Urban Governance and Turning African Cities Around, managed by the Partnership for African Social and Governance Research (PASGR) in collaboration with the African Centre for Cities (ACC).

Source: Alamy Stock Foto/Eric Lafforgue

Huambo

Huambo, which was known as Nova Lisboa (New Lisbon) until 1975, is Angola's second largest city. It is centrally located in the Angolan highlands and linked to the Atlantic port of Lobito and the Democratic Republic of the Congo and Zambia by the Benguela Railway.

Huambo was founded in 1912, by the Portuguese governor general of Angola José Norton de Matos. The city was envisioned by the colonial power as eventually becoming the new capital of Angola, and until independence in 1975, was one of the most important urban centres in the territory. Its structure resembled Portuguese-influenced spatial organisation, and influenced by cities in the British colonies of the time, was based on the idea of a garden city, with racial segregation in residential and social

Pálacio do Governo, in central Huambo

areas in the form of 'indigenous quarters'. The idea of a garden city, first put forward by Ebenezer Howard in 1898, also included the theme of the polygon and radiating plan. In his plan for Huambo, Carlos Roma Machado de Faria e Maia used this theme but restricted it to a single square or roundabout from which eight rectilinear avenues radiated.

Modernism in Huambo (left and above); the Ruacaná Cinema, built during the 1950s

Source: Joost de Raeymaker

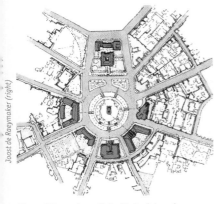

Plan of Praça Agostinho Neto (above); many buildings in Huambo retain scars of the war, but the city is being slowly restored (right)

The simplicity of his design was clear in the final street grid and in the definition and size of the plots of land.

Unusually, there was no church in the original city plan for Huambo, rather there was only a chapel in the cemetery, which was intended for any kind of worship. This plan was designed during the time of Portugal's First Republic (1910–1926) and the state took an intensely anti-clerical stance.

In 1921, the city became a municipal seat, and during the 1930s and 1940s and thereafter, it grew considerably. From 1946 to 1947, Portugal's Office of Colonial Urbanisation (which would later become the Office of Overseas Urbanisation), devised a new urban plan, with the aim of extending the living areas for Europeans, removing the spaces for hotels and parks, and implementing further racial segregation with new 'indigenous quarters'. Throughout the 1950s, the city continued to grow, with many modernist buildings being constructed.

The Angolan Civil War (1975–2002) halted development in Huambo and the whole country, destroying a great part of the infrastructure as well as many buildings. However, both of these are gradually being renewed as the economy improves and businesses reinvest. Huambo is today one of Angola's most rapidly growing cities, with population growth estimated at six per cent annually between 2010 and 2020.   *adp/ed*

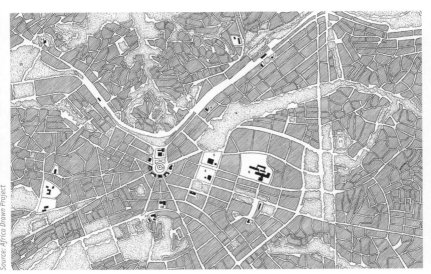

Modernist housing block in Huambo city centre (left); Huambo street grid (above)

Angolan Vernacular Architecture: Linkages and Contemporary Heritage

Caren Melissa Santos da Silva

The year was 2010. It was the very first time I had stepped onto Angolan soil. As a Brazilian Afro-descendant, I was very excited to see the rise of a 'brother country' which had passed through so many years of war. In Brazil, most Afro-descendants – myself probably included – originate from the Bantu ethnic groups in the areas that now make up Angola. In the car, the first impression I had was: Wow, there is so much of Brazil here! But I thought for a second more, and, actually, there was a lot of Angola in Brazil.

In 1888, the Portuguese abolished slavery, and during this period in Brazil, groups of Afro-descendant people who resisted or rebelled against the colonial system and the conditions under slavery started to form independent territories known as *quilombos*, where freedom and common works were the symbol of difference. Today, in certain rural areas of the country, these organised communities remain, preserving their ancestral traditions and maintaining cultural and ethnic identities. The influence of African vernacular building traditions and social structures on the types of structures built in the *quilombos* is clear. Travelling through many different places in Angola strengthened my interest in this relationship between African and Brazilian vernacular architecture. From staying in Namibe (in southern Angola), visiting the Himba people, and travelling the road from Luanda to the city of Porto Amboim, I was quick to observe the similarities between Angolan and Brazilian rural settlements. In both countries, people responded to the scarcity of resources with astonishingly uniform construction methods and use of materials.

One of the great difficulties in studying vernacular architecture in Angola is the lack of documentation of these traditions. Over generations, and through various processes of assimilation, the discarding of that which is seen 'traditional' or 'rural' has been encouraged. Obviously this has a direct influence on the types of structures that are built, with some techniques or materials being substituted. The self-built houses that we find in the provinces today reflect these various cultural interchanges,

Source: Flavio Cardoso

Wooden structure in Bruco, Namibe Province, southern Angola

Source: Coral Gillett

AO

Timber and earthen products used for construction and furniture (Lunda Norte Province)

and as such do not necessarily represent a 'pure' vernacular tradition. The little historical documentation that exists was generated through a colonial methodological framework, which implies a series of limitations. Much of the information that is available today is oral or non-written – heritage that has been passed down through generations. However, this was compromised through cultural influences during colonialism, and, more recently, through the massive displacement of populations during the civil war.

In the traditional constructions that can be seen across Angola, as in most indigenous cultures worldwide, the available local materials and natural resources are fundamental. Earth is used in different forms to create the principle structure of dwellings, most commonly as sun-dried adobe blocks, fired bricks, or through the *pau-a-pique* (or wattle and daub) method, which integrates raw earth into a latticed timber structure. Wood and diverse forms of vegetation are widely used for wall and roof structures, windows and doors, ropes, furniture and fabrics, and decorative elements. Dwellings are usually rectangular in plan, and are clustered together, with external areas for cooking. There are various shared areas and the majority of small villages will have a *jango*, a round open-air structure that serves as a communal space for the whole community.

Source: Coral Gillett

Pau-a-pique wall ready for application of the soil mixture (Lunda Norte Province, 2013)

Source: Coral Gillett

Pau-a-pique (wattle and daub) structure under construction in Lunda Norte

Source: Caren Melissa Santos da Silva

Fisherman and his self-built *pau-a-pique* home for his family in Cabo Ledo, Bengo

Source: Tacum Lecy

Pau-a-pique dwelling in the Rio das Rãs *quilombo* community, Bahia, Brazil

The *pau-a-pique* construction technique consists of a structure made from raw soil and intertwined wood, bamboo, or sisal, and a filling made from mud. This style is common across various regions in Angola, and was taken to Brazil, being used, even today, in the construction of *quilombos*. Despite being commonly thought of as an ephemeral method, and associated with factors such as poverty, *pau-a-pique* is highly resistant and safe when well executed. In Brazil, this is evident not only in dwellings in the *quilombos*, but also in several heritage buildings – some recognised by UNESCO – which are partially, or totally built using this technique. During colonialism, the Portuguese promoted the use of this African method and used it in several public buildings.

In Brazil, the *quilombos* adapted to the new environment, taking on characteristics from both Portuguese and Amerindian influences. While there were obvious departures from African society, many aspects remained – for instance, African spirituality and community organisation as a solid cultural base.

The clustering of dwellings reflected a social organisation similar to that found in villages in various places in Angola: the common use of land and the separation of cooking and rest areas. However, certain other civic buildings emerged in the *quilombos*; examples being the council house, the church, the fortress, and the leisure spaces. Many of the African construction techniques were retained, especially *pau-a-pique*, which is visible in dwellings such as those in the Rio das Rãs *quilombo* community near Bom Jesus da Lapa in Bahia, Brazil. Interestingly, the roof structure changed: rather than the thatch that is common across Angola, clay roof tiles were used in Brazil. Made in situ, these roof tiles, known as *capa-canal*, were shaped over the legs of the slaves during the colonial period. This type of roof was very common and always featured a lack of pattern among the samples (this was because of the different sizes of the women's legs).

Today, the *quilombos* remain, but they face several problems, such as the destruction of historical areas, urban expansion, and a lack of intervention from public institutions. The process of regulating and legalising the properties and the maintenance of the patrimony are new challenges that are only now being addressed in Brazil. We can see parallels in the current situation in Angola. With the economic explosion following the end of thirty years of civil

Source: Mauro Sergio

Wooden foot bridge across the Kikombo River (Kwakra, Kwanza Sul Province)

war, the African country is struggling to maintain its indigenous social, cultural, and architectural influences.

Development in both Angola and Brazil must balance the preservation of these traditions with the inevitabilities of modernisation. To stimulate the survival of African heritage, more concerted efforts are needed to preserve the existing architectures, languages, and traditions in Angola, and to retain the knowledge of building techniques that is at risk of being completely lost.

AO

Source: Flavio Cardoso

Knowledge passed down over generations: wood buildings in Bruco, Namibe Province

São Miguel Fortress

Avenida Dr António Agostinho
Neto/Avenida 4 de Fevereiro,
Ingombota, Luanda
16th–18th century

The São Miguel Fortress was the first of three fortresses to be constructed in Angola's capital. It was built during the rule of the first captain-governor of Portuguese Angola, Paulo Dias de Novais (1575–1588) – initially in earth and clay, and then later, during the seventeenth century, in stone. The plan is the shape of a star with four points, following a bastion system according to the most innovative Italian methods of the time. In the eighteenth century, the construction works came to an end after the building of a battery tower, bomb-proof warehouses, and a cistern – all following a baroque military style. For the city, the fort has always been a landmark that contributed to the organisation of the urban space, and initially delineated the settlement boundary that developed towards Bispo beach to the southeast. It also played a main role in the transport of slaves to Brazil. In 1938, the Portuguese government classified the fortress as a National Monument, and today it welcomes visitors, serving as the Armed Forces Museum. *at et al.*

**View and plan (inset) of the São Miguel
Fortress on the Bay of Luanda**
Source: Africa Drawn Project (plan);
Kostadin Luchansky/Angola Image Bank (all photos)

Nossa Senhora da Nazaré Church »

Praça do Ambiente, Ingombota, Luanda

17th century

Source: David Stanley

The Nossa Senhora da Nazaré Church is located near Luanda Bay, facing Avenida Marginal. The Portuguese governor André Vidal de Negreiros ordered its construction in 1664 to celebrate having survived a shipwreck while travelling between Brazil and Angola. Despite its erudite classical references, the church is a simplified example of religious architecture from the seventeenth century, following Portuguese Plain Style architecture, as George Kubler called it. It is made up of a main nave, with a rectangular shape, and a quadrangular presbytery. In the lateral volumes semi-circular arches support the church's double height, and the main façade has a symmetrical composition that is topped with a pediment. The exterior is clay masonry, with a yellowish colour highlighting the structure's lines, corners, and openings. In the presbytery, the motif on the blue and white, hand painted tiles commemorates the Portuguese victory in the Battle of Mbwila (or Ambuíla) 1665 and also portrays the shipwreck that André Vidal de Negreiros survived. *at et al.*

National Museum of Slavery

AO 03

Morro da Cruz, Luanda Province
17th century

Constructed in the seventeenth century, this building was the primary residence of Captain D. Álvaro de Carvalho Matoso, a knight of the Order of Christ and son of one of the most prominent families of slave traders in the Portuguese empire from the seventeenth to the nineteenth century. The complex includes a small chapel, giving the place the name Morro da Cruz (Hill of the Cross). The building became an important point in the trafficking of slaves in the early nineteenth century: After the British and Portuguese signed a treaty to abolish the slave trade, the trade continued clandestinely, with the main point of departure for slaves moving from Luanda to this location south of the city and behind the Mussulo inlet, where it was hidden from the view of British patrol ships. For at least two decades this building was

Source: Kostadin Luchansky/Angola Image Bank (all pictures)

Source: Ana Tostões

AO

Mabílio M. Albuquerque Building « AO 04

23–29 Rua Major Kanhangulo, Luanda
1894

Located in the historical downtown area of Luanda, in Rua Major Kanhangulo (known as Rua Direita during the colonial era), the Mabílio M. Albuquerque company building was erected in 1894. The façade of the neoclassical building is organised symmetrically and topped by a large cornice and a small parapet, which is decorated with four human sculptures aligned with the four pilasters, which each feature a small capital and volute. This composition emphasises the central door in the axis of the façade. The ground floor has seven doors in semi-circular arches, and the upper floor has five French windows fronted with wrought iron guards. As in the typical *sobrado* houses that made up Luanda's main buildings until the end of the eighteenth century, the ground floor acted as the commercial area, the upper floor was the area designated for nobles, and access was through the centrally located door. *at et al.*

a central node for the Portuguese slave trade – the slaves that were trafficked from the interior of the country were held in its yard and forcibly baptised in the chapel before being loaded onto the slave ships. The Portuguese officially abolished the trading of slaves across the Atlantic in 1838; however, it continued in an illicit fashion. Brazil outlawed the import of slaves in 1850, and the Portuguese only outlawed slavery in all of their territories in 1869. After operating as the clandestine location of the sale of thousands of Angolans, the site was made the National Museum of Slavery in 1977. It still operates as a point of departure for boats – now carrying people across to the popular weekend beach spot of Mussulo Island. *cg/hp*

Source: Joost De Raeymaeker

Luanda City Hall ≿

Largo Irene Cohen, Luanda
Artur Gomes da Silva
1911

AO 05

Designed by the architect Artur Gomes da Silva and built from 1890 to 1911, Luanda City Hall features a classical symmetrical composition, with a central pediment and a cornice around the whole building. The entrance, in the central axis of the composition, juts out. The balcony on the upper floor is supported by circular arc spans that define an exterior entrance area. The City Hall is a symmetrical square volume with two floors around a central courtyard, where a cast iron staircase stands. Located on a high point of the city, the building acquires a monumental character when seen from the Largo do Mutamba. It has been a National Monument since 1981.　　　*at et al.*

Kinaxixe Market

Largo da Kinaxixe, Maculusso,
Luanda (demolished)
Vasco Vieira da Costa
1958

Vasco Vieira da Costa answered his first public commission with a project that was both a square and a building at the same time. Designed from 1950 to 1952 to challenge the colonial power, Kinaxixe Market was a place for trade but it also played a strategic role in the expansion of this area of the city. It was a longitudinal and horizontal volume with two inner rectangular squares, around which the different functional areas were systematised. On the ground floor were service and storage spaces, and on the first floor, commercial areas. The building was lifted from the ground by the pilotis and the double portico – structural and formal gestures that, together with the brise-soleil that adorned the first floor façade, attested to Vasco Vieira da Costa's time in Le Corbusier's office. Circulation was with

Source: Ana Magalhães (all pictures)

stairs and ramps. The promenade's architecture reached its high point in the roof terrace with porticos and sculptural volumes. The market was one of the most important modernist buildings in Angola. It was demolished in 2008. *at et al.*

AO

National Bank of Angola ⌄ | AO 07
135–169 Avenida 4 de Fevereiro/
Largo Saydi Mingas,
Ingombota, Luanda
Vasco Regaleira
1956

The National Bank of Angola stands out in the urban context for its monumentality and richness, which is enhanced by its prominent position on the seafront. Designed in 1956 by Vasco Regaleira, who mainly dedicated himself to religious architecture, it is an icon of the architecture of the Estado Novo regime from the late period of historicism, being inspired by classical architecture. Today, the National Bank of Angola bounds one side of a square – Saydi Mingas – and faces the Avenida 4 de Fevereiro, looking onto Luanda bay. It is predominantly a three-storey building, but on the corner between the square and the avenue, a higher cylindrical volume finished with a dome marks the entrance. Inside the entrance hall there is a monumental marble staircase decorated with traditional Portuguese blue and white tiles that depict the arrival of the Portuguese in the kingdoms of Kongo and N'gola in the fifteenth century.   *at et al.*

Source: Ana Tostões

Cirilo & Irmão Building » | AO 08
10 Rua Major Kanhangulo,
Ingombota, Luanda
Francisco Pereira da Costa,
José Pinto da Cunha
1958

The Cirilo & Irmão Building is the result of an investment in real estate by the Cirilo family, whose wealth came from coffee plantations in northwestern Angola. The young architects Francisco Pereira da Costa and José Pinto da Cunha designed the Cirilo & Irmão investment group headquarters in the capital in a modernist style. Located in Rua Major Kanhangulo, the Cirilo & Irmão Building is a ten-storey block with a double-height commercial area on the ground floor, offices on the first floor, and housing on the upper floors. The spatial generosity of the entrance – also a double-height space – is celebrated with a ceramic wall with African motifs. On the second, third, seventh, and eighth floors, it is possible to find duplex houses, and from the main façade it is possible to identify the kitchen through its tighter concrete grid. On the other floors, the kitchen is located near the horizontal galleries, where a small slab works as shading. The main façade is orientated southeastwards, receiving the morning sun filtered by a second skin. On the ninth floor, the terraces of the houses were once private, but nowadays these are closed and occupied, transforming the original image of the building. The vertical circulation elements – stairs and an elevator – are enclosed in a volume defined by

Source: Kostadin Luchansky/Angola Image Bank

Source: Kostadin Luchansky/Angola Image Bank

owners – the Universal insurance firm – justified the building's monumental character, and the architect was permitted to raise its height beyond the limit defined by the city's urbanisation plan. The main volume has nine floors, but extends sideways into a lower volume with six floors, creating continuity with the existing buildings. On the double-height ground floor, there is a commercial area under galleries that act as sun shades. The intermediate floor, designed for offices, comes out of the façade as a 'box' establishing the transition for five upper residential floors. In both volumes the roof is a large slab placed on top of pillars; this creates community spaces, including ateliers and living spaces in the higher volume, and a community laundry in the lower one. Stairs – within two main cores and on the exterior (the latter a service staircase) – and a horizontal make up the building's circulation elements. The façade is composed of a set of superimposed grids that create balconies and areas of shade. The chromatic differentiation intensifies the layering of various grids: the structure, the balconies, and the handrails. Francisco Castro Rodrigues modernist themes and suggestions for new ways of living can be seen in many aspects of this structure: the organisation of the houses; the mixture of housing, leisure, and work spaces within the same building; the design for an open horizontal gallery; the communal spaces on the roof; and also in the plastic expression of the structural elements, the use of colour, and the grids used to shade spaces and pathways.   *at et al.*

a concrete grid that allows filtered light and natural ventilation. This volume is set 4 m apart from the main building and connects to the horizontal galleries that link to the apartments. The horizontal galleries used to link to a transition hall between the public and private area, but this is now closed.   *at et al.*

Universal Building ⌄   AO 09

Largo Patrice Lumumba, Lobito, Benguela Province
Francisco Castro Rodrigues
1961

Designed by Francisco Castro Rodrigues in 1957, the Universal is a multifunctional, L-shaped building spanning two lots. The main façade faces a square in the downtown commercial area, Largo Patrice Lumumba. This prominent location and the high status of the building's

AO

Source: Ana Magalhães

Francisco Castro Rodrigues: The Architect of Modernist Lobito

Zara Ferreira

Francisco Castro Rodrigues (1920–2015) was born and died in Lisbon, Portugal. But his life belonged to the city that he helped to grow and develop: Lobito, Angola. As a militant member of the Portuguese Communist Party, he was pursued by the International State Defence Police (PIDE) during the Estado Novo (New State) dictatorship and was unable to find employment anywhere in Portugal. Like many other architects in the country at the time, he fought for 'the opportunity for architects to be treated as lawyers or doctors, with free will'. With Le Corbusier and modernist Brazilian architecture as his role models, Francisco Castro Rodrigues wanted to be a Modern architect – something which meant contributing, through urbanism and architecture, to a democratic, healthy, and happy way of living.

That is why, in 1953, he left for Lobito, where he lived for thirty-four years. As part of the Office of Colonial Urbanisation and as a member of the Cultural Committee, Disclosure and Tourism, he was responsible for transforming Lobito into a modern city. In its urbanisation plan, Castro Rodrigues applied the principles of the Athens Charter (which he had translated into Portuguese to be published in the magazine *Arquitectura* in 1948), organising the city according to the four vital functions: housing, leisure, work, and circulation. Through his architecture, he also explored the principles of the modernist movement, together with with local concerns, in social, economic, and climatic terms. In the Universal Building (designed 1957, finished 1961) – which he created as a kind of Unité d'Habitation, combining housing, services, and commerce, and which marked the entrance to the city with its mixed block of monumental scale – we can find an exploration of the Corbusian lexicon adapted to the tropical climate. The Flamingo Open-air Cinema (1963), with its colourful surfaces and undulating walls topped with zig-zag roofs, represents his idea of global design through the synthesis of the arts. In the Nossa Senhora da Conceição Church in Sumbe, we can see similar principles – ones that are clearly connected with the demand for continual fresh air and that take the form of walls ventilated with

Entrance to the Flamingo Open-air Cinema (1963), in Lobito, which features zig-zag forms
Source: EWV Archive / Ana Magalhães

Source: Ana Tostões

Comandante Saydi Mingas School (1967), in Lobito, with its grid walls for ventilation

Inside the Flamingo Open-air Cinema (1963), in Lobito, which is today largely abandoned but sometimes used as an informal primary school

grilles and targeted implementation. In the Comandante Saydi Mingas School (1967), with its permanently open walls, we see the high point of Castro Rodrigues' exploration of social and climatic principles. He advocated teaching fully outdoors where possible, because, should the teaching be bad, students could 'learn more through observing nature than by being subjected to great physical and mental effort'.

Aside from urbanism and architecture, Castro Rodrigues organised exhibitions; actively published in journals and magazines; was a prominent figure in *ciné-clubs*, radio, and other cultural groups; and was a professor at different levels of education. In this way, he contributed continuously to the cultural evolution of Lobito and its people. His cultural activism was a form of political intervention; but, more than that, he was a humanist collaborating with the population in the development of a good city.

Angolan independence did not make Castro Rodrigues return to Portugal like most other architects. Agreeing with the views of Agostinho Neto – who invited him to organise an architecture course in Luanda, in 1978 – Castro Rodrigues was invited to stay by the municipality of Lobito, so he could continue his widely valued involvement the city. He returned to the place of his birth in 1988 for health and family reasons. In the 1990s he received an award from Lobito in recognition of his outstanding contribution to its aggrandisement.

Source: Ana Magalhães (all pictures)

An exploration of Le Corbusier's ideas in a tropical climate: Universal Building (1961), Lobito

AO

Flamingo Open-air Cinema `AO 10`

Lobito, Benguela Province
Francisco Castro Rodrigues
1963

Located in the southwest of the city of Lobito, between the Atlantic Ocean and the mangroves, the Flamingo Open-air Cinema was designed, in around 1960, by Francisco Castro Rodrigues, for an audience of 1,200 people. It was the outcome of a private commission by the president of the Lobito *ciné-club*, the engineer Antonio Vieira da Silva. Displaying the new possibilities of concrete, the innovative building featured a formal freedom that was made feasible by the contribution of the railway structural engineer Bernardino Machado, who calculated the dimensions of the construction that provides the 'roof'. The main elements of this building are the V-shape 'roof' construction, which expands, at maximum length, over 16 m; the huge screen wall, and the console. Over the entrance is a smaller 'roof' structure articulated with the larger one, while a 'wall volume' divides the audience area from the exterior. This wall volume encloses several supporting functions within its wave-like forms and under its pointed roofs, and the colourful pavements establish a ludic and light atmosphere. The Flamingo Open-air Cinema answered the leisure needs of a 1950s colonial society; its functional programme and typology represents the upbeat atmosphere that was

Source: Ana Magalhães

A0

felt among the urban bourgeoisie of the Portuguese colonies before the Colonial War in the 1960s and early 1970s. As a specific response to the tropical climate, this cinema embodies a unique aspect of modernist heritage in Angola. Nowadays it is no longer a cinema, but is used as an informal primary school. *at et al.*

Source: Rui Grilo

Source: Ana Magalhães

Miramar Open-air Cinema ⩗   AO 11
Largo Alioune Blondin Béye,
Ingombota, Luanda
João Garcia de Castilho,
Luís Garcia de Castilho
1964

A classical amphitheatre located at the top of a hill in the Miramar District, the Miramar Open-air Cinema provides magnificent views towards the Bay of Luanda. Awareness of the topographical and geographical conditions of the site is fundamental to understanding the poetic dimensions of this work, which was designed in 1964 by the architects and brothers João and Luís Garcia de Castilho. It does not have the scale or capacity of fellow Luanda open-air cinema the Atlântico; instead, the expressiveness of its design is based on its delicate canopy, which partially protects the supporting services volume at the entrance. This canopy, a light wooden structure, is suspended from concrete columns by metal cables. The volume that houses the ticket office and bar is designed like a wall and defines the audience area. Its modernist architectural language is displayed in its multiple layering and colourful materials. Modernist collective life in Angola was very much connected to outdoor leisure activities, and this open-air cinema represents an exclusively Angolan typology.   *at et al.*

Atlântico Open-air Cinema » ⩗   AO 12
Rua Gregório José Mendes/Eugénio
dos Santos Street, Vila Alice, Luanda
António Ribeiro dos Santos,
Eduardo Paulino
1964

The monumental 1,500-seat Atlântico Open-air Cinema is located in a large square in central Luanda. It sits in the centre of its plot, divided from the street by a 'wall volume' which contains the entrance and ticket office. Formally characterised by a concrete structure that is defined by a system of triangular columns which rise above the roof to support the massive covering, the amphitheatre is open on two opposite sides and closed on the other two by the circulation areas and the screen. The main façade is symmetrically composed and defined by the access system for the top floor seats – ramps and stairs. The bar, cloakroom, and other supporting areas are on the ground floor.   *at et al.*

Source: Ana Tostões

Source: Joost De Raeymaeker

Source: Atelier Mulemba

Source: Joost De Raeymaeker

AO

Source: Joost De Raeymaeker (left); EMV/Paulo Silva (right)

Site plan

Prenda Neighbourhood Unit #1

`AO 13`

Rua dos Funantes, Prenda, Luanda
Fernão Lopes Simões de Carvalho
1965

In 1961, after his internship with André Wogenscky and Le Corbusier, Fernão Lopes Simões de Carvalho led a multi-disciplinary team at the newly created Urbanisation Office for Luanda. Simões de Carvalho worked in a context of demographic expansion and aimed to solve the city's lack of housing and to regulate its rapid and informal expansion. In his master plan for Luanda, Simões de Carvalho defined a hierarchy of use for the roads, assigning different rules for car routes and pedestrian lanes. He argued against zoning through functions, instead creating a system of neighbourhood units where living areas were grouped with the work, equipment, industrial, and commercial functions. This plan was intended not only for the city's new areas, but also for its lower part, where there were extensive traffic problems. Simões de Carvalho envisioned the solution to these as a road network consisting of two major highways – north-south and east-west – connecting the city centre to the interior of Angola and crossing four outer ring roads. Three large surface car parks were planned at the intersection of these major roads, near where one entered the lower part of the city. This plan was never carried out; instead it was used as a starting point for the implementation of the structural axis of the city and for the realisation of the plans for the Neighbourhood Units. Three of these were

designed for the Prenda *musseque*, two of which were constructed. Neighbourhood Unit #1 was proposed as 22 collective housing buildings over ca. 30 ha. Its urban plan, devised from 1963 to 1965 and co-authored by the architect Luís Taquelim da Cruz, was organised according to Le Corbusier's system of seven road types. The unit had two main winding pathways: a commercial street and a smaller one to access housing. Between these, public facilities were planned but never built. Dead ends were designed in order to access the individual family houses or the row housing. Between the collective housing blocks there are small squares. The T1 apartment and office towers are concentrated in the commercial street. Row houses for the middle class are in the northern area; the houses for the most impoverished are in the northeast, with another set of row houses below for the middle class; and in the west are the independent family houses for the wealthier classes. Simões de Carvalho planned 1,150 dwellings and a proportion of one third African to two-thirds European occupants. He hoped that, in time, this proportion would be reversed, contributing to the multiracial society he advocated. The road hierarchy, from the highways to the pedestrian routes, and the spaces created by buildings on pilotis were both designed to promote encounters between members of the community, fostering relationships to establish trust between different classes. *at et al.*

Sagrada Família Church AO 14

Largo da Sagrada Família, Maculusso, Luanda
António de Sousa Mendes, Sabino Luís Martins
1964

Organised by the Movement for the Renewal of Religious Art (MRAR), the Contemporary Religious Architecture exhibition took place in Luanda in 1959, advocating a modernisation of the traditional expressions present in religious architecture. Inspired by the show, a new generation of architects developed their own approach towards religious architecture. Situated in the Ingombota District of Luanda, the Sagrada Família Church is a symbol of this new era. António de Sousa Mendes and Sabino Luís Martins won this public commission in 1964, eventuallly designing the first church in Angola that adopted modernist geometric motifs combined with traditional elements such as mural paintings. *at et al.*

Source: Fabio Vanin

AO

Le Corbusier's Legacy in Angola

Ana Magalhães, Margarida Quintã

One of the common denominators in the works built in Angola during the 1950s and 1960s is a strong bond to Corbusian imagery and grammar. The main reason for this is that two of the most productive authors of the city of Luanda were Le Corbusier's interns in Paris. Vasco Vieira da Costa worked at the Rue de Sèvres atelier between 1946 and 1948, and later, between 1956 and 1959, Fernão Lopes Simões de Carvalho worked at the Boulevard Flandrin atelier as part of a team coordinated by André Wogenscky, developing large projects.   *am*

Vasco Vieira da Costa

The work of Vasco Vieira da Costa was instrumental in the development of Angolan architectural modernity. He was the forerunner of a generation of architects that settled in the country from the 1950s to the 1970s, and who left behind a strong legacy. All of his architectural designs were developed in Angola and dealt with site-specific concerns using both modern construction techniques and climate-responsive design methods. Vieira da Costa was born in 1911 in Aveiro, Portugal, but he soon moved with his parents to Angola, where his family had been living for generations. He worked as an illustrator in Luanda but his contribution to the 1938 Exhibition-Fair of Angola earned him a scholarship to complete

his education in Portugal. Therefore, in 1940, aged twenty-nine, he began studying architecture at the Escola de Belas Artes do Porto (EBAP). After completing the curriculum, he moved to Paris to study urbanism and graduated from the Sorbonne University of Paris in 1948. During these years, he was part of the founding group of the Atelier des Bâtisseurs, an interdisciplinary team set up by Le Corbusier for the commission for the Unité d'Habitation in Marseilles.

In 1949, he graduated from the EBAP with a master plan for a satellite city on the outskirts of Luanda. Satellite City #3 offered a solution to Luanda's urban development based on the establishment of autonomous peripheral towns designed according to modernist principles. At that time, design constraints imposed by the local climate were already at the top of Vieira da Costa's concerns. Therefore, Luanda's weather data was closely examined for input into the urban planning and architectural design.

Also in 1949, he moved back to Luanda to start his architectural practice and to act as a consultant architect for Luanda's town council (1949–1959). During this period, he filled several prominent public positions in the country. This continued not only during the Portuguese colonial period but also after Angola's independence in 1975. He worked for the Engineering Laboratory of Angola (LEA), both as

Source: Ana Tostões (all pictures)

Angola Engineering Laboratory (Vasco Vieira da Costa, 1965), Luanda

Public Servants Building (Vasco Vieira da Costa, 1965), Luanda

Source: Simões de Carvalho Archive, EWV

Caputo Market (Fernão Lopes Simões de Carvalho, 1962–1965), Cazenga Quarter, Luanda

a lecturer and an architect (1960–1982), and he founded the Angolan section of the National Syndicate of Architects (1970) and the Faculty of Architecture at Agostinho Neto University (1979).

Vieira da Costa developed exceptional works in Angola for about thirty years. He took public and private commissions and tackled different typologies and locations, among which a few stand out: the Kinaxixe Market (Luanda, 1950–1958, demolished in 2008), the LEA (Luanda, 1963–1965), the Public Servants Building (Luanda, 1965), the Ministry of Urbanism and Public Works (Luanda, 1965–1969) and the Academic Veterinary Hospital (Huambo, 1970–1974).

He created an articulated collection of systems for passive environmental control using a modernist lexicon and a plain rationality. Solar protection, natural ventilation, and rainwater drainage were central topics for the development of all of his designs. Vieira da Costa's thoughts on the relevance of local climate for the development of his architectural practice are expressed in all of his project descriptions. His writings on urbanism also show similar concerns. The notion of compromise can be found in a broader sense in Vieira da Costa's work. He mastered the art of making precise concessions in order to find the best possible design solutions and used the available construction techniques and materials with a radical economy of means. His architectural designs established successful compromises between climate and city, function and form, and reason and emotion.   *mq*

Source: Ana Magalhães

Rádio Nacional de Angola (Fernão Lopes Simões de Carvalho et al., 1967), Luanda

Source: Simões de Carvalho Archive, EWV

CTT Housing Block for post office workers (Fernão Lopes Simões de Carvalho, 1968)

AO

Fernão Lopes Simões de Carvalho

Fernão Lopes Simões de Carvalho, who was born in 1929 in Luanda, completed his architecture degree at the Escola de Belas Artes de Lisboa in 1955. After training at the Office of Colonial Urbanisation, he took an interest in urban issues, and in 1956, with a scholarship from the French government, he decided to go to Paris, where he joined Le Corbusier's atelier until December 1959. There he worked on the detailed project for the Unité d'Habitation in Berlin, and subsequently the Briey-en-Forêt Housing Unit. He also participated in the La Tourette Convent project and the Maison du Brésil. At the same time, he studied at the Sorbonne with Robert Auzelle.

These two vectors would be the basis of the consolidation of Simões de Carvalho's training and a determining factor in his work in Angola. On the one hand, there was the stark imprint of the large projects developed at Le Corbusier's ateliers during that period (and not only those in which Simões de Carvalho took part but also Chandigarh or Firminy) – the experience of building with *béton brut* and applying the Modulor system. On the other hand, there were the teachings of Auzelle, a critic of the Athens Charter. Simões de Carvalho's urban planning degree was completed in 1965 upon submission of a master plan for a fishermen's borough on the Ilha de Luanda. This project was based on the study of a wider urban structure within the zoning principles of the Athens Charter, yet it also reveals a sensitive understanding of the pre-existing elements and an attentive study of popular housing on the site.

In 1961, Simões de Carvalho founded the City of Luanda Urban Planning Office, leading a large multidisciplinary team and coordinating Luanda's urban plan. It was within this context that he designed the Neighbourhood Unit #1 (1963–1965) in the Prenda District. There he combined the Corbusian model – the 7V traffic hierarchy and a mixture of different housing typologies – with Auzelle's ideas – the integration of the population seen from a more humanistic and ethical perspective.

Simões de Carvalho's architectural work is closely connected to the plastic expression of *béton brut*, as is clearly shown in the Rádio Nacional de Angola Broadcasting Station (1963–1967), which is his most iconic project; in the terraced houses in Quilundo (1960), which are marked by the Catalan vault roofing; or in the works developed in Luanda's Cazenga Quarter – the Caputo Market (1962–1965), the Chapel (1962–1964), and the Care Complex, which included a social centre, health centre, crèche, and kindergarten (1963–1965); or in the CTT Housing Block for post office employees (1968). *am*

Source: Ana Tostões

Angola Engineering Laboratory ⚏ ⇗   `AO 15`

Rua Labouratório de Engenharia,
Prenda, Luanda
Vasco Vieira da Costa
1965

Located in a street specially designed to access it (Rua Labouratório de Engenharia), near the Prenda *musseque*, the Angola Engineering Laboratory covers a vast scale. The complex – designed by Vasco Vieira da Costa from 1963 to 1965 – occupies 7 ha of land, organised through orthogonal axes of planned green areas. The hierarchy of roads and footpaths on the site is defined by both the gutters that integrate and irrigate the green space, and the small squares between the built volumes that act as open community spaces. The built and open areas were determined by the organisation of the main function – the laboratories – and influenced by the topographical conditions, which necessitated a parallel implementation with the contour lines in order to minimise high earthworks. The complex is made up of four different typological groups. First, the various pavilions – such as geotechnical, roads and aerodromes – and structures that are set 30 m apart from each other for tests at the northern boundary, and limited by the construction materials pavilion in a perpendicular axis. Second,

the building housing the administrative departments and library, and the chemistry pavilion. The former is a three-floor horizontal volume of 135 × 15 m broken by the vertical volume for the stairs, and the latter a single-floor building designed as a wall. Third, the minor laboratories that face the entrance and shape the expressive main façade. These are oriented east to west, and small patios form their entrances. Fourth, the workshops for mechanical experiments in the northern area, near the secondary entrance. Despite these different typologies, the site still has a unity to it, as Vasco Vieira da Costa designed common elements for it, including the colours used for certain aspects of the volumes (orange, green, and white), the concrete grids, the shading slabs, the gargoyles, the structural components, and the wooden slats.   *at et al.*

Public Servants Building ⇙   `AO 16`

Rua Amílcar Cabral,
Maianga, Luanda
Vasco Vieira da Costa
1965

The Public Servants Building (Edifício Servidores do Estado) is one of Vasco Vieira da Costa's most important designs. Dated 1965 and designed to house Portuguese public employees who worked in the colony, the structure is oriented

Source: Ana Tostões

northeast to southwest, between Rua Amílcar Cabral, a street with heavy traffic, and Rua do Padre Francisco Gouveia, a smaller road that makes the transition to small scale housing. Requirements to complete the project at a low cost necessitated imaginative solutions and resulted in a rigorous design based on constructive accuracy and an approximation of the 'dry construction' concept. The structure's grand scale is provided by a long volume on top of a massive ground floor, which profits from the slope between the two streets, creating an open public space and almost doubling the building's volume. Access is from Rua do Padre Francisco Gouveia through two staircases connected with long distribution galleries. These galleries – semi-private corridors set 1.5 m away from the apartments' volume – establish a shadowing system. The gap between them and the main volume is interrupted only to allow the access to the apartments through a private space. The impression that the building is very long is strengthened through various methods: a play on light and dark volumes; the use of advanced and recessed plans; the inclusion of rough concrete grids; and a structure of transversal beams that extends beyond the building's limits. The latter also confers a rhythm and a brutalist expression on the structure. There are three different apartment typologies coordinated to maintain a constant volumetric game. The composition reflects the economy of space, featuring open living spaces with substantial dimensions, occupying almost half of the apartment's area. One of this building's innovations is the relation between living room and balcony: the large living room is a sheltered environment with doors that allow its isolation from the balcony; and the balcony – also large – is an indoor/outdoor environment. From the west, air enters through the balconies and bedrooms. From the east, the rooms open onto the exterior galleries. Today, the building has been extensively modified. Its public and semi-private spaces have been occupied and turned into either small apartments or commercial establishments. *at et al.*

Jessica Bonito

Typical floor plan

Source: Hans Engels

Source: Ana Magalhães (left and right)

Nossa Senhora da Conceição Church « ⌃   AO 17

Sumbe, Cuanza Sul Province
Francisco Castro Rodrigues
1966

Designed by the Portuguese architect Francisco Castro Rodrigues from 1960 to 1966, the Nossa Senhora da Conceição Cathedral overlooks the sea in in the city of Sumbe (formerly Novo Redondo). The church is composed of three main volumes: a rectangular prism for the bell tower, a triangular prism for the main area of the church, and a low cylinder for the baptistery. All three are united by a continuous base made from coated brick. The monumental gabled roof structure designed by the engineer Oliveira Resende is the church's most striking element, comprising massive concrete girders and coated fibre cement sheets. On the exterior are a series of triangular forms in reinforced concrete. As there is no glass in the roof openings, the interior space is not completely closed, allowing natural ventilation – a solution that is much explored in the work of Castro Rodrigues. A metal grid composed of triangular combs, the main façade lets in a film of light, while large, open stained-glass windows behind the altar allow the sea view to come through. The baptistery, a curved plane coated in relief tiles decorated by the sculptor Clotilde Fava, protects the baptismal font, seeking, according to the Modern Movement doctrine, global design through the integration of the three arts. The Nossa Senhora da Conceição Cathedral stands as an icon of modernist Angola. *at et al.*

Comandante Saydi Mingas High School   AO 18

Compão, Lobito, Benguela Province
Francisco Castro Rodrigues
1967

Comandante Saydi Mingas High School opened in 1967 in Lobito. Drawn by Francisco Castro Rodrigues, the initial plan defined a set of fourteen buildings that were developed with a progressive construction strategy. Only the first phase was built, however: two classroom blocks, the administrative building, and one of the gymnasiums. Located in the Compão Neighbourhood, on Avenida Sá da Bandeira, the school's four buildings lie in a northwest to southeast direction, perpendicular to the dominant winds. The administrative building is a two-storey horizontal volume situated at the entrance to the school enclosure. The classrooms are in two parallel blocks, each with three floors: the ground floors are defined by pillars, which help create covered yet fully ventilated exterior playgrounds; and on the first and second floors, the classrooms are perpendicular to the circulation gallery and the open concrete grid ensures the flow of air through the rooms. Situated in the northeast of the grounds, the gym is a large concrete portico structure – open but delimited by the locker room building. Its lower level is faced with brick tiles – the dominant material in the compound – and a fibre-cement roof marked by huge gutters completes the structure. The galleries, the lightness of the raised volumes, and the grid-faced façades not only provide an effective response to climatic issues, but also ensure the high school's functionality within the framework of modernism. *at et al.*

Source: Ana Tostões

Source: Ana Magalhães

technical and storage purposes. The main volume's northwest façade, where the main entrance is located over a bridge, is asymmetric: on one side, there is a series of vertical concrete elements that serves as a brise-soleil, extending the grid of the side façades; and on the other, there is a large opaque surface faced with glazed brick tiles. The building's inner structure is organised along a longitudinal corridor and through a sequence of patios. This is where the main work areas are. A secondary corridor, parallel to the main one, marks out the service areas, which are also limited by patios. The presence of such patios permits greater clarity in the organisation of the programme, while also ensuring, through light shafts, the lighting and ventilation of the circulation elements on the underground floor. On the side façades, a long grid wraps the rising volume. This concrete grid, set away from the glass façade, allows for ventilation and interior shading. *at et al.*

Rádio Nacional de Angola `AO 19`
Avenida Comandante Gika, Luanda
José Pinto da Cunha,
Fernão Lopes Simões de Carvalho
1967

Although it is an unfinished project, the Rádio Nacional de Angola Broadcasting Centre has a strong presence in downtown Luanda. Today's structure corresponds to the first stage of the original project, and contains a main studio block and a smaller workshop building. The studio block is a large rectangular volume, which is situated at the centre of the plot allowing for green areas around it. The topography of the land meant the building could have a main floor at street level and a semi-underground floor; the latter is used for

Source: EWV/Paulo Silva

Floor plan of the studio block

Ministry of Urbanism and `AO 20`
Public Works »
Largo da Mutamba, Ingombota, Luanda
Vasco Vieira da Costa
1969

Created from 1965 to 1969, the Ministry of Urbanism and Public Works Building has had various names. It has been known as the Alfredo Matos Building and the Mutamba Building, as it is on Largo da Mutamba, a main square in Angola's capital that in home to the Finance Ministry and Luanda City Hall. The construction is made up of several blocks and exhibits parallelepiped forms (three-dimensional shapes made up of six parallelograms). Taking the front facing north, towards the square, as the main façade, one can recognise a ten-storey parallelepiped block that is partially supported by pilotis. The end walls of the building are three narrow bodies, with the horizontal central body receding and underneath the other two. The nine floors of the tall volumes stand on top of three storeys of the horizontal volume, which is elevated on pilotis that seem to be organised asymmetrically when seen from the street. Inside this horizontal

Source: JJoost De Raeymaeker

AO

volume is an inner courtyard of around 300 m². When viewed from the south, the horizontal volume has two different fronts – the west part being short and narrow, and the east part being longer and wider. A gallery with a height of 4 m surrounds the base of the building, protecting pedestrians from the sun, providing ventilation, and allowing access to the commerce and service compound spaces. The south-facing side and the inside of the plot are interrupted by the staircase and lift zone. On the outside of the two vertical volumes is a sort of second skin that sits about 90 cm apart from the façade. Made up of concrete plates, this structure acts as a sun shade, while also obscuring the floors from outside view. It is therefore difficult to see how many floors the building has from outside. On some floors of the horizontal volume, the brise-soleil comes in the form of wooden slats. Inside the offices, there are small openings on the doors to improve the airflow. Solutions such as these highlight Vasco Vieira da Costa's two main concerns while working in the Portuguese colonies: ventilation and protection against excessive exposure to the sun. *at et al.*

AO 19   Rádio Nacional de Angola

AO

Academic Veterinary Hospital | AO 21 |

Avenida Nuno Álvares, Huambo,
Huambo Province
Vasco Vieira da Costa
1974

Huambo's Academic Veterinary Hospital (Hospital Escolar Veterinário do Huambo) is located in an expansion area of the city 3 km from the centre in a southeasterly direction. Its location was defined by the zoning strategy of the 1972 master plan, which respected the radial matrix of the city and predicted a major expansion to the south due to the topographical conditions and the railway line to the north. Designed by Vasco Vieira da Costa in 1970, this veterinary hospital was commissioned by Luanda University to integrate with the first higher education buildings in Angola. It is situated 300 m from Avenida Nuno Álvares, which links Huambo to Caconda, and set on a plot of 1,200 ha where the Institute of Veterinary Research of Angola (IIVA) already stood. The plan is organised in an 'H' shape, and despite the complex being composed of different volumes that enclose diverse functions in diverse formal gestures, the general perception is of a set of horizontally oriented volumes that stand in a northeast–southeast direction. Each one is 170 m in length. The functional programme is composed of classrooms, auditoriums, observation rooms, surgery rooms, and wards with cages of varying sizes to house the facility's animals. Between the months of October and April, torrential rain occurs on an almost daily basis in Huambo, so Vieira da Costa designed the complex to work with the climate. The guttering and downpipes concealed in the buildings are large enough for the storm water run-off. All of the exterior circulation is under the cover of large slabs that sit on inverted beams placed at intervals of 4.5 m. Seen together with the structure of the main volumes, these decisions expose the project's formal and technical strategies. There is a continuity between interior and exterior areas, and the roofs are often extended; the concrete grids have a certain transparency to them; all of the volumes are horizontally oriented; and the chosen materials – exposed concrete and orange and red brick – have a rough appearance that contributes to the assimilation of the buildings into the landscape.   *at et al.*

Source: Margarida Quintã (all pictures)

Dr António Agostinho Neto Memorial (MAAN)

AO 22

Praia do Bispo, Ingombota, Luanda
USSR Projects Institute et al.
1982, 2011

The MAAN Complex was initially designed and developed in the early 1980s by the USSR Projects Institute, after it was commissioned by the Angolan government as the final resting place for the first president of Angola. The construction process was interrupted due to the complex financial and social situation resulting from the civil war. The project was re-evaluated and partially redesigned in 1998, with construction restarting in 2005 and finishing in 2011. It officially opened on 17 September 2012. The memorial focuses on research and the preservation of Agostinho Neto's legacy, promoting the dissemination of knowledge of African culture and the arts. The complex's most striking element is the 120 m high central tower, which is flanked by two 60 m long building wings that house, among other things, the mausoleum, museum, archive, exhibition gallery, workshops and training areas, a small library, conference and press rooms, and a suite of protocol rooms that support state events. The outdoor areas cover a total of 18 ha, and include a 500 m long parade with seating for 2,000 people, a car park, and the main square.   *cg/hp*

Source: Kostadin Luchansky/Angola Image Bank

AO

Source: Kostadin Luchansky, Angola Image Bank

Source: GCIS South Africa

A Concrete Utopia: The Memorial to Neto

Nadine Siegert and Fabio Vanin on the Dr António Agostinho Neto Memorial in Luanda, which manifests (post)socialist dreams and memories

Since the end of the Angolan civil war in 2002, Luanda's inner city has been dominated by commercial high-rise buildings, which shape the profile of its coastline. Despite the fact that it has lost its status as highest building in the Angolan capital, one architectural structure still stands out: the Dr António Agostinho Neto Memorial (MAAN). This towering concrete edifice is the posthumously erected mausoleum of a man who was a doctor and a poet, and who led the Popular Movement for the Liberation of Angola (MPLA) during the struggle for national independence (1961–1974), eventually becoming the first president of the Republic of Angola in 1975. When Neto – who was politically aligned with both the USSR and Cuba – died in Moscow in 1979, the USSR was commissioned to construct a monumental mausoleum symbolising the greatness of the president in line with socialist tradition.

In 1980, Russian designers from the USSR Projects Institute started the conception of the building. Two years later, in 1982, the laying of the cornerstone took place, but because of several reasons – such as the long-lasting civil war, the economical and political crises in Angola, and the collapse of the USSR – the completion of the construction was postponed for more than twenty years. In 1998, before the end of the conflict, the Angolan government decided to restart the works, transforming the mausoleum into a cultural centre. Since then, a Brazilian architecture office, Willer and Associates, has led the conceptual redevelopment of the original plans. However, it was only after the necessary funds were obtained in 2005 that the works were taken up again, and the North Korean company, Mansudae, completed the construction in 2011. Mansudae, with a style that one could interpret as a translation of socialist aesthetics into a contemporary form for totalitarian regimes, is a well respected actor on the African continent. It has been commissioned for a number of monuments and commemoration sites in countries such as in Namibia, Zimbabwe,

Source: Erik Cleves Kristensen

The Dr António Agostinho Neto Memorial as a backdrop for the state and a city landmark: during the inauguration of João Lourenço in 2017 (left), and in Luanda's cityscape (above)

AO

Interior of the Dr António Agostinho Neto Memorial Complex:
central hall at the base of the tower
Source: Claudio Chocolate

and Senegal, and the interior design of the mausoleum clearly reflects the company's neo-socialist realist aesthetic.

The monument opened in 2012, and today its 120 m high concrete structure is still a public venue, as well as one of the most visible landmarks in Angola's capital. Situated in an area close to the bay in the Praia do Bispo Neighbourhood, and in front of the new National Assembly, the Memorial is in the new institutional monumental axis that was built following the processes of reconstruction and gentrification that have taken place since the end of the civil war in 2002.

Inside the mausoleum are Neto's remains. His body was embalmed by the same team of specialists that took care of Lenin's body in the prototype of the socialist mausoleum at Red Square in Moscow. As such, this commemoration centre freezes the ambivalent socialist past in a unified official history and becomes a form of national heritage. As in Lenin's mausoleum, Neto's sarcophagus is stored in a central block that also forms the pyramidal base for a constructivist tower made of juxtaposed concrete elements. The contrast between the rough and brutal elegance of the memorial's exterior and the airport-like interiors or the Dubai-like design of the surrounding area reveal the long history of the project and the shifting paradigms between the early independent government and the current one.

The basement is divided into three wings. At the central main entrance, a gallery displays twelve Mansudae-manufactured bronze sculptures representing different professions in neo-socialist realist style, and Neto's signature, engraved in bronze, is flanked by two of his most famous poems: *Pathway to the Stars* and *Farewell at the Moment of Parting*. In the corridor around the room that hosts Neto's body, forty-eight engraved bronze plates feature the eulogy to the former president and extracts of the speech he delivered on the day Angola was proclaimed independent, 11 November 1975. That wing also accommodates the other public rooms. The conference rooms, library, and other spaces appear to be mostly unused and seem like show rooms in an interior design store rather than a public centre that is in use.

We could claim that the current memorial to António Agostinho Neto is an ambiguous and almost schizophrenic object. Seen from a certain distance, the mausoleum is a completely abstract construction, a gigantic landmark that sits on the boundary

between sculpture and architecture. Its geometric shapes built of an indestructible material seem to be firmly skewered yet ready to move. The monument reveals a neutral iconography with no ornamentation, only plastic shapes. Contrastingly, the interiors and some of the elements of the outdoor space – such as the huge statue depicting Neto when national independence was declared and the flag hoisted – are devoted to the cult of the national hero, with relics, images, and statues representing the great leader.

If, on the one hand, Neto's memorial talks about a specific Eastern European tradition of monument building, in line with the purest constructivist tradition, then, on the other hand, the redevelopment of the area that hosts the memorial and the newly designed interiors present a visual language that reveals a symbolism and a world view which have both shifted. The cultural centre has to be a crowd pleaser, a place of a static memory that forces visitors to forget today's social contradictions in Angola. The bright socialist future embedded in the engraved words and in the beauty of the monumental building's original design clashes with the current social issues facing the country and its capital.

At present, the building could be seen as an architectural metaphor for a failed utopia or for the modernist melancholia of late socialism, when architecture was monumentalised to project oneself into the future. Moreover, it could be interpreted as part of Soviet modernism, referring to space travel and hyperbolic modernity. The building's most popular nickname is, unsurprisingly, the 'space rocket' (*foguetão*), and the same idea can be found not only in public discourses but also in contemporary artworks such as Kiluanji Kia Henda's *Icarus 13*, where the artist uses fiction to assign an alternative narrative to the memorial, transforming the mausoleum into a rocket named Icarus with a mission to travel to the sun. The work reflects a post-independence utopia, where socialist countries endeavoured to be as powerful as their Western antagonists.

This art project and others illustrate how the mausoleum – a monument and, as such, part of the cityscape – serves as a constant reminder of Angola's socialist past and its part in Cold War history, yet also refers back to previous ideas of the future – ideas that were epitomized in the Space Race, a gigantic power-driven military and scientific project on both sides of the Iron Curtain. As such, the Dr António Agostinho Neto Memorial is a post-socialist and even Afro-futuristic imaginary space that connects us to a recent past, when building and dreaming big were connected not only to economic power but also to political and architectural ideology.

AO

Source: Cláudio Chocolate

Source: Soares da Costa

BFA Headquarters AO 23
Avenida Amílcar Cabral,
Maianga, Luanda
Vinagre & Corte Real
2003

Built immediately after the civil war for the Banco de Fomento Angola (one of Angola's largest private banks), this building was one of the first of a wave of construction projects financed by private institutions during the opening up of the country's economy to international investment after the conflict ended. It is near the National Assembly and the emerging government quarter. The programme of this fourteen-storey building includes a branch on the ground floor, office space, three apartments, and underground parking. The façade treatment references some of the characteristics of Luanda's Tropical Modernist buildings – specifically the use of curtain wall glazing set behind horizontal elements that act as both shading to control heat gain and as light shelves, and the inclusion of a ground-level pedestrian colonnade that softens the street edge. The corner of the façade facing the main intersection incorporates an installation by the Angolan-born sculptor José Rodrigues – an aspect reminiscent of the integration of murals into many of Luanda's modernist buildings. *cg/hp*

Source: Kostadin Luchansky/Angola Image Bank

AO

Ponte 4 de Abril AO 24

Avenida Paulo Dias de Novais,
Catumbela, Benguela Province
Armando Rito, Pedro Cabral
2009

The Ponte de 4 de Abril (4th April Bridge)
is named after the date in 2002 when
the peace treaty that ended the civil war
in Angola was signed – a symbolic gesture given how many bridges were destroyed during the war to cut off connections between key territories. The project is representative of the massive
reconstruction of the national road network that has been underway in the post-
war period. Linking the important coastal
cities of Lobito and Benguela, and with
a large scale and prominent location in
relation to its surroundings, the bridge
has become an important local landmark. It is a full suspension cable-stayed
bridge with a semi-fan arrangement of
stays. The main span is 160 m long and

the two side spans are both 64 m long.
The stays are arranged in two planes and
constituted by bundles of individual pre-
stressed steel strands. They connect to
the pylons crossing them through sad-
dles, with the exception of the first three
stays, where traditional anchorages are
used. The structure was cast entirely
in situ. Armando Rito and Pedro Cabral,
the bridge's engineers, received the Secil
Prize for it – the first time this important
engineering prize was awarded to a structure on the African continent. *cg/hp*

Source: David Stanley

Pululukwa Resort

AO 25

Mapunda, Lubango City, Huíla
Art' Cittá
2012

With the reconstruction of the regional transport infrastructure after the civil war, a small tourism industry is beginning to emerge in Angola, and Pululukwa is considered to be one of the best tourism destinations of its kind in Angola. It also, unlike many other tourism ventures, explicitly references an 'African' aesthetic in its architecture and construction.

Settled within a stunning landscape, the property covers an area of 100 ha and incorporates accommodation, a restaurant, a spa, sporting and communal areas, staff lodgings, and a 'pedagogic farm'. The impact on the surrounding environment has been considered, with on-site water treatment and partial energy generation through solar and hydroelectricity. The central building, which houses the restaurant, reception, and communal areas, is composed of two wings, both with thatched roofs. The accommodation is split into three themed 'villages':

A0

the Kimbo Muhole houses, loosely based on the vernacular architectural tradition of the Lubango Region; the Santana village, which references the architectural traditions of the island of Madeira, the birthplace of the farm's owner; and, curiously, the Zulu Umuzi, apparently based on the structure of traditional Zulu villages. Though this resort is a welcome addition to the Angolan architectural landscape, it is a pity that the end result does not reflect a more in-depth engagement with the vernacular traditions of the area.   *cg/hp*

Source: Art'Città (all pictures)

A Brief Analysis of Angola's Housing Facilities from Independence to Today

Maria Alice Vaz de Almeida Mendes Correia

During the main part of Angola's colonial period, only public servants could purchase houses. In the late 1960s, this opportunity was extended to all Angolans and the Housing Foment Fund was created. However, the fund imposed financial conditions, and so buying a home was only affordable for a minority and largely did not benefit the indigenous population, who lived predominantly in rural areas with poor housing, infrastructural, and living conditions, and in informal settlements in large cities.

In the months leading up to independence in 1975, the worsening of the war between the major national liberation movements caused the flight of the bulk of the Portuguese to Portugal and with it the abandonment of their homes. This gave suburban and rural populations the chance to occupy these dwellings, offering better living conditions and job opportunities. This massive influx into Angola's big cities caused problems with the adjustment to urban life.

After independence, the population of Portuguese descent in rural areas moved to coastal cities such as Luanda and Benguela in a quest for stability and safety during the civil war, which lasted from 1975 to 2002. Despite the intense conflict, rural and urban plans for rebuilding were drafted with the intention of developing the most affected areas, focusing on education and healthcare. In the late 1980s, Luanda Province, one of the first areas to benefit from this intention, gradually started showing

Centralidade Housing Project in the northern province of Uíge
Source: Joost De Raeymaeker

architectural development, with unfinished buildings left by the Portuguese completed and houses distributed to civil servants. From the 1990s to 2000, many new buildings were constructed to house public servants. Joint ventures with private companies, including Cuban and Italian ones, generated new edifices in Luanda city, and in the privately owned neighbourhood of Talatona, banks financed the building of detached houses. The approval of high-rise buildings in Luanda's historic city centre before the end of the war favoured new private investment and led to many projects characterised by international collaboration and high tech construction techniques.

In recent times, social housing has been erected through donation and resolvable income. For example, in new cities such as Zango, which was built by private partnerships and Chinese investment. Recently there have been government initiatives in the capital targetting the poor living conditions in the Sambizanga, Cazenga, and Rangel districts.

Today, 62.3 per cent of the population lives in urban areas and 37.7 per cent in rural areas. The buildings registered over many of the country's provinces – from Uíge in the north to Huíla in the south – are a sample of the state's intention to minimise the housing problem and help combat property speculation. However, more action is required to develop the provinces to the sustainable level seen in Luanda today – for instance, improving education and creating master plans.

Informal settlements and one of the Prenda Neighbourhood
Units (Fernão Lopes Simões de Carvalho, 1965) in Luanda

Housing in Luanda: Metamorphosis

Filomena do Espírito Santo Carvalho

Luanda's tropical and semi-arid climate is characterised by high humidity (generally above 80 per cent) but relatively low rainfall (annual average 350 mm) and an average annual temperature of 24°C. The hot season, the longest of the year, is defined by elevated temperatures and humidity, accentuating thermal discomfort; however, the dominant southwesterly and westerly afternoon breezes create a favorable situation for achieving thermal comfort naturally in urban areas, with the use of architectural devices to provide ventilation. The centre of Luanda is the bayside downtown (also the historical centre), though the city has grown both north to south along the coast, and inland to the east. The majority of housing stock was built across three distinct eras: The Colonial Modern era before independence (1940–1975); the period of the civil war (1975–2002), and the postwar era (since 2002).

The late colonial period saw the creation of the Office of Colonial Urbanisation (1944), an official department that would create new urban plans and housing programs for the Portuguese colonies, and the deploying of a strategy of

Housing units in Luanda's Prenda District

differentiated housing for public servants, Portuguese settler merchants, and local populations. Typically, a public servant's house was composed of a principal space with annexes in the backyard for the servants. Portuguese settlers' houses tended to be built with local materials and adjusted to requirements, usually with commercial space on the ground floor and living space on the first floor; while housing for the local population was predominantly the in the *musseques* (slum neighbourhoods), in ground-level constructions in compounds with a yard and annexes. Urban

AO

Public Servants Building (Vasco Vieira da Costa, 1965), Luanda

housing was a key factor in the ideals of the Modern Movement. Luanda was a laboratory for modernist experimentation, with inhabitatation considered an essential concern when adapting the environment to the user. Some examples of this are the Neighbourhood Unit #1 in Prenda – collective housing blocks planned as a pedestrian-oriented, self-sufficient settlement – and the Public Servants Building, where climatic issues and a regard for social quality of life are evident in the use of slender columns, open spaces, continuous spans, sun shading and optimal solar orientation, as well as in the way the breeze is captured and used for natural ventilation.

The period of civil war following independence saw the gradual degradation of the existing housing stock through general ageing and lack of maintenance, damage resulting from the armed conflict,

Cuban-built housing erected using the Sandino System (Tecnogirón Construction, 1980s)

Source: Pedro Vemba Cidad

Aerial view of various new private housing projects made up of gated condominiums in Luanda's Talatona Neighbourhood
Source: Kostadin Luchansky

overcrowding due to the lack of housing and the resulting changes in the use of space and the alteration of building elements according to the different demands of the new users. New housing was essentially provided by the state and its international partners. High-rise buildings, mostly prefabricated, were built with the application of the Sandino System (consisting of concrete block walls with precast concrete stairs) and the Tunnel System (a precast building method where walls and slabs are simultaneously assembled in situ). Examples of both methods can be seen in Luanda's Cuban-built housing.

In the period following the end of the civil war in 2002, housing construction has had three strands: Firstly, large public sector projects; secondly, the private sector as an active player in a real estate market targeting large corporations and wealthy consumers; and thirdly, the continued growth of informal neighbourhoods in the peripheries. There has also been an increasing trend towards verticalisation, reinforced by the emergence of large state housing projects around Luanda, such as the Morar and Sapú projects (single storey), and the new cities

of Kilamba, Sequele, and Zango, which feature a mixture of medium buildings of four floors and higher and buildings of twelve to fifteen floors. These structures all share a typical spatial organisation and construction typology with medium sized interior spaces, small openings, simple walls of cement block masonry, basic aluminium framed openings, and a roof of sheet metal or concrete slabs. This presents a challenge in terms of interior thermal comfort, encouraging artificial rather than natural ventilation.

In Luanda city centre there is a proliferation of high rises with unshaded glass façades that are exposed to direct sunlight; these buildings are sealed off with centralized cooling systems and have no natural ventilation. This attempt to create generic (international) isolated interior spaces represents a total disregard for local climatic factors. Fans and air conditioning are necessary to reduce the discomfort inside a building, as its exterior (façade systems, wall types etc.) plays a lesser role in moderating the effect of the outside climate on the interior environment, and natural ventilation is disregarded. In Talatona to the south of the city, the private sector introduced

Aerial view of southern Luanda: the neighbourhoods of Belas, Talatona, and Benfica
Source: Kostadin Luchansky

Source: Joost De Raeymaeker

Emerging social life on the streets of the new city of Kilamba, Luanda Province

something new and (until recently) uncommon in Luanda – diversified examples of multi-family and single-family dwellings in gated condominiums. This housing applies construction methods suited to different cultural and climatic situations and reflects a decontextualised reality in the face of climatic, environmental, and user requirements.

Source: Pedro Vemba Cidad

New glazed high-rise, Luanda city centre

In the post-war period, informal neighbourhoods have grown rampantly, both in the interstices of (formal) urban areas and in the periphery, and reflect poor living conditions, with cement blocks generally the most used material. This is the most accessible and economical material available, yet it has a high transmission coefficient and a high degree of moisture absorption, both of which are disadvantages for thermal comfort. Minimal construction and habitability rules are not applied, bringing about poor functional organisation, reduced setbacks, spaces with insufficient ventilation and illumination, a lack of shading, and high thermal conductivity, and eventually resulting in unsustainable buildings. Existing norms and regulations are often ignored in this unchecked occupancy of space – particularly in the areas between buildings – meaning that the city becomes less porous and is unable to take advantage of the natural breezes, a situation that, combined with the use of generators, contributes to a reduction of air quality in the urban area. Further research on the development and modernisation of the production processes for construction materials and traditional building practices is necessary in order to develop sustainable and locally inspired responses to current and future housing issues.

The residential ciy of Kilamba is home to mixture of medium buildings (over four floors high) and taller buildings of twelve to fifteen floors

Source: Joost De Raeymaeker

Multi-use Pavilion
Kilamba, Luanda
Berger Arquitectos
2013

Constructed for the Hockey World Cup in 2013 (the first time the event was hosted by an African nation), the Pavilion can hold up to 12,000 spectators. One of the main driving ideas in the design and construction of this building was to ensure the future flexibility of use for various types of events (both sport and non-sport related), and has so far been relatively successful in this respect. This stands in contrast to the football stadiums built for the 2010 African Cup of Nations, which remain under-utilised due to their large size and relative inflexibility in usage, a problem that is persistent in the infrastructure built for these types of events throughout the world. Berger Arquitectos (based in Portugal) and Omatopalo (Angolan head contractor based in Lubango, Angola) delivered the project on a short time frame with a limited budget, the design solution being driven by the logic of functional low-tech operation. Energy consumption was minimised through the integration of natural lighting and ventilation strategies. The building's programme is organised vertically across four distinct levels: the central 'arena' is located on the below ground level surrounded by a perimeter of retractable seating (configured according to the event requirements), with technical and support facilities, underground vehicle access, and storage to the rear. The ground level is a large open concourse facilitating the majority of pedestrian circulation into and through the building — two thirds of the seats can be accessed directly from this ground floor concourse, minimising accessibility issues and lift requirements. The first floor houses the VIP and press rooms, leaving the remaining general seating areas on the second level. The building's visual identity is largely determined by the façade composition, which can be understood as a negotiation between rapid and cost effective solutions (both technical and spatial) and the desire to create an iconic landmark, given the international

Source: Fernando Guerra (all pictures)

exposure associated with the initial event. Functionally, the façade is a series of perforated metal screens that form a skin to shade interior spaces while regulating the natural ventilation, and refined simplicity is evidenced in the resolution of the details. The play of repetition and variation in the composition of the metal panels creates an engaging undulating effect, playing with the colour of the light with varied effects during the day and night. The final product can ultimately be understood as a design that is the marriage of the constraints of the project with the desire to create a strong aesthetic statement. *cg/hp*

Source: Art' Cittá/IMSA

Masuika Office Plaza AO 27

Talatona, Luanda
Art' Cittá
2014

This office building is the first phase of the Masuika Development, a development that will eventually include a total of three buildings, with a mixture of office, commercial, and residential space. It shows some new approaches to the typology of real estate development that has typically appeared in the new Talatona business district of Luanda in the last decade. Contrary to the typical approach that has emerged in this area of securing developments within high perimeter walls with one centralised entry and exit, this complex proposes a contrasting approach. The street frontage is opened up to the pedestrian through handrails, garden beds, and changes of level to define the property's perimeter and the creation of a small plaza area in front of the building. It will be interesting to

Source: Joost De Raeymaeker

Mwana pwo mask from the Lunda/Cokwe ethnolinguistic group, which symbolises the beauty of the Cokwe woman; it served as inspiration for the building's design

see how these outdoor spaces are used upon completion of the whole complex, and if this nod to a more inclusive public interface influences the area's future developments. The forms, materiality, and colours used and the graphic references integrated into the exterior refer the building's location in the Angolan context – again, this is not typical in Talatona, where most new buildings emulate distinctly international aesthetics. The most explicit illustration of this is the playful referencing of a Cokwe mwana phwo mask in the design of the eastern and western façades. *cg/hp*

Source: Art' Cittá/IMSA

Source: Joost De Raeymaeker

Vilavi Casas Evolutivas

AO 28

Vilavi, Huambo Province
2014

This cluster of ten houses was built in the town of Vilavi near the city of Huambo. It is one of many state-initiated social housing projects that fall within the Angolan government's *200 fogos* programme to build 200 dwellings in every rural municipality in the country. Many of these are based on the *casa evolutiva* (evolving house) model – with varying degrees of success. This model proposes that a basic structure is built initially and the inhabitants receive basic guidelines on how to best extend or add to it over time. This particular project is interesting as it uses local materials such as timber and adobe brick (the most common self-built construction method in this area); however, the typology has been modified by adding a large foundation of concrete-earth mixture, as well as wider overhangs in order to avoid the weathering of the adobe structure. This venture received the patronage of the local governor, and represents an attempt to achieve a higher quality and more contextually relevant typology than the standard responses emerging throughout the country. There is a didactic element to this project, as it demonstrates alternative methods of building with adobe that increase durability – hopefully these details will be replicated amongst the local communities in the future. *cg/hp*

Kapalanga School

Kapalanga, Luanda
Paulo Moreira, PARQ Arquitectos
2014

This school is located in Kapalanga, an informal neighbourhood on the outskirts of Luanda. The project emerged from a prolonged period of community work involving local residents and an NGO, and included rehabilitating an existing building comprising a front porch, two small offices, and three classrooms. These rooms have been renovated and one of the dividing walls was replaced with a movable wall, allowing two classrooms to be transformed into a single assembly hall, intended for student gatherings and community meetings. Each of the new classrooms is an independent building that faces the site's prevailing winds so as to allow air to flow through and around the rooms. Natural light and ventilation have been optimised, meaning the temperature is significantly lower inside the buildings. The landscaping attempts to consolidate existing uses. The broad shadows of the trees growing in front of the school are used as gathering places. At the back, a flat cement surface provides a good place for children to play games. A perforated perimeter wall increases the perception of security at the school, an issue that previously worried parents and teachers. The building was constructed using local materials and labour. Building techniques consisted of concrete frame structures and cement blocks for the walls, and steel structures and corrugated metal sheets for the roofs. The walls are finished with a type of plaster made from cement mixed with reddish earth. This material gives the school a textured appearance and creates a strong link between the various buildings and the ground. Both the materiality and the arrangement of the buildings allow the school to blend into the surrounding context. *pa*

Source: Paulo Moreira

Source: Paulo Moreira

Banco Económico Headquarters

AO 30

Avenida do 1º Congresso do MLPA, Ingombota, Luanda
Costa Lopes Arquitectos
2015

Source: Kostadin Luchansky / AIB

AO

Where the Banco de Fomento Angola (BFA) Headquarters represents one of the first new private commercial high-rise developments in Luanda following the end of the civil war, the more recent headquarters of the Banco Económico, an Angolan investment bank, represents a more recent example that is ambitious in scale. The building was designed by Costa Lopes, a prominent Angolan architecture firm who have been commissioned to design many new buildings in Luanda in the postwar period. The ground and first floor form a podium encased in curtain wall glazing, and house public areas including a bank branch and a multifunctional art gallery space. The higher levels of this twenty-six-storey building are wrapped in zig-zagging white panelling and made up of commercial office areas. The building faces an important intersection that connects the downtown with the government precinct and the National Assembly, and the ground levels are slightly recessed, producing a larger pedestrian space oriented toward this node. Previously on the site was the Escola 189, a heritage colonial school and public property that was sold and demolished in order to build this project – a process not uncommon in the creation of the new Luanda.   *cg/hp*

Understanding Informal Neighbourhoods: The Case of Chicala

Paulo Moreira

Studies on African cities, in particular on the subject of informal settlements, have suffered from over-generalisation in recent architectural practice and scholarship. Despite the obvious inclusion of Angola's capital, Luanda, in the 'sub-Saharan Africa' geographic context, I am developing a study on the type of urban order that is specific to this city. Within the complex urban and architectural topography of Luanda, the Chicala Neighbourhood is my chosen case study.

Chicala is a central informal neighbourhood, located in close proximity to the ocean. Such geographical circumstances have had unequivocal material consequences over the years. The area began to change rapidly and profoundly as civil war broke out (1975) and thousands of internally displaced people moved across the country in search of security and prosperity in the capital. Since 2002, when the war finally ended, the site has continued to grow. But in the context of the great urban ambitions that followed the end of a long-lasting conflict, it became subject to multiple pressures.

Chicala is representative of the irreversible transformations seen in Luanda in the post-war period: the neighbourhood is situated at the confluence of several large scale urban regeneration projects and it is now experiencing a gradual process of evacuation and replacement by high-standard financial, residential, and leisure districts. My research emerged from dissatisfaction with the results of the strategy of clearing this entire neighbourhood and relocating its inhabitants to peripheral resettlement colonies. As the dispersal process continued, I considered it urgent to record and understand Chicala before it was destroyed.

Given the magnitude of Luanda's current oil-fuelled boom, the city has attracted the attentions of numerous architects, planners, and researchers in recent years. But the bulk of ongoing urban projects and studies often lacks discussion of the contribution of informal settlements to the city. Instead, existing studies mostly focus on Portuguese colonial architectural and planning heritage. Those accounts that do pay attention

Chicala and its surroundings photographed from its highest building
Source: Paulo Moreira

Source: Paulino Damiao

Members of the Chicala Observatory, an archive of the history and urban culture of Chicala

to informal settlements, mostly from a social sciences perspective, primarily emphasise the explanation of current events. I found that often the historical context of any particular informal settlement is framed in as little as a chapter, or half a page, or a paragraph, or even a sentence, in existing research on Luanda. There is a void in the way the history of the city is being told. The widespread misconception that Luanda did not produce any significant human settlements (or that Angola did not produce any significant cities) before the arrival of

the Portuguese is the result of the denial of African history by nineteenth and twentieth century colonialists. My aim is to challenge this vision.

Through the deciphering of this particular case, Chicala, I try to present informality as a coherent possibility, which deserves to occupy its rightful place in Luanda's post-colonial history. I question the impacts of Angola's current neoliberal trajectory, which shows little consideration for local forms of territorial appropriation. Hidden within the conception of a purified world-class city

A vibrant stall in the lively market in Chicala's main street

Source: Paulino Damião

lies a cruel indifference to the plight of the underprivileged citizens, which manifests itself in coercive evictions and displacements to colonies outside the city. Given this context, how can a socially and ethically-engaged architect intervene? There are no magic formulae for approaching the informal city. But a collaborative and inclusive approach seemed to be the right way to tackle the subject. In 2011 and 2012, I organised workshops with architecture schools. These workshops involved the mobilisation of many constituents of the complex fabric of Chicala and Luanda: the local authorities in supporting our work, the residents in consenting to describe their lives and show us their houses, the students in empathising with the people and documenting their experiences. In 2012, during the second workshop, I was invited by Dr Isabel Martins, the head of architecture at Universidade Agostinho Neto, to apply to the university's annual research fund. The fund would institutionalise our initial collaborations. Together, we formed the Chicala Observatory research cluster as a guarantee of institutional legitimacy in Angola.

The Chicala Observatory is an archive of the history and urban culture of Chicala. The project takes the form of various open access components, which complement one another: a physical archive (displayed at the architecture school),

an interactive website (www.chicala.org), and public presentations (lectures, exhibitions, and publications). All of these elements are running simultaneously. Their aim is to present the urban and social character of this area of the city, which is gradually disappearing, and about which there is still a widespread lack of knowledge. The study also seeks to understand the nature of the neighbourhood's reciprocal relationship with the city as a whole.

Chicala, along with any other Luanda neighbourhood, exists because of a history of urban development that is worth documenting. This study does not simply present a study of informal urbanism. It seeks a broader understanding of cities as hybrid territories, conceived of as spatial, political, and social networks. In this respect, Chicala can be compared to segregated neighbourhoods elsewhere, and Luanda is no different from Johannesburg, London, New York City – or any other city in which the urban poor have been progressively pushed to the outskirts for the sake of a homogenised global culture.

The project contributes to highlighting the proactive role that architects and the academic community can play in the context of rapid transformation in Luanda. It is in itself a means of communication with the population of Chicala, Angolan civil society, and the outside world. The Observatory has fomented civic responsibility and social solidarity among participants (students, residents, and professionals within and beyond the neighbourhood). The solidarity which it so readily instigated appears to have generated some promise of symbiosis between the neighbourhood and the city.

The Observatory adopts a different approach to that of most recent work on the history and urban development of Luanda with regard to both the characteristics of the study site and the methodology employed. The project brings together architectural research practices (including technical representation of architectural and urban forms) and social science techniques (using surveys and participatory methods).

The Chicala Observatory has contributed to increasing the inclusion of informal neighbourhoods in the teaching and professional practice of architecture. It has also helped to encourage public debate on the place of urban informality in Luanda. Some of the primary spatial and social characteristics of the Chicala neighbourhood recorded in this study have already vanished, due to the ongoing urban transformation process.

Source: The Chicala Observatory/Prompt Collective

3D-model of part of Chicala's main street

The Chicala Observatory, hence, contributes to strengthening and consolidating the collective memory of the city of Luanda. Besides the documentary nature of the project, focusing on this specific neighbourhood, we hope that the manual of participatory practices formulated by the Chicala Observatory may be adapted to other urban contexts in Angola, Africa, and beyond.

AO

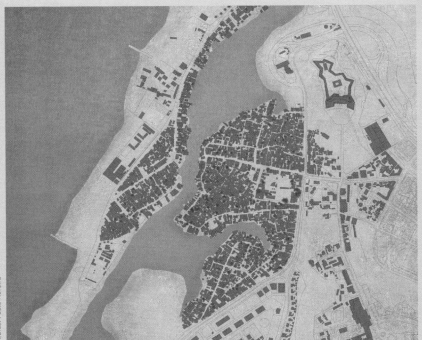

Source: Paulo Moreira

Chicala, in the Angolan capital, Luanda, is in close proximity to the city centre and the sea

Working against the Tabula Rasa

Helder Pereira and Coral Gillett on the importance of context

Historically, the modernist project as it was implemented in Angola was intimately tied to colonialism, and the 'universalist' ideals it embodied effectively meant the further erasure of that which existed physically, socially, and culturally. Angola and other Portuguese colonial spaces were seen as a *tabula rasa* (blank slate) for the creation of a new society or a new world. Today, in the post-independence and post-war reconstruction, the built environment is changing at incredible speed, with the majority of the large construction projects underway designed by actors with very little experience in Angola and conceptualised within a void – Angola remains a *tabula rasa*. Rather than reflecting an exploration of local culture(s), climates, or existing architectural heritage, these new buildings could exist anywhere in the world, and as such belong to no place: the universalism present in the Modern Movement continues under capitalism.

We assert that there is an imperative for design practices in Angola today to take context as the starting point for any intervention. In our own practice, we attempt to create the possibility for the emergence of contemporary identities and aesthetic languages that are born out of local references and to bring the social, cultural, and economic realities that are lived every day into conversation with design and architecture. In attempting to counter universalist tendencies we are influenced by Arturo Escobar's idea of the 'pluriverse'[1] – there are other ways to be 'modern' or contemporary without negating the past or the present, acknowledging that the culture(s) that exist in a place do not need to be extinguished in order to become modern. The following projects are attempts to put these ideas into practice: two small-scale ephemeral interventions that attempt to create a platform for dialogue about identity.

The temporary pavilion that was created to house the Angolan representation at the World Urban Forum in Medellín, Colombia, in 2014 used scaffolding to create a geometric skeleton. Not only a pragmatic way to create a structure that could be demounted and reused at other events, the materiality references the omnipresent scaffolding in many of Angola's urban centres today and the lived reality of these centres being cities under (re)construction. Panels with graphic content were integrated into the geometry to create a shell: the patterning on the exterior nods to the *samakaka* (a pattern originally used in traditional fabrics from southern Angola but now found across the country in the colours of the national flag – in the popular imagination it represents something particularly Angolan, surpassing differentiation based on region or ethnic group), presenting a singular gesture and alluding to the necessity to build a cohesive nation with uniform values. The experience of the interior, however, reveals the complexity of the structure and the diversity of experiences and realities lived in such a nation – paired panels show on one side the housing projects and on the other portraits of their residents, attempting to give a human face to the individuals that make up this 'nation under (re)construction'.

Source: Sergio Gómez

Angolan Pavilion, World Urban Forum 2014

Source: Joost De Raeymaeker

Exhibition at the National Museum of Anthropology, Coqueiros, Luanda

AO

The second exhibition design project is housed in the National Museum of Anthropology. The driving idea was to bridge the gap between conservation and innovation – to create a dynamism that challenges the notion that it is only that which existed in the past or is 'dead' that ends up in a museum. We symbolically drew on the 'traditional' in order to inspire the creation of the contemporary and desirable, to create a dynamism that posits these objects and the culture and traditions that they embody as part of (and inspiration for) vibrant, living, and evolving cultures. Photographs were employed in a didactic manner to bring the pieces on display to life – pieces which are still found in use when travelling through the countryside today. Motifs were selected from various pieces and abstracted to create the graphic language of the exhibition. The project involved the partial recuperation of the interior of one wing of the historic building, itself is an interesting reflection of the changing social and political dynamics in Luanda: a seventeenth century house probably built with slave labour, it has been an aristocratic house; housed the colonial era diamond company Diamang and now houses the National Museum of Anthropology. The intervention into the existing built structure was minimal, with exhibition elements reading as 'insertions' within this historic shell. The display structures were fabricated on a tight time frame with local material and labour, negating the possibility of importing structures (which is so often the easiest solution). How can small-scale interventions such as these inform a different type of practice? Much of the development that is underway in Angola is defined by visions borrowed from elsewhere: again, the *tabula rasa*. While this can be considered appropriate in the face of a short-term necessity to rapidly rebuild, the outcome will always be unsustainable if it is not adequately adapted to this historic, economic, social, cultural, and environmental context. We have arrived at the point in the reconstruction process that demands reflection on what is being (re)built: we now need to reimagine and redefine the long term vision that determines what sort of futures we are creating, and whether they are appropriate to our context. There must be local creative input into this vision, ideas that are generated and debated here: this is the only way that 'development' or 'progress' can have a meaningful and effective impact. In order to be able to participate in this conversation, we architects and designers must move our practices beyond instrumentalist service-provision and equip ourselves with the skills necessary to communicate with and engage other disciplines in the creation of a critical multidisciplinary community and platform for possible futures.

Notes
1   Arturo Escobar, 'Sustainability: Design for the Pluriverse', *Development*, 54/2 (2011), pp. 137–140.

Mixed used residential, office and retail building
in Lubango, Huíla Province (Promontorio, 2016)

Source: Fernando Guerra/FG+SG

Sixth floor residential plan

Source: Promontorio

AO

Selected Bibliography

This list contains literature directly cited or referenced in this volume.
A full bibliography for all volumes is available in volume 1.

Ahyi, Paul, 'Préface' in Yves Marguerat, *L'architecture française et l'oeuvre de Georges Coustère au Togo* (Paris and Lomé, 2000).

Almeida, André Freire de, 'Arquitectura em Clima Tropical: Viagem à Obra de Francisco Castro Rodrigues em Angola', master's dissertation, University of Coimbra, 2012.

Aravena, Alejandro, 'It's Time to Re-think the Entire Role and Language of Architecture', *The Guardian* (20 Nov. 2015), www.theguardian.com/cities/2015/nov/20/rethink-role-language-architecture-alejandro-aravena, accessed 26 April 2016.

Babina, Lucia, et al., *Douala in Translation: A View of the City and Its Creative Transformative Potentials* (Rotterdam, 2007).

Baduel, Pierre Robert (ed.), *Habitat, État, Société au Maghreb* (Paris, 1988).

Bangui, Thierry, ,L'habitat des quartiers aéroportuaires des métropoles africaines (Bamako, Bangui, Brazzaville et Dakar): L'exemple de Bangui (Rép. Centrafricaine)', doctoral thesis, University of Provence, Aix-en-Provence, 2004.

Bangui, Thierry, 'L'architecture coloniale du centre-ville de Bangui (Rép. Centrafricaine): Essai sur un patrimoine urbain en décadence', *Les Cahiers d'Outre-Mer* 261:1 (2013), pp. 105–122.

Beeckmans, Luce, 'Agency in an African City: The Various Trajectories through Time and Space of the Public Market of Kinshasa', in Karel A. Bakker (ed.), *Proceedings of African Perspective 2009, The African City CENTRE [Re]sourced* (Praetoria, 2010), pp. 115–129.

Bourriaud, Nicolas, *Relational Aesthetics*, trans. Simon Pleasance and Fronza Woods, with Mathieu Copeland (Dijon, 2002).

Castelo, Cláudia, 'O Luso-Tropicalismo e o Colonialismo Português Tardio', Buala (5 March 2013), www.buala.org/pt/a-ler/o-luso-tropicalismo-e-o-colonialismo-portugues-tardio, accessed 29 Nov. 2014.

Centre Pompidou and Cinqalbre, Olivier (eds), *Jean Prouvé: La Maison Tropical – The Tropical House* (Paris, 2009).

Coquery-Vidrovitch, Catherine, *Histoire des villes d'Afrique Noire: Des origines à la colonisation* (Paris, 2016).

Corkin, Lucy, *Uncovering African Agency: Angola's Management of China's Credit Lines* (Farnham, 2013).

Cotarelo, Ramón, 'Las construcciones religiosas en Guinea Ecuatorial', minutes of the Patrimonio Guinea 2020 symposium, 2015.

D'Olivo, Marcello, and Mainardis De Campo, Piero, *Ecotown Ecoway: Utopia ragionata* (Milan, 1986).

Delpey, Roger, *Affaires centrafricaines: Quand la Centrafrique bougera, l'Afrique explosera ...* (Paris, 1985).

Dequeker, Paul, et al, *L'Architecture tropicale: Théorie et mise en pratique en Afrique tropicale humide* (Kinshasa, 1992).

Domingos, Nuno, and Peralta, Elsa, 'A Cidade e o Império', in Nuno Domingos and Elsa Peralta, eds, *Cidade e Império: Dinâmicas Coloniais e Reconfigurações Pós-Coloniais* (Lisbon, 2013), pp. IX–L.

Dulucq, Sophie, *La France et les villes d'Afrique noire francophones: Quarante ans d'intervention, 1945-1985* (Paris, 1997).

Ellong, Epée, and Chehab, Diane, *The African Dwelling from Traditional to Western Style Homes* (Jefferson, NC, 2019).

Escobar, Arturo, 'Sustainability: Design for the Pluriverse', *Development*, 54/2 (2011), pp. 137–140.

Fernandes, Ana Silva, Fernandes de Sá, Manuel, and Fernandes Póvoas, Rui, 'A Bittersweet Inheritance: The Cocoa Islands of São Tomé and Príncipé from Colonial Hegemony to Developing Microstate', minutes of the 2nd Conference of the Portuguese Network of Urban Morphology: Urban Morphology in Portuguese-speaking Countries, Lisbon, ISCTE, 5–6 July 2012.

Fernandes, J. M., 'As Roças de São Tomé e Príncipe: Valor urbanístico e arquitectónico', in José Manuel Fernandes (ed.), Arquitectura e urbanismo na África Portuguesa (Lisbon, 2005), pp. 37–53.

Fernandes, Walter, and Hurst, Miguel, Angola Cinema: A Fiction of Freedom – Uma Ficção da Liberdade (Göttingen, 2015).

Frobenius, Leo, Ethnographische Notizen aus den Jahren 1905 und 1906, vol. iii: Luluwa, Süd-Kete, Bena Mai, Pende, Cokwe, ed. Hildegard Klein (Stuttgart, 1988).

Fry, Tony, Becoming Human by Design (London, 2012).

Geary, Christraud M., and Ndam Njoya, Adamou, Mandou Yenou: Photographies du pays Bamoum, royaume ouest-africain, 1902-1915 (Munich, 1985).

Geary, Christraud M., and Smithsonian National Museum of African Art, Images from Bamum: German Colonial Photography at the Court of King Njoya, Cameroon, West Africa, 1902-1915 (Washington, DC, 1988).

Gondola, Charles Didier, Villes miroirs: Migrations et identités urbaines à Kinshasa et Brazzaville, 1930-1970 (Paris, 1996).

Guaita, Ovidio, La maison colonial (Paris, 1999).

Guilloux, Tristan, 'The Maison "Tropique": A Modernist Icon or the Ultimate Colonial Bungalow?', Fabrications: The Journal of the Society of Architectural Historians, Australia and New Zealand, 18/2 (December 2008), pp. 6–25.

Guionie, Philippe, and Kelman, Gaston, African Ex-soldiers (Aubagne, 2006).

Guionie, Philippe, Swimming in the Black Sea (Paris, 2014).

Hamadeh, Shirine, 'Creating the Traditional City: A French Project', in Nezar AlSayyad (ed.), Forms of Dominance: On the Architecture and Urbanism of the Colonial Enterprise (Aldershot, 1992), pp. 241–259.

Henriques, Isabel de Castro, Percursos da Modernidade em Angola: Dinâmicas comerciais e transformações sociais no século XIX (Lisbon, 1997).

Henriques, Isabel de Castro, and Pais Vieira, Miguel, 'África – Visões do Gabinete de Urbanização Colonial, 1944–1974: Uma Leitura Crítica', Buala (17 March 2014), www.buala.org/pt/cidade/africa-visoes-do-gabinete-de-urbanizacao-colonial-1944-1974-uma-leitura-critica, accessed 27 Nov. 2014.

Houvounsadi, Jonas, et al., Douala, capitale économique: L'architecture (Douala and Lyon, 2011).

Jan van Eyck Academie (ed.), Brakin: Brazzaville-Kinshasa, Visualising the Visible (Zurich and Maastricht, 2006).

Kultermann, Udo, Neues Bauen in Afrika (Tübingen, 1963).

Lagae, Johan, and De Raedt. Kim, 'Building for "l'Authenticité": Eugène Palumbo and the Architecture of Mobutu's Congo', Journal of Architectural Education, 68/2 (Oct. 2014), pp. 178–189.

Lagae, Johan, and Touliers, Bernard (eds), Kinshasa (Brussels, 2013).

Lagae, Johan, et al., Claude Laurens: Architecture Projets et Realisations de 1934 à 1971 (Ghent, 2001).

Lauber, Wolfgang, 'Klimagerechte Architektur in den afrikanischen Tropen. Eine Untersuchung am Vorbild der traditionellen Architektur des Regenwaldes in Kamerun und der Savanne in Mali', Dr. Ing. dissertation, Fachhochschule Konstanz, 2003.

Lauber, Wolfgang, *Paläste und Gehöfte im Grasland von Kamerun: Traditionelle Holzarchitektur eines westafrikanischen Landes* (Stuttgart, 1990).

Leprun, Sylviane, and Sinou, Alain (ed.), *Espaces coloniaux en Afrique noire* (Paris, 1984).

Lulle, Thierry, 'Le Togo', in Jacques Soulillou, ed., *Rives coloniales: Architectures, de Saint-Louis à Douala* (Paris, 1993), pp. 170–205.

Marguerat, Yves, *L'architecture française et l'oeuvre de Georges Coustère au Togo* (Paris and Lomé, 2000).

'Maison préfabriquée type tropique', *Techniques et Architecture*, 5–6 (1952), p. 12.

Malaquais, Dominique, *Architecture, pouvoir et dissidence au Cameroun* (Paris, 2003).

Martins, Maria João, 'No Sobrado Sobre a Baía: Retrato da Burguesia de Luanda no final do Século XIX', *Camões: Revista de Letras e Culturas Lusófonas*, 1 (April–June 1998), pp. 46–53.

Mbembe, Achille, 'Decolonizing Knowledge and the Question of the Archive', WISER: Wits Institute for Social Research, University of the Witwatersrand (2016).

Mbembe, A., *Sortir de la grande nuit: Essai sur l'Afrique décolonisée* (Paris, 2010).

Milheiro, Ana Vaz, 'Africanidade e Arquitectura Colonial: A casa projectada pelo Gabinete de Urbanização Colonial (1944–1974)', *Caderno de Estudos Africanos*, 25 (2013), pp. 121–139.

Milheiro, Ana Vaz, 'Casa portuguesa? Sempre! Mas portuguesa e ultramarine: Gabinete de Urbanização colonial e as habitações tropicais', paper, 9th Docomomo Brazil seminar, 'Interdisciplinaridade e experiências em documentação e preservação do patrimônio recente', Brasília, June 2011.

Monte, Maria Manuela Alfonso da, 'Urbanismo e Arquitectura em Angola: De Norton de Matos à Revolução', PhD thesis (revised), Technical University of Lisbon, 2013.

Nascimento, Augusto, *Poderes e quotidiano nas roças de São Tomé e Príncipe de finais de Oitocentos a meados de Novecentos* (Lisbon, 2002).

Nelson, Steven, *From Cameroon to Paris: Mousgoum Architecture in and out of Africa* (Chicago, 2007).

Njoh, Ambe J., and Bigon. Liora, 'Germany and the Deployment of Urban Planning to Create, Reinforce and Maintain Power in Colonial Cameroon', *Habitat International* 49 (2015), pp. 10–20.

Njoh, Ambe J., *Planning in Contemporary Africa: The State, Town Planning and Society in Cameroon* (Ashgate, 2004).

Njoya, *Histoire et coutumes des Bamum [History and Customs of the Bamum]*, trans. Henri Martin, Populations 5 (Douala, 1952).

Pabois, Marc et al., *Architecture coloniale et patrimoine: L'expérience française* (Paris 2005).

Osayimwese, Itohan. 'Architecture and the Myth of Authenticity during the German Colonial Period', in *Traditional Dwellings and Settlements Review*, 24:2 (2013), pp. 41–52.

Pape, Duarte, and Andrade, Rodrigo Rebelo de, *As Roças de São Tomé e Príncipe* (Lisbon, 2013).

Pereira, José Maria Nunes, 'Mário de Andrade e o Lusotropicalismo', Centro de Estudos Afro-Asiáticos, Universidade Candido Mendes, Rio de Janeiro, 2000, bibliotecavirtual.clacso.org.ar/ar/libros/aladaa/nunes.rtf, accessed 12 December 2014.

Pinther, Kerstin, et al., *Afropolis: Kairo, Lagos. Nairobi, Kinshasa, Johannesburg* (Cologne, 2010).

Pinto, Alberto Oliveira, *História de Angola: Da Pré-história ao Início do Século XXI* (Lisbon, 2015).

Plissart, Marie-Françoise, and De Boek, Filip, *Kinshasa: Tales of the Invisible City* (Leuven, 2005).

Rodrigues, Francisco Castro, *Um Cesto de Cerejas: Conversas, Memórias, uma Vida*, introduction and notes by Eduarda Dionísio (Lisbon, 2009).

Rodrigues, Inês Lima, 'Quando a habitação colectiva fez cidade: O caso de Luanda Moderna', in Roberto Goycoolea Prado and Paz Nuñez Martí (eds), *La Modernidad Ignorada: Arquitectura moderna de Luanda* (Alcalá, 2011).

Rubin, Robert, 'Preserving and Presenting Prefab: Jean Prouvé's Tropical House', *Future Anterior, Journal of Historic Preservation, History, Theory, and Criticism*, 2/1 (Summer 2005), pp. 30–39.

Sinou, Alain, et al., *Les villes d'Afrique noire: Politiques et operations d'urbanisme et d'habitat entre 1650 et 1960* (Paris, 1989).

Soulillou, Jacques (ed.), *Rives coloniales: Architectures, de Saint-Louis à Douala* (Paris, 1993).

Sousberghe, Léon de, 'Kombo-Kiboto. Near Njinji (Kasaï)', 1955, Eliot Elisofon Photographic Archives, National Museum of African Art, Smithsonian Institution, EEPA 1999-100086.

Strother, Z. S., 'Architecture against the State: The Virtues of Impermanence in the Kibulu of Eastern Pende Chiefs in Central Africa', *Journal of the Society of Architectural Historians*, 63 (2004), pp. 272–295.

Tati, Gabriel, 'Brazzaville', in Simon Bekker and Göran Therborn, *Power and Powerlessness: Capital Cities in Africa* (Cape Town and Dakar, 2011), pp. 103–118.

Thornton, John K., and Heywood, Linda M., *Central Africans, Atlantic Creoles, and the Foundation of the Americas, 1585-1660* (Cambridge and New York, 2007).

Tostões, Ana (ed.), *Modern Architecture in Africa: Angola and Mozambique* (Lisbon, 2013).

Toulier, Bernard, and Renoux, Bernard, *Brazzaville-la-Verte Congo* (Brazzaville and Nantes, 1996).

Toulier, Bernard, et al., *Kinshasa: Architecture et paysage urbains* (Paris, 2010).

Vaisse, Christian, and Barat, Christian, and Augeard, Yves, *Maisons créoles de la Réunion* (Paris, 1993).

Vansina, Jan, *How Societies are Born: Governance in West Central Africa before 1600* (Charlottesville, VA, and London, 2004).

Viallet, Michel, *Douala autrefois: Recueil de cartes postales anciennes de Douala* (Biarritz, 2002).

Villien, François, et al., *Bangui, capitale d'un pays enclavé d'Afrique centrale: Étude historique et géographique* (Bordeaux, 1990).

Zoctizoum, Yarisse, *Histoire de la Centrafrique*, vol. i: *1879–1959: Violence du développement, domination et inégalités* (Paris, 1983).

Index of African Places

By page number and with country code. City portraits are in bold.

Index of Architects

By page number and with country code. Projects and articles are in bold.

Index of Other Key Person:

By page number and with country code.

Authors and Contributors

By page number and with country code. Biographies are in bold.

A
Arnaut, Daniela .... ST 119; AO 317

B
Basabose, Nicolas-Patience .... CD **234**, 260–261, 298–301, 310–313
Bangui, Thierry .... CF **12**,26–34
Boer, René .... GA **161**, 170–175
Brose, Andrew .... CD **234**, 306–309
Bullinger, Winfred .... CF **12**, 18–21

C
Carvalho, Filomena do Espírito Santo .... AO **316**, 422–429
Chehab, Diane .... CM **47**, 48–57, 63–75
Correia, Maria Alice Mendes .... AO **316**, 420–421
Croese, Sylvia .... AO **316**, 359–361

D
DeLancey, Mark D. .... CM **47**, 58–61
De Raeymaeker, Joost .... AO **316**, 336–319
Dresse, Anaïs .... CF **13**, 35–37

E
Ellong, Epée .... CM **47**, 48–51, 56, 63, 65, 72–73
Essesse, Amélie .... CM **46**, 62
Essimba, Ulrich .... CG **188**, 190–231
Exchanging Worlds Visions .... AO 317; ST 119

F
Ferreira, Zara .... AO **316**, 380–383
Franca, Enerlid .... ST 118

G
Gillett, Coral .... ST 19; AO **316**, 318–333, 372–373, 407, 416–419, 430–435, 440–441
Guenguebe Mbari, Mesmin .... CF **13**, 14–17
Guillevic, Karine .... CD **234**, 282–287
Guilloux, Tristan .... CG **188**, 190–231
Guionie, Philippe .... CG **189**, 212–217

K
Krapp, Stefan .... CD **235**, 262–269
Kruschwitz, Claudia .... CD **235**, 262–269

L
Lagae, Johan .... CD **234**, 236–313

M
Magalhães, Ana .... AO **316**, 392–394
Maïssa, Jean-Pierre .... GA **161**, 162–187
Memba Ikuga, Laida .... GQ **77**, 78–117
Minang Ntang, D. N. .... GQ **77**, 116–117
Molitor, Jean .... CD **235**, 282–287
Moreira, Paulo .... AO **316**, 434, 436–439
Mulimilwa, Claudien ..... CD **234**, 236–313
Müller, Sabine .... CG 230–231

N
Neto, Edwlne .... ST **118**, 130–135

P
Pape, Duarte .... ST **119**, 120–123, 136–139, 144–155
Pereira, Helder .... ST 19; AO **316**, 318–333, 372–373, 407, 416–419, 430–435, 440–441

Q
Quednau, Andreas .... CG 230–231
Quintã, Margarida .... AO **317**, 392–395

R
Rodrigues, Cristina Udelsmann ..... ST **119**, 140–143

S
Siegert, Nadine .... AO **317**, 410–415
Silva, Caren Melissa Santos da .... AO **317**, 366–369
Strother, Z. S. .... CD **235**, 250–253

T
Tomás, António .... AO **317**, 352–357
Tostões, Ana .... ST 117; AO **317**, 340–348, 70–379, 384–391, 396–406
Toulier, Bernard .... CG **189**, 190–231

V
Vanin, Fabio .... AO **317**, 410–415
Vannucci, Riccardo .... CF **13**, 40–45
Villaverde, Montserrat .... GQ **77**, 78–117

W
Westerheide, Rolf .... CD **235**, 262–269

Editors

Philipp Meuser, PhD, born 1969, architect and publisher. Studied architecture in Berlin and Zurich, with a focus on architectural history and theory. Honorary professorship in Kharkiv, Ukraine. International planning and construction projects, among others in Western Africa and Central Asia. His research focus is on prefabricated architecture.

Adil Dalbai, MA, BSc, born 1985. Studied architecture at the Technical University of Berlin, as well as history and cultural studies at the Humboldt University of Berlin, with a focus on the cultural and architectural history of Eastern Europe, Central Asia, and (post-)colonial contexts. He works on architecture projects in Western Africa.

With Diane Chehab in Frankfurt (2015)

Challenges of online communication (2015)

Official visa for Angola (2014)

Epée Ellong with Amélie Essesse (2014)

Claudien Mulimilwa in Kinshasa (2016)

N. P. Basabose in Brazzaville (2019)

The *Deutsche Nationalbibliothek* lists
this publication in the *Deutsche National-
bibliografie*; detailed bibliographic data
are available at *http://dnb.d-nb.de*

ISBN 978-3-86922-086-4 (Volume 6)
ISBN 978-3-86922-400-8 (Set)

© 2021 by DOM publishers, Berlin
www.dom-publishers.com

This work is subject to copyright.
All rights are reserved, whether the
whole part of the material is concerned,
specifically the rights of translation,
reprinting, recitation, broadcasting,
reproduction on microfilms or in other
ways, and storage or processing on data-
bases. Sources and owners of rights are
stated to the best of our knowledge;
please point out any we might have
omitted.

Publisher's Note
When editing, we have endeavoured to
keep place names and spellings consistent, while also respecting regional
differences. Where possible, we have
used the current names of locations
rather than the colonial designations
(though these are also referenced).
Efforts have been made to keep language gender neutral and to use loaded
or pejorative terms, such as 'mud hut'
and 'natives', with the due care and
attention. The political views presented
here do not necessarily represent those
held by the publisher. Facts have been
checked as far as is practicable, though
information has often been scarce, non-
existent, or contradictory.

Publishing Director
Philipp Meuser

Editorial Director
Adil Dalbai

Associate Editor
Livingstone Mukasa

Copy and Content Editor
Amy Visram

Translation
Amy Visram, Laura Thépot,
Clarice Knowles

Editorial Assistance
Ingrid Stegmann, Laura Thépot

Design
Atelier Kraut

Design Assistance
Masako Tomokiyo, Sarah Zahradnik,
Inka Humann

Printing
Tiger Printing (Hong Kong) Co., Ltd
www.tigerprinting.hk